1857: THE GREAT REBELLION

Encyclopaedic History of India Series

1857: THE GREAT REBELLION

Dr. Mahesh Vikram Singh
Professor, Deptt. of History
Mahatma Gandhi Kashi Vidyapeeth
Varanasi (UP)

Dr. Brij Bhushan Shrivastava
Head of Deptt., Ancient History, Archeology & Culture
SMMTPG College, Ballia (UP)

CENTRUM PRESS
NEW DELHI-110002 (INDIA)

CENTRUM PRESS
H.O.: 4360/4, Ansari Road, Daryaganj,
New Delhi-110002 (India)
Tel: 23278000, 23261597, 23255577, 23286875
B.O.: No. 1015, Ist Main Road, BSK IIIrd Stage,
IIIrd Phase, IIIrd Block, Bangalore-560085 (INDIA)
Tel: 080-41723429
Email: centrumpress@gmail.com
Visit us at: www.centrumpress.com

1857: The Great Rebellion

First Edition, 2011

ISBN 978-93-80836-85-0

PRINTED IN INDIA

Printed at Mehra Offset Press, Delhi

प्रो. विपिन चंद्रा
अध्यक्ष
Prof. Bipan Chandra
Chairman

नेशनल बुक ट्रस्ट, इंडिया
नेहरू भवन
5 इंस्टीट्यूशनल एरिया, फेज़-II, वसंत कुंज, नई दिल्ली-110 070
फोन/ Phone: 011-26121880 फैक्स/ Fax: 011-26121883
NATIONAL BOOK TRUST, INDIA
Nehru Bhawan
5 Institutional Area, Phase II, Vasant Kunj, New Delhi-110 070
ई-मेल / E-mail: chairman@nbtindia.org.in
वेबसाइट / Website: www.nbtindia.org.in

FOREWORD

The term 'history' is derived from the Greek word 'historia' that means knowledge acquired through investigation. Obviously, this knowledge can be correct if the method of investigation is objective and not vitiated by any kind of bias. In other words, if the study of human past is comprehensive and obtained through scientific inquiry, it can provide perspective on the present day problems and help one plan for the future.

A true historian has to identify the sources that can be most useful in a given context. Documents, coins, archaeology, anthropology, geography, travel accounts, oral traditions, mythology and so on can be useful but they can be used only after their veracity is tested and they are critically examined. They should be checked and counter-checked.

Over the centuries, one finds the study and writing of history vitiated by biases. There are numerous instances in which historical data have been distorted to support or oppose certain preconceived ideas and purposes. Strictly speaking such history is just like fiction to accord with preconceived notions and serve some ulterior purposes.

The study of the past has never been static. Conclusions go on changing because of the discovery of new materials and tools of investigation. To give a concrete example, the carbon 14 or radiocarbon dating test has revolutionized the study of civilizations and settlements, especially of prehistoric times, for which written documents, coins, etc. are seldom available. This method has enabled historians to determine more accurately than before the time period of a particular civilization or settlement. This method was discovered only 70 years ago by American scientists.

In our country, excavations brought to light the Indus Valley Civilization and its various features, hitherto unknown. Similarly, no complete text of Kautilya's Arthashastra was available before it was discovered by Shamasastry, the chief of the Mysore Government Oriental Library in the first decade of the last century. Likewise, people's knowledge of the history of the Buddhist period got extended after excavations at Sarnath and the ruins of the Asokan period at Patna. In the future, if the Harappan inscriptions are deciphered, our knowledge of the Indus Valley Civilization will increase enormously. All these instances underline the fact that our knowledge of history is never static and its frontiers go on extending.

In the light of what has been said above the encyclopedic history is going to be of great help to students interested in Indian history. It is comprehensive and as far as possible free from biases. It includes the latest materials, and objective conclusions.

Prof . Bipan Chandra

Professor Emeritus, JNU

Chairman, National Book Trust, India

Contents

Preface

The people of India have had a continuous civilization since 2500 B.C., when the inhabitants of the Indus River valley developed an urban culture based on commerce and sustained by agricultural trade. This civilization declined around 1500 B.C., probably due to ecological changes. During the second millennium B.C., pastoral, Aryan-speaking tribes migrated from the northwest into the subcontinent. As they settled in the middle Ganges River valley, they adapted to antecedent cultures.

The political map of ancient and medieval India was made up of myriad kingdoms with fluctuating boundaries. In the 4th and 5th centuries A.D., northern India was unified under the Gupta Dynasty. During this period, known as India's Golden Age, Hindu culture and political administration reached new heights. Islam spread across the Indian subcontinent over a period of 500 years. In the 10th and 11th centuries, Turks and Afghans invaded India and established sultanates in Delhi. In the early 16th century, descendants of Genghis Khan swept across the Khyber Pass and established the Mughal (Mogul) Dynasty, which lasted for 200 years. From the 11th to the 15th centuries, southern India was dominated by Hindu Chola and Vijayanagar Dynasties. During this time, the two systems—the prevailing Hindu and Muslim—mingled, leaving lasting cultural influences on each other.

The first British outpost in South Asia was established in 1619 at Surat on the northwestern coast. Later in the century, the East India Company opened permanent trading stations at Madras, Bombay, and Calcutta, each under the protection of native rulers. The British expanded their influence from these footholds until, by the 1850s, they controlled most of present-day India, Pakistan, and Bangladesh. In 1857, a rebellion in north India led by mutinous Indian soldiers caused the British Parliament to transfer all political power from the East India Company to the Crown. Great Britain began administering most of India directly while controlling the rest through treaties with local rulers.

In the late 1800s, the first steps were taken toward self-government in British India with the appointment of Indian councillors to advise the British viceroy and the establishment of provincial councils with Indian members; the British subsequently widened participation in legislative councils. Beginning in 1920, Indian leader Mohandas K. Gandhi transformed the Indian National Congress political party into a mass movement to campaign against British colonial rule.

—*Authors*

1

The Rebellion of 1857

The Situation Preceding the Rebellion: In the 1840es, the EAST INDIA COMPANY, facing financial difficulties, expanded rapidly into Hindustan and the Punjab. A huge force of Indian soldiers called SEPOYS (sipahis), commanded by British officers, was to protect and secure the newly acquired territories.

The Cource of Events: The *Lee-enfield Rifle* had been newly introduced in 1857. The complex process of loading required that Sepoy soldiers would have to use teeth to pull bullets out of their cartridges. These had been greased in animal fat (pig fat, beef tallow), to the horror of both Hindu and Muslim soldiers. Beginning in Meerut, the Sepoy soldiers rebelled. *Nana Sahib,* son of the last Maratha prince, was denied by the EIC succession to his father; he then lead an army of rebellious Sepoys against EIC troops in the *Battle of Kanpur* (Kanpur, May-June 1857); the battle turned into a massacre. Nana Sahib was victorious; by July he controlled Gwalior. Siege was laid to Lucknow (taken August 31st, where another massacre took place). Delhi fell in early September.

EIC (British) forces then retook Delhi (Sept. 20th) and laid siege to Lucknow, which fell in November. Peace was signed on July 8th 1858. Nana Sahib died in battle in 1859.

Legacy: One consequence was that the EIC was broke; its attempt to avoid bankrupcy by an aggressive policy of expansion had thus failed. The EIC was succeeded by the British government, which held on to the recent EIC acquisitions in the Ganges and Indus valleys. Britain established direct colonial rule over the more productive provinces of India, while being content with

INDIRECT RULE over the remaining principalities of the subcontinent.

British diplomacy was somewhat more subtle than that of the EIC in the 1840es and 1850es, considering Indian religious traditions and respecting the rights of native dynasties.

Mutiny or First Indian War of Independence?

The profound hypocrisy and inherent barbarism of bourgeois civilization lies unveiled before our eyes, turning from its home, where it assumes respectable forms, to the colonies, where it goes naked. Did they not, in India, to borrow an expression of that great robber, Lord Clive himself, resort to atrocious extortion, when simple corruption could not keep pace with their rapacity? While they prated in Europe about the inviolable sanctity of the national debt, did they not confiscate in India the dividends of the rajahs, who had invested their private savings in the Company's own funds? While they combated the French revolution under the pretext of defending "our holy religion," did they not forbid, at the same time, Christianity to be propagated in India, and did they not, in order to make money out of the pilgrims streaming to the temples of Orissa and Bengal, take up the trade in the murder and prostitution perpetrated in the temple of the Juggernaut? These are the men of "Property, Order, Family, and Religion."

The story of the Sepoy (sepahi) War of 1857, (an attempt at a compromise between two more controversial titles, 'the Sepoy Mutiny of 1857' and 'the Sepoy Rebellion of 1857,' though "insurgency" might also fit) began long before March of 1857. The history of the war delves deep into the colonization and conquest of India and the cultural and religious oppression imposed on Indians by British rule. Furthermore, the telling of the history of the war is, to this day, an ongoing battle between two competing narratives, the history belonging to the British that won the war, and the history claimed by the Indians who were defeated. In a time when the history of India is being retold everyday, this web page is an attempt to present a history of the Sepoy War that is derived from various points of view, accounting for the context of the histories related, and the points of view of the historians relating them.

The East India Company was a massive export company that was the force behind much of the colonization of India. The power of the East India Company took nearly 150 years to build. As early as 1693, the annual expenditure in political "gifts" to men in power reached nearly 90,000 pounds (Marx 23). In bribing the Government, the East India Company was allowed to operate in overseas markets despite the fact that the cheap imports of South Asian silk, cotton, and other products hurt domestic business. By 1767, the Company was forced into an agreement that is should pay 400,000 pounds into the National Exchequer annually.

By 1848, however, the East India Company's financial difficulties had reached a point where expanding revenue required expanding British territories in South Asia massively. The Government began to set aside adoption rights of native princes and began the process of annexation of more than a dozen independent Rajes between 1848 and 1854 (Marx 51; Kaye 30). In an article published in The New York Daily Tribune on July 28, 1857, Karl Marx notes that "... in 1854 the Raj of Berar, which comprise 80,000 square miles of land, a population from four to five million, and enormous treasures, was forcibly seized" (Marx 51).

In order to consolidate and control these new holdings, a well-established army of 200,000 South Asians officered by 40,000 British soldiers dominated India by 1857. The last vestiges of independent Indian states had disappeared and the East India Company exported tons of gold, silk, cotton, and a host of other precious materials back to England every year.

Religion

Historians like J.A.B. Palmer and John Kaye trace the origins of the soldiers' rebellion at Meerut, in which South Asian soldiers rose up against their colonial officers, to the Lee-Enfield Rifle. It was developed at the Enfield arsenal by James P. Lee and fired a.303 caliber ammunition that had to manually loaded before firing. Loading involved biting the end of the cartridge, which was greased in pig fat and beef tallow. This presented a problem for native soldiers, as pig fat is a haraam, or forbidden, substance to Muslims, and beef fat is, likewise, deemed inauspicious for certain Hindus. Thus, the revolt occurred as a reaction to this particular intrusion into Hindu and Muslim culture, and then caught on as a national rebellion. Palmer dramatically relates this discovery, according to Captain Wright, commanding the Rifle Instruction Depot:

Somewhere about the end of the third week in January 1857, a khalasi, that is to say a labourer, accosted a high Brahmin sepoy and asked for a drink of water from his lotah (water-pot). The Brahmin refused on the score of caste. The khalasi then said, "You will soon lose your caste, as ere long you will have to bite catridges covered with the fat of pigs and cows," or, it is added, "words to that effect."

Furthermore, historians taking similar positions argue that British legislation that interfered with traditional Hindu or Muslim religious practices were a source of antagonism. Palmer and Kaye also argue throughout their respective work that the prohibition practices such as saathi (often transliterated "sati"), or the ritual suicide of widows on their husbands' funeral pyres, became a source of outrage. In other words, the growing intrusion of western culture became the impetus for rebellious soldiers, fearful that their culture was being annihilated.

The long-belaboured significance of the Lee-Enfield cartridge is challenged by the work of historians like Marx, Collier, Majumdar, Chaudhuri, and Malleson. These historians argue that the actions of soldiers at Meerut was the "last straw" for South Asians who had been victims of British cultural and class based oppression and antagonism, and discard the notion that religion played an overwhelmingly vital role in fomenting revolt. For them, the root causes of the insurgency cannot be traced to a single, well-defined set of events and causes, but rather stemmed from an on-going set of conflicts.

Divide and Conquer

Col. G.B. Malleson argues that forcing Western ideas on an Eastern people fundamentally backfired, and the "divide and conquer" tactics employed by the British in India ultimately sowed the seeds of the rebellion. He notes, "action of a different character... so dear to the untravelled Englishman, or forcing the ideas in which he has been nurtured upon the foreign people with whom he has brought into contact, assisted... to loosen the bonds of discipline, which, up to that period, had bound the [Sepoy] to his officer" (Malleson 8). In other words, the Sepoy soldiers found themselves constantly pit against their countrymen in an army governed by what common soldiers came to feel were outside influences.

In a colonial setting, this is the prime breeding ground for a coup, (or in this case, a revolt) because any soldier's allegiance is governed by competition with other soldiers in currying favour and accumulating power, not by discipline or obedience to the orders of superior officers, and he begins to affiliate himself with his own people rather than the military ethics forced on him.

Expansionism

Greater still was the influence of British expansionism on the Sepoy Rebellion. Richard Collier explains how rapidly increasing territorial conquest also intesified Indian unrest:

> *... these annexations were a source of discontent and anxiety to many people besides the sepoys. In eight years, Canning's predecessor, the despotic Lord Dalhousie, at 35 the youngest Governor-General India had ever known, had annexed over 250,000 square miles— an area three times the size of England and Ireland. The Punjab, Sattara, Nagpur— Dalhousie's hands had stretched out to embrace them all. 'An Indian Governor General,' stormed The Hindu Patriot, 'is chartered to destroy dynasties with a scratch of his quill.' Indignities were heaped upon crowned heads: the jewels of the Royal Family of Nagpur were publicly auctioned in Calcutta.*

Partcipating in the military conquest of local authorities, then, and having first-hand knowledge of the effects of British expansionism would have fomented resistance in the Sepoys.

Torture and Oppression

On August 28, 1857, Marx published an article in The New York Daily Tribune in order to "show that the British rulers of India are by no means such mild and spotless benefactors of the Indian people as they would have the world believe". Marx cites the official Blue Books — entitled "East India (Torture) 1855-57" — that were laid before the House of Commons during the sessions of 1856 and 1857. The reports revealed that British officers were allowed an extended series of appeals if convicted or accused of brutality or crimes against Indians. Concerning matters of extortion in collecting public revenue, the report indicates that officers had free reign of any methods at their disposal.

Torture became a financial institution in colonial India, and was challenged by a petition from the Madras Native Association presented in January of 1856. The petition was dismissed on the basis of a lack of evidence, despite the fact that, according to the Marx, "there was scarcely any investigation at all, the Commission sitting only in the city of Madras, and for but three months, while it was impossible, except in very few cases, for the natives who had comnplaints to make to leave their homes" (Marx 74). Marx also refers to Lord Dalhousie's statements in the Blue Books that there was "irrefragable proof" that various officers had committed "gross injustice, to arbitrary imprisonment and cruel torture".

In addition to torture, the Company levied extremely large taxes on the Indian people. Collier describes taxes as "a cynical outrage. A man could not travel twenty miles without paying toll at a river ferry, farmed out by the Company to private speculators. Land Tax, often demanded before the crop was raised, was made in quarterly instalments... the annual rent for an acre of land was 3s[hillings]., yet the produce of that acre rarely averaged 8s[hillings]. in value."

Marx's position, as illustrated by the introductory quote to this page, is that the Indians were victims of both physical and economic forms of class oppression by the British. In Marx's analysis, the clash between the soldiers and their officers is the inevitable conflict that is the result of capitalism and imperialism.

The Rebellion

The military history of the rebellion is straightforward. Prior to the "mutiny" at Meerut on May 9th, 1857, fires broke out on January 22nd near Calcutta. An incident occurred on February 25th of that year when the 19th regiment mutinied at Berhampore, and the 34th Regiment rebelled at Barrackpore on the 31st of March. At Berhampore, the regiment allowed one of it's men to advance with a loaded musket upon the parade-ground in front of a line and open fire on his superior officer; a battle ensued. April saw fires at Allahabad, Agra, an Ambala, but the spark that lit the powder keg went off on May 9th in Meerut.

Members of the 3rd regiment of light cavalry were awaiting sentencing and imprisonment for refusal to obey orders and put the Lee-Enfield. caliber cartridge into their mouths. Once imprisoned, the 11th and 20th cavalry assembled and broke rank and turned on their commanding officers. After liberating the 3rd regiment, chaos ensued in Meerut, and the rebels engaged the remaining British Troops. Meerut was the single-most evenly balanced station in India in terms of the numbers of British and Indian soldiers. Troops and rebels were on near-even terms with 2,028 European Troops versus 2,357 sepoys, which certainly made the British side's capacity to defend its interest and defeat the Sepoys that much more likely. Furthermore, the British had 12 field guns and the sepoys had no artillery. Both Collier and Marx indicate that the rebellion would have ended there had Major-General William Hewitt cut off the rebel army at the bridge between Meerut and Delhi, some 40 miles away, with added weapons.

As the 38th, 54th, and 74th regiments of infantry and native artillery under Bahkt Khan (c.1797- c.1859) joined the rebel army at Delhi in May. June 1857 marked the battle of Kanpur. The last Maratha prince, Baji Rao II, decreed his title and 80,000 pound annual pension to his son Nana Sahib (c.1820-c.1859) and was refused twice. Despite Sahib's attempts to push his claim, Lord Dalhousie refused the Hindu nobleman. Thus, in June 1857, Nana Sahib led the sepoy battalions at Crawnpore against the British. Nana Sahib sent word to Sir Hugh Wheeler, commander of the Britsh forces at Kanpur warning of the attack, guaranteeing him safe passage. On June 27, Nana Sahib broke the pact and trapped Wheeler in his palace. The events leading up to Wheeler's surrender and death have been recorded as the Kanpur Massacre.

The Kanpur Massacres

In the words of Sir Colin Campbell, leader of the British forces during the war: never was devised a blacker scheme than that which Nana Sahib had planned. Our miserable countrymen were conducted faithfully enough to the boats-officers, men, women, and children. The men and officers were allowed to take their arms and ammunition with them, and were escorted by nearly the whole of the rebel army. It was about eight o'clock a.m. when all reached the riverside-a distance of a mile and a half. Those who embarked first pushed off from the shore; but others found it difficult to get their boats off the banks, as the rebels had placed them as high as possible. At this moment the report of three guns was heard from the Nena's camp. The mutineers suddenly levelled their muskets, guns opened from the banks, and the massacre commenced. Some of the boats were set on fire, volley upon volley was fired upon the poor fugitives, numbers of whom were killed on the spot... A few boats crossed over to the opposite bank, but there a regiment of native infantry (the 17th), just arrived from Azimghur, was waiting for them; and in their eagerness to slay the "Kaffirs," rode their horses belly deep into the river to meet the boats, and hack our unhappy country men and women to pieces.

Andrew Ward's historical narrative, Our Bones Are Scattered, also relates an account of the terrible and bloody massacre that followed the rebellion at Kanpur, as well as Delhi and Meerut. By July, when Nana Sahib had captured Gwalior, he was reinstated as prince.

The Siege of Delhi

The siege of Lucknow lasted roughly from July 1st to August 31st. The commanding British officer, Sir Henry Lawrence, died early on during the siege. By July 25th two-thirds of the Britsh forces had retreated across the river and Delhi had been taken by early September. Bahadur Shah, the last surviving Mogul ruler was installed as ruler and the devastating battle between rebel and British forces for control Delhi ensued. Soldiers faced down the horrific sight of the impregnable walls of Delhi and "more than fifty guns and mortars belching fire at Delhi's northern walls from the water bastion on the east to the Mori bastion on the west."

As the siege wore on the Punjabi forces fighting for the British began to weary and there was talk of a retreat. Under General John Nicholas, Delhi had toppled by September 20th, at the cost of 3,835 soldiers, British and Indian, and 378 horses (Collier 264). Rebel forces retreated to Lucknow where the siege was approaching three months in length. There the war lasted until late November, until the rebels were driven to defeat in the Ganges Valley in

December and January by Hugh Rose and Colin Campbell. By July 8, 1858, a peace treaty was signed and the war ended. By 1859, Rebel leaders Bahkt Khan and Nana Sahib had been slain in battle.

Conclusion

Though the Sepoy War has been dismissed as a chaotic, disorganized peasant uprising, several facts go undisputed that offer a counter-argument. The "unorganized peasants" of India fought one of the most powerful empires in the world to near defeat with limited resources and even more limited training. Nevertheless, the lesson of the Sepoy War is not one of victory or justice, but failure.

Though the exact cause of the Sepoy War has yet to be agreed upon, and it is likely that there were many complex causes rather than one, it is clear that British interference governments and the oppression of the Indian people, religious and economic, created a bloody revolution. If there is a lesson to be learned from any of this, it is that a people, once pushed into a corner, will fight for nothing more than the freedom to fight, and live, if not for religion then for their basic right to live in freedom. Furthermore, in the desperate vengeance of a people reduced to pure indignity, lives a coldness that rivals that of their oppressors.

What's in a Name?

One hundred and fifty years after the events of 1857, there is still great debate in what they should actually be called. The British authorities firmly regarded the event as a mutiny by large sections of the Bengal army. Indeed the British were fortunate that it was only the Bengal Army, with a few exceptions, the Bombay and Madras armies stayed remarkably quiescent. The British recognised that there were a number of fellow travellers who joined in and took advantage of the collapse of authority throughout Northern India, notably Ghazis and Gujars.

Post 1947 Indian Nationalists have thought to refer to the events as India's First Nationalist Uprising. It is clear why they would like to brand this event as a nationalist uprising. It was unusual in that it did attract Muslims and Hindus to the cause, but the event was clearly confined to Northern India in general and Bengal in particular.

The truth was obviously somewhere in between. Undoubtedly, the Bengal Army took the lead through their initial mutinies, but they quickly tried to politicise and widen the event through asking the last Mughal Emperor to reassert his claims and reestablish the old Mughal Empire. This did attract wider support but the old Emperor did not have the energy or the resources to fully take on the power of the British in India. The hoped for general Indian uprising never did take place and despite attempts to escalate the events through various atrocities and sieges, the British were able to reorganise their forces in the Indian subcontinent and slowly but surely reestablish their control over the Bengal and other affected areas. Therefore, you could claim to call these events a mutiny that escalated into a rebellion but it never did hit the hoped for nationalist uprising status. For the sake of convenience and familiarity, I will use the term mutiny throughout although with the understanding that it did escalate further.

Causes

Again, there is much debate into why the mutiny did break out in India in 1857. For generations, British schoolboys and girls were told that it all had to do with a misunderstanding and mistakes over a new kind of cartridge issued to the Sepoys and Sowars. Indians were told that 1857 was the 100th anniversary of the Battle of Plassey and that British rule would come to an end on that date. These events certainly did occur and were significant in their own right. However the causes of the mutiny were far more varied and interconnected with one another in quite unforeseen and complicated manners.

Religion

The common thread that will tie most of the factors together and bringing an unlikely alliance between the Muslims and Hindus was the perceived threat to the native religions of the Indian subcontinent. The threat was the increased religious overtones of the East India Company and of the Europeans operating in the subcontinent. In the eighteenth century, the East India Company had been interested only in profit and commercial areas. As the nineteenth century progressed, religion began to play a more important role. Consequently, East India personnel took more interest in religious affairs and allowed more missionary work to be carried out under their aegis. This increased religiousity did not make much of a direct impact in terms of converts, but it was certainly noticed by a growing percentage of the Indian population and definitely by the East India Company's employees the sowars and sepoys. Indeed, more and more EIC officers were making unsubtle attempts to expose their soldiers to Christian teachings.

Losing Touch

In fact, the East India Company Officers had a good reputation for mucking in with their soldiers and were known to lead from the front. In the eighteenth century, EIC officers had been real swashbucklers keen to make their fortune at whatever personal cost. They frequently underwent the same privations and dangers as their charges did. This earned the respect and awe of many Indian company soldiers. As time went on, newer generations of EIC officers were not so hungry for success. There were more British officers for starters and so it was easy for them to stay within the company of like minded officers rather than with their soldiers whose needs and wants they increasingly saw as foreign and peculiar. The officers' language skills consequently suffered which further took them out of the loop of understanding. When families started joining the officers, the break down in contact was almost complete. Officers were having to rely on their Indian NCOs who were very often as aggreived as the soldiers themselves.

Over-Confidence of EIC

Hand in hand with the loss of touch was the over confidence of the East India Company officials. They had become dangerously complacent about their own invincibility. Winning countless small battles at incredible odds had made the EIC seem impregnable. The fact that they were often using far better technology and were better organised only seemed to confirm their right to rule the subcontinent. Over the past century, the EIC had got side-tracked from making money from the ports of Calcutta and Bombay by supplying exotic goods to the people of Britain and the rest of the Empire. In fact scandal and corruption had already converted the East India Company from a trading company to a provider of government services. Ostensibly, this had been done to stamp out corruption and end the monopoly of the EIC over supplying goods.

Actually, it would have the long term effect of changing the dynamics of EIC income. Their income would now come from direct taxation. The only ways to increase income was to increase taxation or to rule over an expanded empire. Neither of these methods would be popular with the Indian population. Whilst the company was making itself more unpopular in the areas it controlled, it would soon find that its armies were tied down in the newly conquered areas and their borders. The ratio of Europeans to Indians in the armed forces in the existing Indian Empire was reaching perilously low levels.

Dalhousie's Reforms

In 1848, James Ramsay, the Earl of Dalhousie, became Governor General of India. It was thought that he would represent a steadying influence on the colony and would control its budget. Dalhousie though attempted to spur on the modernisation and Europeanisation of the Colony. A department of Public Works was set up; telegraphs, railways, ports were all to be built or to be upgraded. The Ganges canal was to irrigate huge swathes of central India. Metalled roads were to be built. A postal system was set up. New engineering colleges were set up. Promotion was to be on merit rather than seniority. Tea plantations were encouraged and provided with the infrastructure to take away their products. He encouraged Christian missionaries and societies to provide missions to care for the needy and low caste Indians. These reforms, and many more, were intended to improve the efficiency of colony in the long run. The short term investment costs though would prove unpalatable and put yet more strain on the taxation system. He would also preside over the resurrection and implementation of the infamous 'doctrine of lapse' which will be expanded upon below. He retired due to ill health in 1856-just before the mutiny-and was expecting a heroes welcome for his reforms but instead found himself having to defend himself against the charges of having stirred up the socio-economic structure of India to beyond breaking point.

Technology

EIC soldiers and other Indians would view many of the technological changes with trepidation. Steam trains and steam ships seemed to be some ungodly creature that defied the laws of nature. The new communications systems threatened many existing castes and businesses. Boatmen would be put out of the haulage business, farmers would find their local monopolies being challenged by cheaper imports from elsewhere in India or even further afield. Mass produced British made goods could be imported far more cheaply and efficiently than the locals could produce themselves. Severe strains were being placed on the existing economic systems by the very tools that were supposed to make India more efficient. Soldiers would have the added complication of new equipment and tactics to adapt to. With the expansion of the Indian Empire, soldiers were travelling further and further from their homes. Expeditions in Burma, the Middle East and further afield also required soldiers to travel over water. For high born Brahmins, this meant the loss of their caste. Technological change brought as many fears as benefits to the Indians in the 1850s.

The Doctrine of Lapse

Simply put, the doctrine of lapse allowed the company to annex the principality of any Indian ruler who died without natural heirs or one who was manifestly incompetent. It was thought that this would be a fairly painless way for the company to expand its Indian Empire (and therefore its tax base) by avoiding any direct confrontations or military annexations. It was hoped that the Indians did not really mind who their rulers were and would fatalistically live with the changes far above their heads. It was hoped that they would appreciate British efficiency and incorruptability. Satara was the first state to be annexed this way, Jaitpur, Sambalpur, Nagpur and Jhansi would follow suit. The practice of Indian princes adopting heirs was conveniently placed aside by Dalhousie. In 1856 the EIC would pick up the richest of the states in this manner. It was declared that the Oudh was being mismanaged by its incompetent ruler and so was annexed. Oudh was a very rich and probably corrupt Indian state but it was one that was understood and appreciated by its population. The British were thought of as inflexible and alien. It was also not appreciated just how large a proportion of the EIC sepoy army came from Oudh. They had been happy to take the King's shilling as any mercenary would, but many of them were horrified to find that their own homes had been annexed in such an underhand and unfair way.

Overstretch

The decade before the mutiny had been a busy decade for both the British and EIC armies. The British army had just been involved in the hugely complicated and disastrously run Crimean campaign from 1854 to 1856. Apart from the manpower costs of this campaign, it was hardly an advertisement to the world on the efficiency of the British Army. Many observers felt that the British might be a paper tiger after all. Azimullah Khan who would later advise the infamous Nana Sahib was just one such observer. He felt that the Turks or the Russians might provide better long term allies for the Indians. The EIC armies had been busy in 1848/9 in the annexation of Punjab and Sindh with the Anglo-Sikh Wars. There had been war in Burma and many smaller scale battles along the frontiers. The Santal Expedition had shown how even poorly equipped peasant armies could cause huge logistical problems for the EIC army. On top of all this was the stationing of the EIC armies in the newly acquired lands. This policy was thought prudent lest the newly acquired peoples rose up against their new masters. The EIC assumed that those areas it had ruled for decades or more were firmly under their control.

Cartridges

The infamous cartridge difficulties combined religious sensibilities with technological change. For years the EIC had relied on a simple but inaccurate smooth bore musket. It was decided to introduce a more accurate muzzle loading Enfield Rifled Musket. One way to speed up the loading process was the introduction of a paper cartridge with the bullet sitting on the exact quantity of powder needed. The loader was required to bite open this paper cartridge to expose the powder. The original cartridges were made in Britain and had been covered in tallow to help protect the cartridge from the elements. Unfortunately the tallow had been made from a beef and pork fat. To the British users of these cartridges, this made no big deal. Hindu and Muslim users were horrified at the defiling fat. The EIC quickly realised its blunder and replaced the animal fat with vegetable fat but the damage had already been done. To Hindus and Muslims alike, their worst fears of being ritually humiliated had been confirmed. Many assumed that this had been a deliberate policy by the Europeans who were looking to impose their own religion on the subcontinent. Battalion after battalion refused to use the new cartridges. Some even refused to handle the cartridges when officers had allowed them the option of tearing open the cartridges instead of biting them. As far as the officers were concerned, refusing to obey an order was tantamount to mutiny as it was. Different commanders handled the situation in different ways-some with more sensitivity than others. The first shots were to be fired by (an inebriated) Mangal Pandy on March 29th at Barrackpore. He protested against the disbanding of a unit that had disobeyed orders to use the cartridges. He shot at a British sergeant-major and a lieutenant and then engaged them in a sword fight. He saw the two of them off but then shot himself in the chest when General Hearsey arrived in the parade ground. The authorities at Barrackpore were forutunate to have the European 84th regiment to hand so that the disarming of the Indian battalions could be done with the threat of force for any sepoys thinking of refusing to hand over their guns. Not all stations would be so fortunate.

The Uprising

Ever since the victory of Plassey in 1757 AD, and putting the French East India Company to its political doom, the British East India Company established its rule in Indian and gradually tightened its grip over the major part of the country. The British introduced significant changes in thedifferent spheres, which proved disastrous to the solidarity of their rule. The rival forces joined their hands, thus leading to the great upheaval in 1857 AD.

Divergent views are held on the nature of the 1857 uprising, whether it was a military mutiny or the first national war of independence, or a Hindu-Muslim voice against the impending danger of Christianity-is a matter of controversy among the historians. Sir John Lawrence and James Seeley feel that the uprising of 1857 was a "wholly unpatriotic and selfish Sepoy Mutiny with no native leadership and no popular support." This opinion is accepted by Trevelyan, C. Raikes, P. E. Roberts, and Edwards and Garratt. The contention of these writers is that the uprising was influenced by the sepoys, who had their own grievances and held the British government responsible for the same. The revolt had started from the cantonments and remained effective around the same. Obviously, it was the case of greased cartridges which sparked the fire. On the other hand, the civilians, by and large, remained unaffected by all these developments. Indeed, the Indian rulers, who had grievances against the British, rose to the occasion after the sepoy uprising; otherwise they had no courage to take such a step.

Kaye and Malleson name it an organised Hindu-Muslim rising, which Reese prefers to call it a war of religious fanaticism against Christianity. J. Outram is of the opinion that "it was a Mohammedan conspiracy making capital of Hindu grievances." However, Benjamin Disraeli observes that it was a well-planned, well-organised and vigilant event.

There is a nationalist approach to this event, forwarded by V. D. Savarkar, K. M. Panikkar and Ashok Mehta, who observe that it was the First National War of Independence, in which Indian masses from all walks of life participated. The grievances of the people, as a consequence of one hundred yeas of British rule, forced them to stand in unison, putting aside all their differences, as matters caste and religion. The evidence came when even the Hindus acknowledged Bahadur Shah II as their ruler. The Hindus and the Muslims swore by the Ganges and the Holy Quran to get rid of the British rule, which was the common objective of the rebels everywhere. The event was confined not only to the military Mutiny, but spread rapidly and achieved the character of "a popular rebellion and a war of Indian Independence."

After going through the above analysis, one comes to certain conclusions:

(a) It was a military mutiny.

(b) It was a religious war of the Hindus and the Muslims against Christianity.

(c) It was a national war of independence aimed at the freedom from the alien rule, and in which Indians from all walks of life participated.

However, there are certain limitations in accepting any of these views. In fact, the movement was never religious in character.

Christianity was being supported by the British government, which was posing a general threat to the Hinduism and the Islam. But in this struggle those who were defeated were the followers of a religion and not religion itself. Secondly, it was not on the whole, a sepoy mutiny. Though the sepoys provided boon to other elements to operate, they did not take part in it from all over the country. In many places, many of them even supported the British cause. Thirdly, the revolt did not cover the whole of the country, but its scope was limited only to certain parts. The majority of the North and the Deccan remained entirely unaffected or fought on the side of the foreigners against the rebels.

The revolt had nothing constructive as its objective rather than the anti-British base. There is a recent approach towards the character of the mutiny, led by Dr. R. C Majumdar. He holds the view that "the so called First National War of Independence of 1857 is neither first nor National, nor a War of Independence." According to him, those who participated did so not out of any nationalist consideration, but only to further their self-interests.

In fact, the population was, by and large, unaware of nationalism during 1857. The struggle was much less for the freedom of India, but for Jhansi or Oudh etc. It is the general contention that the civilians also participated in the revolt along with the sepoys, and that the former were punished to death in great number because of this reason. But it is significant to understand the social stratification of the civilians in this uprising.

The major role in the rural areas was played by the peasant, who held the moneylenders as the source of their agony. These moneylenders were supported by the British which caused unrest among the peasants against the government. However, the revolt was strong in the rural areas only where the moneylenders' position was weak and the hereditary caste and clan groups were strong. There were certain castes and tribes in the Central and Northern India, which had been subdued, found an opportunity when the British rule was shaken. They again returned to their traditional profession of loot and plunder, and there was nothing national in it. As matters the feudal lords, they had an intention of regaining their old status of the medieval times.

From the above survey, it is not proper to name this event either the military uprising, because it remained active in and around the cantonments; or the first war of independence, because people from all walks of life took active part in it without any distinction of caste or religion. People lacked the sense of national consciousness, and those who rebelled did so influenced by a variety of grievances. The revolt, however, sowed the seeds of national awakening, which were to be observed in the coming years.

The major reason regarding the outbreak of the revolt is associated with the greased cartridge controversy. The soldiers were provided with the new Enfield Rifles and the cartridges were allegedly greased with the fat of cow and pig. These cartridges were to be opened with the mouth before using in the rifles. It enraged the Hindus and the Muslim soldiers, because it hurt their religious sentiments. When the soldiers objected to its use, they were court-martialled, thus "falling as a spark on dry tinder." However, the cartridge issue was not the whole important. Obviously, it had only enraged the soldiers and gave the military feed to the discontented general masses and the ruling classes, who hated the British rule for its political, economic, socio-religious and military policies. In fact, "the first century of British rule in India set the stage for the great tragic drama which was to celebrate the centenary of its foundation in the blood and tears."

The British came to India as traders and took advantage of its political weaknesses, created by its lack of unity and mutual distrust. As a consequence of the French defeats in the Carnatic Wars, and the British victories at Plassey (1757) and Buxar (1764), the East India Company established its rule in Bengal. Apart from defeating the Marathas and the Mysore, the British made a successful bid to hold their political control over different States in India. The Subsidiary Alliance System, formed by Lord Wellesley, set up the British influence in many States including Oudh, Tanjore, Carnatic, Hyderabad, Mysore, Nagpur, Indore, Gwalior, Baroda, Jaipur, Jodhpur and Bhopal, and annexed many parts into the Company's Empire.

The work of the political conquests was carried on by Lord Hastings, William Bentick and Ellenborough. The crises reached its climax under Lord Dalhousie. The Doctrine of Lapse gave the authority to the Company Empire to annex all the States of the heirless rulers. The adopted sons of such rulers could not succeed unless permitted by the East India Company. Luckily or otherwise, the States of Satara, Jhansi, Nagpur, Jaitpur, Sambalpur, Udaipur and Bhagalpur fell a prey to this policy which caused restlessness among the ruling classes. The titles and pensions of the Raja of Tanjore, the Nawab of Carnatic and Nana Sahib, the adopted son of Peshwa Baji Rao II were abolished. Dalhousie's imperialism crossed all the limits, when in 1856, Oudh was annexed to the Company's rule on the pretext of mal-administration. Even the Mughal Emperor, Bahadur Shah II, was informed that his sons would be deprived of the title, fort and palace, which hurt the Muslim sentiments in the country and added fuel to the fire. The Mughal Empire was, in fact, looked upon as the pillar of Islamic State in India and the loss of the Empire was, in other terms, a loss to the position of the Muslims.

The administrative set up was also a cause of discontentment to the Indians. The British ruled the country from England. They had no sentiments, and no sense of gratitude for the Indians. The natives were deprived of the high posts in the administration. Though the Charter Act of 1833 mentioned that caste, creed or colour would not become a barrier to appointments, it was not implemented. No doubt, Lord William Bentick had appointed Indians on lower posts, but the key posts were reserved for the Europeans.

The Charter Act of 1853, recommended for the competitive examinations for those aspiring to higher administrative positions, but the Indians found its terms too harsh for themselves to get through. The examinations were conducted in England, and the maximum age limit was 22 years. The highest office any Indian could aspire for, was that of a Deputy Collector in the Executive and a Sadar Amin in the Judiciary. The natives could not approach their English officers easily, and were ill-treated by them. They were considered inferior "even to the backward persons of the most backward of the European countries." Sir Syed Ahmed Khan exposed in The Causes of the Indian Revolt that the absence of Indian representatives in the Governor-General's Legislative Council was an important factor leading to the revolt. The

Government could not understand the feeling of the subjects. In his opinion, it was in the general interest of the government to have the representative voice in its Council.

Suspicions and hatred towards the British rule increased on the socio-religious grounds. The government allowed the Christian Missionaries in 1813 to spread their religion in India, and they did so with much zeal. Even the government supported their cause. Missionary schools were opened with this very object. During a severe famine in 1837 in Upper India, the relief work was left with the charitable institutions, and it gave an opportunity to the missionaries to undertake their proselytizing task. Those who converted to Christianity were fed properly. The Disabilities Act of 1856 guaranteed the rights over inheritance, even after conversion, but only to Christianity.

The spread of Western education, the introduction of female education and the establishment of railways and telegraph system were looked upon by the Indians an instrument to crush their religion. They government also started interfering into the social structure of the Indians. The abolition of Sati and female infanticide, and the introduction of secular legal system was a danger to the prevailing structure. The abolition of Persian in the courts also offended the Muslims. The new system affected the priestly classes to a large extent and they toyed with the fears of the common masses in instigating them against the government.

Here the blame rests not with the common masses, as they were ignorant of the objectives and utilization of all these innovations, but with the officials themselves. They issued certain statements, which raised the fears in the minds of the natives. Mangles, the Chairman of the Board of Directors, declared in the House of Commons, "Providence had entrusted the extensive Empire of Hindustan to England in order that the banner of Christ should wave triumphant from one end of India to the other. Every one must exert all his strength — in continuing in the country the grand work of making all Indians Christians." The statement of Major Edwards that "the Christianization of India was to be the ultimate end of our continued possession of it," made the Indians deadly against the British rule.

The British officials, military as well as civil, used abusive language for Lord Rama and the Prophet, and prevailed upon their subordinates to convert to Christianity. The Indians were discriminated even in the courts where they were meted out harsh punishments even for minor crimes, while the Christians received mild punishments for complex crimes.

The economic policies of the British had grave consequences on the Indian public, which stood to revolt. The economic exploitation of India started since the British established their rule here. The British economic policy proved beneficial to England, while it had drastic results over India. The Indian trade was kept in the hands of the British traders and were given many concessions, which had a negative impact on the economy of Indian traders.

The Charter Act of 1813 brought to an end the monopoly of the East India Company to trade with India, while the Company rule began to serve the commercial interests of the English traders and the industrialists. To start with, the British opened their trade in spices, cotton, etc. but after the industrial revolution their policy in trade matters also changed. "India became a milch cow, while her own sons were gradually pushed to the starvation wage." India exported raw materials to England at cheap rates, while became a ready market for the sale of finished goods at high prices. The government aimed at destroying the Indian trade and manufactures; therefore it imposed heavy custom duties on Indian made goods in England, while a nominal duty was imposed on British manufactures in India. The result was that India became an economic colony for the British.

Not only were the trade and industry of India destroyed, but also the British rule led to the deterioration of agriculture. The revenue policy of the British did no favour either to the peasants or the zamindars. Revenue was imposed on the rent-free lands given in the form of religious grants as well. To make the matters worse, Lord William Bentick had confiscated land from a number of landlords who could not prove that these were assigned to their forefathers by the then rulers.

The army's role in the revolt was very significant, but the soldiers had their own grievances. The inequality in the status of the Indians and European soldiers was disliked by the Indian troops. All the commissioned ranks were reserved for the

Europeans, and the highest rank in the army an Indian could aspire for was that of a Subedar with a salary of Rs. 60 per month. However, their European counterparts used to draw the salary 7 to 8 times more than the Indians. The additional bhattas (allowances) of the soldiers was also stopped. The efforts of the British Generals to propagate Christianity among their ranks, was also a cause of misery to the Indian mercenaries. The number of the Indian soldiers in the army was much larger as compared to the Europeans. The heavy losses that the British had to suffer in Afghanistan encouraged the Indian soldiers. Discipline among them was waning and Lord Dalhousie had informed the authorities in England about it. To make the matters worse, the soldiers were abandoned to send the revenue free letter according to the Post Office Act, 1854. They had been enjoying this privilege so far. The General Services Recruitment Act, 1856, required the new recruits to serve any part they were sent. Though the new Act did not affect the old incumbents, it became very unpopular, because service in the Bengal Army was almost hereditary. It was felt against the social and religious beliefs to go across the sea. Earlier too, the Barrackpore Regiment was disbanded in 1824, when the soldiers had refused to go to Burma.

In the meantime, the controversy regarding the greased cartridges caught much fire, ultimately leading to the mutiny. Soon, it spread among the civilians as well, who were waiting for an opportune moment to strike.

The banner of revolt was raised at Barrackpore on March 29, 1857. A young Brahmin sepoy Mangal Pandey, refused to use the greased cartridges and killed his European officers. The government disbanded the 34 N.I. Regiment and punished the guilty rebels. The mutiny spread like wild fire and in May 1857, 85 sepoys of 3rd Cavalry Regiment, at Meerut, were court-martialled on their refusal to use the cartridges. On May 10, the rebels killed many European officers and got their fellows released. Even General Hewlett, at the command of 2200 soldiers, could not dare resist the mutineers.

On May 12, the rebels attacked Delhi. Lt. Willoughby surrendered after putting some resistance. Bahadur Shah Zafar was declared the Emperor of India, to which he hesitantly accepted.

The loss of Delhi was very tragic to the British position. Soon the rebellion centred around Lucknow, Kanpur, Barreily, Benaras, Jhansi and many towns in the Central and Northern India. To crush the revolt, Lord Canning felt the expediency of re-establishing the British authority over Delhi. Military assistance was sought from the Presidencies of Bombay and Madras and the Chief Commissioner of Punjab Sir, John Lawrence. The British got valuable services from the Gorkhas, the Sikhs and a number of rulers from the Indian states. Delhi was besieged under Sir Henry Bernard and Wilson, while the rebels fought bravely under Mirza Mughal and Bakht Khan. However, General Nicolson succeeded in recapturing Delhi on September 14, but soon after succumbed to his injuries received during the battle. Bahadur Shah was arrested from the tomb of Humayun by Lt. Hudson, while his two sons and a grandson were publicly shot. The loot and plunder of Delhi by the British troops continued for three days and surpassed even the loot of Nadir Shah.

The revolt broke out in Lucknow on June 4, 1857. The rebels attacked the British Residency and killed its Resident, Sir Henry Lawrence. The efforts of Havelock and Outram to recover Lucknow failed. Later on Sir Colin Campbell at the head of the Gorkha Regiment, entered the city in March 1858, but the guerilla activities continued till September.

In June 1857, the revolt broke out in Kanpur also and the rebellious troops occupied the city. Nana Sahib declared himself the Peshwa and forced Sir Hugh Wheeler to surrender on June 27. Taking revenge of the atrocities committed on the Indians by General Neil at Allahabad and Benaras, the Indian troops murdered many English men and women in Kanpur. On July 17, Gen. Havelock defeated Nana Sahib and forced him to retreat towards Fatehgarh, but after

The decisive battle was fought in the first week of December, when Sir Colin Campbell defeated the rebels on December 6. Nana Sahib fled towards Nepal, while Tantia Tope escaped and joined Lakshmibai, the queen of Jhansi. Lakshmibai, the widow of King Gangadhar Rao, led the rebels in Jhansi in June 1857. On April 3, 1858, Sir Hugh Rose attacked Jhansi and recaptured it. Lakshmibai fled to Kalpi, where assisted by Tantia Tope, inflicted many losses on the enemies. Ultimately, the British defeated the rebels on May 24. Lakshmibai and Tantia Tope fled to Gwalior and sought Sicindia's help. But Sicindia, showing loyalty to the British refused to assist them. However, the troops of Gwalior revolted against Scindia and forced him to flee towards Agra. Sir Hugh Rose attacked Gwalior on June 11, and after a fierce battle of 8 days, captured the town Rani Lakshmibai gave a fine expression of her bravery, but died on the battlefield. Tantia Tope, who had fled to the South, was arrested in April 1859.

The death of Lakshmibai proved to be a death knell to the revolt. Though there were rebellions in Rohilkhand, Bareilly, Shahjahanpur, Bihar, parts of Rajputana, and the Maratha territories, these had no impression on the destruction of the alien rule and were very easily crushed. By December 1858, the British were able to re-establish their authority all over India.

The rebels had shown the signs of their extreme bravery, but the British had their day. Varieties of factors are held responsible for the failure of this upheaval from the Indian point of view. The superiority of the British arms, discipline in their troops and their control over telegraph system played a very significant role in the Company's success over the rebels. At this critical juncture, the British secured valuable support from many Indian States including Patiala, Jind, Nabha, Kapurthala, Gwalior, Hyderabad, Rampur etc. Even Canning observed that the British would have been forced to pack, had Scindia joined the rebels. Even the warrior

The political diplomacy of the British had its own role in this success. They created the communal differences among the Hindus, the Muslims and the Sikhs to a great extent and successfully played on these. On the other hand, they won the support from the rulers of the States. In his analysis, Dr. R. C. Majumdar observes, "A race which could successfully employ the sepoys against the Sikhs, and then the Sikhs against the sepoys, the sepoys against the Pathans and the Gurkhas, and then the Pathans and the Gurkhas against the sepoys, certainly deserves a Empire."

A serious drawback on the part of the rebels, was the lack of any common solid objective. Apart from their limited resources, indeed, the rebels had an anti-British attitude in common, but they had nothing national in them. Each party had its divergent interests and had only to fulfil the same. While Bahadur Shah, Lakshmibai and Nana Sahib were eager to achieve their political interests, they were not serious towards the hardships of the peasantry and the menial classes. Their unity with the sepoys was also only to strengthen their military positions. Moreover, inefficiency of the rebel leaders against the British was also observed. Obviously, they fought bravely, but it was their strategy that mattered.

Last but not the least important factor was the attitude of the civilians towards the sepoys. The plundering activities and the reckless destruction on their part had alienated the general masses from them. Civil population did not help them at any stage, which was ultimately a factor of the failure of the cause of the revolt.

The Mutiny was suppressed, but it had the long-drawn consequences over the Indian history, which affected almost each and every sphere of life. P. E. Roberts writes, "The suppression of the Mutiny was deemed a fitting time for the Crown finally to take over the control of the Indian government." The suppression led, on the one hand, to the end of the Mughal rule in India, and on the other of the East India Company, which had established its political authority with the conquest of Plassey (1757). The Company protested against the decision and held that she established the rule in India at a time when the Crown was losing her significant colonial government in the United States.

John S. Mill even filed a petition against the decision but of no use, and the administration passed over to the Crown on November 1, 1858. Sir H. S. Cunningham remarked that it was "a formal than a substantial change." According to the Act of 1859, the Board of Control and the Court of Directors were abolished, and their place was taken over by the Secretary of State for India. The Council of India was formed consistently of seven members. The Indian administration was to be supervised by the Viceroy of the Crown. "For a few years, Crown and Parliament showed a keen desire to supervise Indian affairs, but this gradually diminished. Towards the end of the sixties hardly a dozen members took any active interest in India." Soon certain factors strengthened the importance of the Secretary of State and his position in the Cabinet increased his authority over the finances and political activities of the government of India.

A very significant aspect of the aftermath of the revolt was the enactment of Indian Councils Act of 1861. As the British had acquaintance of the Indian reaction towards the government's policies, the Indians were nominated to the Legislative Council. The annexationist policy of the East India Company, especially the Doctrine of Lapse, was a prime factor of many States raising the banner of revolt, even though the Company's officials deny this fact. The timely assistance provided by other States helped in crushing the revolt and consequently deeply affected the policy of the Government towards the Indian States during the future course. Lord Stanley, the Secretary of State for India, expressed his views before the House of Commons: "I think also that the Government, whether in India or in this country, have profited sufficiently by the recent and costly experience, not to feel inclined to pursue that policy of annexation, which, whether well or ill-founded, has undoubtedly, in a great degree, been the cause of the present disaster."

The valuable support of the Indian States had defended the British cause. Sir John Lawrence, the Chief Commissioner of Punjab, reported to Lord Canning, "Had they (the Sikh chiefs of cis-Sutlej territories) deserted our cause any time before the fall of Delhi, the communications with the Punjab would have been cut off.. These chiefs not only remained staunch, but acted vigorously on our behalf." Those who supported the government at this critical juncture were announced many rewards-monetary, territorial as well as titular. To conciliate these Princes, the Queen in her proclamation assured of the safety of their territories and to respect their rights, dignity and honour. They were given the rights of adopting sons and nominating them as their political heirs. Lord Canning realized both at home and in the Council. Metcalfe assesses that "should British power ever in the future be challenged by a foreign foe, or British resources be drained from India to fight a European war, the support of these princes would be worth more to the Empire than any number of British troops."

The revolt had a serious impact on the Indo-European relations, which caused racial bitterness on both the sides. While the Indians were furious over the British atrocities committed on them, the British could not forget the Indians "behaving like brutes and killing English men, women and children" during the days of the revolt. The Queen had declared that everybody would be granted equal protection of the law and that recruitment to different services and promotions were to be made on the basis of merit, though it was not implemented. The bureaucrats were not willing to treat the Indians on the same footing. Wells, a judge in the Calcutta High Court, explained in the Legislative Council, "It is insulting to place the Europeans on the same level, and subject them to the same regulations as those tainted with the spirit of rebellion.

Between the Indians and the Europeans there could be no equality." The only policy of the British was to increase the respect for the Europeans and to treat the Indians as a subject race. Efforts were made to keep the Indians away from the higher administrative services.

A very serious effect of the revolt was on the Hindu-Muslim relations as well. Though both the communities had actively participated in it, but the Muslims showed more zeal and vigour. The British officers in Agra, Aligarh and Rohilkhand had also reported that the Muslims were "for the most part against us, " while the Hindus remained "almost universally friendly." Similar views were held by the Government of Punjab. On the other hand, the Hindu and the Muslim leaders blamed each other for not extending full cooperation. The British took full advantage of those differences and adopted the policy of divide et imperis. They adopted the strategy of political counterpoises, which continued throughout their rule. All the avenues of progress and enhancement were opened in the Hindu dominated areas, while the Muslims lagged behind in the political, economic and cultural spheres.

The British learnt a lesson from the sepoy mutiny and felt it expedient to do away with the practices originally responsible for it. The Indian soldiers out-numbered their European counterparts by more that 5 times, and some cantonments were held only by the Indians. Consequently, the number of the Europeans was increased to such an extent that they should not be less than half the number of the Indians. Artillery was put strictly under the control of the Europeans. In order to check the possibility of the break-out of any such revolt, the units were divided on communal basis, *e.g.* the Jat regiment, the Sikh regiment, the Gorkha regiment etc. The number of the Brahmans and the Muslims in the army ranks was reduced, while those who had supported the British at this juncture, were recruited in great numbers. Moreover, the sepoys were forbidden to read the Indian newspapers.

Another relatively significant aspect was that the government showed no more interest in the social and religious reforms. It became also very much cautious in extending its support to the Christian missionaries.

The post mutiny period paved the way for the reorganization of the fiscal system. The government's finances were greatly shattered in her efforts to crush the revolt.

Experts in the fiscal affairs were called from England and economic reforms were introduced, which began a new era in Indian economy. Annual budgets, income tax etc. were introduced. Additional taxes, apart from the land-revenue, on the landholders were also introduced.

While free trade policy was adopted for exports on the raw material and tea, the custom duties were reduced on imports. The government undertook the steps to check the expenditures. However, the new commercial policy became highly detrimental to the Indian interest.

Now, the basic aspect of the policy was the economic exploitation by the British as a whole. The Indian trade and industries had already been hampered, and the agriculture ruined. The British now created a wedge among the social classes, appeasing those who could be helpful for the continuance of their rule. The government supported the interests of the landlords and the feudal lords, while divided the peasant by granting certain concessions to the larger peasant farmers, and by enacting laws under which peasant lands could be bought and sold.

The Revolt of 1857 proved to be a turning point in the British rule in India. It was a cumulative result of a number of factors, each having its own importance. The revolt had created a sense of national awakening among the Indians, who in the future raised the banner of independence from the British rule. The revolt had failed in 1857, but it gave many lessons to the Indians to learn from its failure.

The Story of the Storm

Columnist Hamid Hussain looks at the 1857 War of Independence Dispassionately

'If this be the policy it will be working its own ends and purpose... Oudh will become another "Cabul" the scene of our national disgrace, dishonour and bloody massacres. I speak with a warning voice, because I have opportunities of seeing and hearing what the people think of the policy now pursued' Englishman, 16 January 1857 1

1857 is an important landmark in the history of Indian subcontinent. This landmark event has been called mutiny, rebellion, war, uprising and war of independence depending on who described the event. Several different factors were at play long before the rebellion but the sudden outburst of violence and its rapid spread gave the movement a transient unity of purpose despite stark differences and diversity of India. Various individuals and different groups joined the rebellion for different reasons. The presence of so many different factors makes the task of comprehensive analysis of 1857 in any single work impossible. In 1857, different regions of India not only differed in geography and composition of inhabitants but also in terms of local customs, relationship between different communities and political scene. Eighteenth and nineteenth century was an era of dramatic change in India. Old guards were coming down crumbling and new realties sometimes very harsh were being created. Dislocations, social upheaval and anxiety accompanied with such changes was felt everywhere. Gradual decline of old central authority and emergence of a new alien power of East India Company had resulted in resurgence and emergence of religious, caste, ethnic, clan and family feuds to the forefront in many localities.

A large number of writings about the 1857 rebellion started to emerge right during the rebellion. With time the volume of such writings steadily expanded. Almost all the writings are narrative of events. What happened when and who did what? Every author had his own convictions and prejudices which reflected on the historical work. General perceptions of anger, hatred, betrayal and cruelty influenced the people who wrote about the rebellion either immediately or long after the event. Same event was seen with a different perspective thus giving it a different interpretation. It is, therefore, critically important to evaluate each work in proper perspective and not to make a final judgment on the basis of anyone or for that matter several works relating to the events of 1857. It will be futile to explain the complex events of 1857 on the basis of one single concept or theory. Benjamin Disraeli, then member of the Parliament had rightly stated that, 'The rise and fall of empires is not an affair of greased cartridges'. A non-judgmental, non-biased approach to the subject will give one a better appreciation of the scenario. 'The main duty of a historian is not composition of eulogy or invective but interpretation of the complex processes and conflicting ideas in the most objective way'. This article will briefly review the writings of 1857 rebellion and highlight some important areas of the conflict. For detailed description of events, the reader should refer to the excellent narrative work done by different authors.

History of the Historians

Most of the early writings about rebellion were by British who were involved in the historical process. The soldier saw it as the epic of his bravery and valour, the missionary saw the rebellion as a conflict between 'truth and error' and 'displeasure of God on the British' while others saw it as a conspiracy either by Muslims or Hindus or both together. The veterans of these campaigns against the rebels saw themselves as heroes. 'The Mutiny thus furnished an excellent medium for a display of the magnificent and shining exploits of British valour'.

The works of these authors though helpful in terms of particular details of battles, lack the objectivity. It was narration of personal experience which was obviously heavily influenced by the emotions and excitement which is an essential component of any conflict. The writings by the military participants of the conflict are a good source for those who are interested in the military aspect but have very limited value in comprehensive analysis. There was no serious analysis of rebel leadership.

The reason for this is obvious. After all if the brave and self-righteous British were fighting for a just cause, then the rebels were only a bunch of murderous mob led by some blood thirsty, debauch and corrupt leadership. In this view of a British historian there is not much room for any mention of rebel leadership except just few passing comments.

Sir George William Forrest wrote the history of Indian mutiny. He was the director of records of Government of India. His father was Lt. (Later Captain) George Forrest who won Victoria Cross defending the magazine in Delhi. It is quite natural to expect how he would have viewed the events. His father's exploits and valour were to influence his narrative. Several officers who participated in the battles of rebellion wrote their memoirs. Major Norman, Colonel Baird Smith and Colonel Keith Young narrated the events at Delhi. Captain R.P. Anderson and W. Forbes-Mitchell wrote about siege of Lucknow. The civilian British administrators who wrote their version of the events included Edwards (Badaun), Greathed (Delhi), Robertson (Saharanpur), Taylor (Patna), Gubbins (Lucknow) and Sherer (Cawnpur). All these narratives are good in documenting the events of the respective areas.

There are no significant authentic original accounts of the rebellion by the natives. The diaries kept by Mirza Moinuddin Hassan Khan, Munshi Jivanlal and Chunilal give some account of happenings inside Delhi while diary of Nanakchand give some glimpse of events in Kanpur through native eyes. It will be too naive to expect that these natives looking for reward or not to implicate themselves after the British victory would write anything good about the rebels. Moinuddin was a sub-inspector of police in the suburb of Delhi at the time of rebellion. He fled to Persia and returned after two years. He came as he was sure that he would not be punished as he had saved the life of Theophilus Metcalf. At the request of Metcalf, he wrote his experience of the rebellion but gave the manuscript to Metcalf on the condition that it should be published after his death. The apologetic work by Sir Syed Ahmad Khan went at length explaining the benefits of English rule and portraying rebels as a murderous mob and stating that there was no participation by the noble class. The life of Syed Ahmad and his thought process was based on his experience. As a child he had sat in the lap of Major General David Ochterlony, the British resident in Delhi and played with the gold buttons of his uniform. His maternal grandfather, Khwaja Farid-ud-Din, who made an early childhood impression on Syed had served the British in several important assignments. Syed had accepted the permanent status of power of British in India and any attempt to subvert it was seen as a challenge to a legitimate authority. In addition to that, Syed admired Syed Ahmad Saheed, a reformer who died fighting the Sikhs. His Afghan comrades betrayed him. Syed had held Afghans in contempt. In Rohilkhand (including Bijnor and Bareilley), the descendants of Afghans were in the forefront of the rebellion. Syed's work is a rare example of a thorough account of the events in Bijnor and Muradabad as he was the witness and an active participant in the events. He was in Bijnor at the time of rebellion.

In April 1858, he was posted in Muradabad as Principal Sadar-e-Amin. He served a member of the commission appointed to investigate the disposition of properties seized from notables who sided with rebels. It is extremely helpful in knowing the exact details of events in that area but cannot be used for comprehensive analysis due to obvious bias of Syed in favour of British. In early part of twentieth century, India was experiencing the emergence of nationalist ideas. In Bengal a violent campaign against British was in progress. The English educated Bengali intelligentsia which was freshly infected by the European nationalist ideas at the early part of twentieth century went to other extreme and tried to portray the rebellion as a grand show of national struggle by a hypothetical Indian nation against alien rule. In this backdrop, Vinayak Damodar Savarkar published his work on rebellion in 1909. It was titled 'History of the War of Independence'. These works were more like imposing one's own ideological bent on a historical situation. In 1957, government of India sponsored work by Surendranath Gupta titled Eighteen Fifty-Seven reviewed a good portion of literature on rebellion with some favourable comments about rebel leadership.

A recent addition to this catalogue is A.H. Amin's 'The Sepoy Rebellion'. It is an excellent work looking at different aspects of the rebellion in depth and more balanced. His work is free of generalized, rhetorical statements of many later Muslim writers who tried to portray 1857 as a grand show of Muslim martial spirit. He does another fine job of evaluating the effects of the rebellion on the Indo-Pakistan political scene. An area where he is a bit carried away is that he puts a label on the future generations of the natives who participated in the rebellion. From social point of view, it is critical to analyze the background of people who participated in later Indo-Pakistan politics. Ideas do not occur in a vacuum. Our thoughts and actions are moulded by the ideas, actions and experiences of our parents, friends and acquaintances. We are affected by our perceptions of events which are happening around us. Having said that it is also important to evaluate each individual on the basis of his own actions. If someone's father or grandfather committed a crime, his progeny cannot be held responsible for the sins of their forefathers. He should be judged according to his own actions. Surely, Nawabzada Liaqat Ali Khan could be criticized for many of his policies and actions during his political career. Knowing his background will help to understand his thought process but it cannot be used as a broad based broom to beat him up for his acts of omission or commission.

Military Aspect

The company's native army had performed very well for over a century winning large part of India for the company and bringing stability. Company's army was not a static entity but a self-sustained living cosmos which was itself undergoing a significant change. The usual ripples accompanied with these changes were also occurring whether someone was noticing it or not at that time. Overall, there has been a gradual change in the Company's army. The native army which conquered India for the John Company was composed of autonomous regiments. The British officers posted in these regiments were for life. They saw themselves as 'fathers' of the native sepoys. The 'commanders could reward or punish their sepoys with almost complete impunity'. By 1840s, there were significant changes.

The young officers of the company started to distance themselves from the native sepoys. One factor was the arrival of increasing numbers of European women. Earlier British officers lived with native concubines and even married native women. Most British officers were well versed with native languages, knew the cultures of their regiments and mixed with native officers and sepoys. Now the younger generation of officers, both bachelor and married developed their own little white worlds, increasing the gulf between them and their native sepoys. 'The men were badly treated, sworn at, and called "niggers" and "pigs". The annexation of new territories needed new administrators and several military officers were posted to civilian jobs. Officers coveted these civilian jobs as they brought more money, fame, honour and a break from monotonous garrison life. In early 1850s, Colonel Frederick McKesson was civil commissioner of Peshawar while Lieutenant Harry Lumsden was serving as deputy commissioner and Captain James an assistant commissioner. Similarly many officers like Nixon in Bhurutpur and McPherson in Gwalior were serving at civilian posts. Old and infirm officers were left behind to command the regiments. The centralization and reform decreased the authority of officers of the regiment as the list of regulations kept proliferating. Any measure of extra money for sepoys going on far away campaigns advocated by military officers were fought furiously by company bosses in Calcutta. In July 1856, general enlistment order was proclaimed which stated that sepoy would serve anywhere if ordered. This meant that a Hindu might have to cross the dreaded 'Black Waters' at the cost of losing his caste. In early 1857, rumours were rife among native sepoys in many cantonments. The sepoys of 2nd Bengal Native Infantry (BNI) told their Colonel that there were unmistakable signs that the company was bent on destroying the religion of the natives. They pointed to contamination of salt, ghee and sugar of its sepoys with the bones of pigs and cows. Hindu soldiers interpreted the reddish colour of the salt from the dye of the sack as cow's blood.

A.H. Amin has discussed in some detail the perception of company's military effectives by the native sepoys. We with the benefit of command of different languages and historical hindsight can see these things more clearly but the perception of sepoys in 1857 needs a more careful evaluation. Surely, the setbacks of company's army in late eighteenth and early nineteenth century would have affected the perception of native participants of these battles. The overall impact about half a century later on a new generation of native soldiers, mostly illiterate and with no means of information or communications with other parts of the country would have a limited impact. Even the more recent campaigns against the Sikhs were viewed in the light of overall victory of British arms and sepoys were not in a position to do a critical analysis of the setbacks in individual battles. More important is the fact that the scenes which they witnessed after the start of rebellion had a more pronounced effect on the sepoys. Murder of British officers, refuge of civil and military officers in entrenchments and general breakdown of law and order in affected areas would be a more powerful signal to the wavering native troops that the company's rule was about to end. Having said that, it is also true that at least there was dent in the aura of invincibility of the British arms with defeat in First Afghan War and setbacks against Sikhs. More important than the military setbacks in Afghanistan was the psychological trauma of sepoys. Subedar Hidayat Ali, a third generation of loyal sepoy of the company wrote in 1858 to his British superiors about the troubles of sepoys during Afghanistan campaign. Hindu sepoys were fearful of losing their caste. Their colleagues refused to smoke or dine with them as they were considered outcasts.

Although in later part of rebellion there was general disaffection in most regiments of Bengal army but in the early part of the rebellion, the regiments which started the mutiny in their stations need to be carefully studied. They had particular historical background and specific immediate causes of unrest. Only A.H. Amin has looked into this aspect in some cases. The 3rd Cavalry which started the rebellion in Meerut had run into problems in September 1855 when stationed at Bolarum near Hyderabad.

During Muharram, Colonel Mackenzie had issued a cantonment order of prohibiting noisy procession at midnight. After realizing that it was Muharram, the order was cancelled. The procession in which several cavalrymen participated proceeded along the route and in front of Colonel Mackenzie's house there was a heated conversation between Colonel and some participants of the procession. Later, there was an attempt on Colonel Mackenzie's life. Some cavalrymen later told Colonel Carpenter that they were loyal to the government but their religion has been insulted. In an inquiry all native commissioned officers of 3rd Cavalry were with two exceptions dismissed. The 2nd Native Cavalry stationed at Kanpur had an interesting history.

It was raised in 1787 and had fought bravely in various campaigns. In 1840, two companies of the regiment fled when confronted by a small body of Afghan horsemen. The exact cause was never established. One possibility is the origin of troopers of the regiment which were mainly Afghans of Qandahar origin who had settled in Lucknow and they may not wanted to confront their ethnic kin though separated by a time span of sixty years. The outraged commander disbanded the whole regiment and all European officers were transferred to 11th Native Cavalry. In 1850, one of the old officers captured the Sikh standard in Multan. Impressed by this feat of bravery, the Company restored the old number of 2nd Cavalry. Nana Sahib's commander of the guard, Jawala Prasad worked on the disgruntled Risaldar Teeka Singh and won him and his house in the lines became the centre for all disaffected sowars. The 56th BNI at Banda was involved in operations against Santals in 1855-56.

The operations against Santals were different than earlier campaigns against many local armies. This was a scorched earth policy in which sepoys burned villages and hanged Santals. It was more a counter-insurgency operation rather than the romantic headlong charges on enemy forces. This gave the sepoys their first encounter in suppressing civilian population on a large scale. The wife of Captain William Halliday of 56th BNI had Bible printed in Urdu and Nagri and distributed among the sepoys convincing them that the British were there to convert them to Christianity. 10th Native Infantry stationed in Fatehgarh which rebelled had officers like Major William Lindsay who had spent most of his career as a staff officer with little interaction with his sepoys. It was commanded by a mediocre sixty years old Lt. Colonel George Smith who had served most of his life in 47th BNI and had taken charge of 10th at Fatehgurh. He had seen his last action in the battlefield about thirty-eight years ago. The sepoys did not know him. His second-in-command was fifty one year old Captain Robert Munro who had managed to serve in the Indian army for thirty years without ever fighting a battle.

The 10th BNI also had a peculiar experience. This regiment had served in Burma travelling in ships. Brahmins called the sea, 'Black Water' and believed that they will lose their caste by crossing the sea. The regiment had agreed when their officers had promised rewards which never came. Locals jeered the regiment as Christian Regiment. The local scene was spiced by the affair of pensioned Nawab with the wife of an ensign Reginald Byrne. The ensign when seeing his wife with Nawab, had kicked him out of the door. The 19th and 34th Bengal Native Infantry were at Lucknow at the time of annexation of Oudh. It was quite natural that sepoys were affected by the general discontent which was aroused with the annexation.

In February 1857 both these regiments were in Barrackpore. When 19th BNI came to know about new cartridges, they refused. The Colonel confronted them angrily with artillery and cavalry on the parade ground but then accepted their demand to withdraw the artillery and cancel next morning parade. On March 29, Mangal Pandey of 34th BNI (the regiment was thoroughly disaffected due to the zealous Christian preaching by its commandant Colonel Wheler) shot at two British but when the General John Hearsey (an officer of old school) came himself thundering on the parade ground alone, Mangal turned his musket to himself and wounded himself in chest. Two days later, when 19th BNI was being disbanded, the sepoys were weeping in front of Hearsey and blessing him for his mercy. Lt. Colonel George Smith who was not popular among the officers and men commanded the 3rd Cavalry which rebelled at Meerut. When the condemned sepoys were marched off to jail, they threw their boots at Lt. Colonel Smith. Quite a contrast to how the disbanded sepoys behaved to General Hearsey.

Several regimental officers who had spent long years with their sepoys trusted fully their native sepoys. Colonel Thomas Pierce of 6th Light Cavalry stationed at Nasirabad sent his eight-month pregnant wife to sleep in the quarters of native officers families. His sowars had a bloody skirmish with the rebellious 15th Bengal Native Infantry. Later they switched sides but didn't harm their officers. Colonel Wart had vowed that if his regiment mutinies it may walk over his body, but he will never leave it. 47th BNI at Mirzapur remained loyal as it was commanded by a wise old Colonel David Pott greatly respected by his men. Colonel George Sherer of 73rd BNI stationed at Jalpaiguri was of the view that disarming native regiments was counterproductive. He never even carried any personal weapon with him while with his troops in line Patrick Grant of Madras Army had avoided the problem of greased cartridges by allowing his soldiers to lubricate their cartridges with Ghee, clarified butter rather than animal fat. 31st

BNI at Saugor remained staunchly loyal, without any support from British soldiers, under their own native officers they chased and defeated the mutinous 42nd BNI and captured their colours and arms.

The Ist and 3rd Cavalry and 2nd Infantry were stationed in Aurangabad. These regiments were composed mainly of Muslims. In late June 1857, when the troops came to know that they might be part of the force of General Woodburn to advance on Delhi, there was disaffection among the Ist Cavalry. The prompt arrival of Woodburn, disarming of small number of mutineers and escape of one troop stabilized the situation.

The troops remained loyal to British and 3rd Cavalry under Captain Orr fought well against Holkar's troops. Many native officers like Risaldar Major Bhawani Singh of Ist Cavalry, Jemadar Khoda Buksh of 56th BNI remained loyal even when their regiments mutinied. Sebedar Ram Bukhsh begged to be allowed to join the garrison at the entrenchment of Cawnpur but was not allowed. He tried to carry the regimental record in a cart to safety but was looted by a band of peasants. 53rd and 56th BNI at Cawnpur were steadfast. They were repeatedly taunted, abused and threatened by the rebel troopers of Ist Cavalry and even then only part of the regiments joined the rebels.

In fact several sepoys of 53rd assembled on parade ground with their arms to help British officer quell the mutiny but by now General Wheeler was not sure himself and he ordered artillery fire on the sepoys thus assuring their desertion. Similarly, in Benaras when native regiments were being disarmed, Ludhiana Regiment (consisting of Sikhs) mistakenly thought that they were also being disarmed and rebelled.

After the uprising at Meerut, the situation for British became very difficult. In fact, the very instrument of disarming of native regiments to prevent the rebellion became the main immediate cause of outright mutiny by native soldiers. The attempts at disarming and dismounting of native regiments caused panic and panic quickly escalated to revolt. Whenever disarming was attempted, the sepoys thought they have lost the confidence of the British and European troops will mow them down without any qualm.

The British officers and men fought with a determination and passion as they were defending their own homeland. This is the reason that even today, it is considered a glorious chapter of British military history. In the later part of rebel operations, as the atrocities on women and children by the rebels were known, revenge became the force multiplier. In many battles of the rebellion, 'interior impulses, largely vindictive, made the British fight with a demonic energy and contempt for the odds which were often stacked against them'. The British won the day due to the presence of dare-devil young officers who led from the front. In several instances brave officers were able to weld the wavering sepoys together and prevent the mutiny.

One such officer was Captain Edmund Vibart of 2nd Native Cavalry. In May 1857, he was passing through Fatehgurh to Naini Tal. When the riot in prison started, the sepoy guard just watched. Captain Vibart was hit on his face by a brick. The enraged, bleeding Vibart ordered the sepoys to charge on the prison. The sepoys fired, killing several prisoners and chased remaining into their cells. One gallant officer by his action was able to rally wavering sepoys which even didn't belong to his regiment. In Delhi, it was the tenacity of Richard Baird-Smith which prevented the timid General Wilson to retreat from the ridge. Officers like Hodson, Nicholson and Collin Cambell saved the day for the British.

It is very difficult to assess and analyze why in one place the sepoy rebelled while in another place he remained staunchly loyal. What factors influenced him in the critical hour of making that decision of dishonour his oath and colours. One cannot generalize the motives of all the sepoys. The colonel of 47th BNI devised an ingenious plan telling his men to loan their pay to locals at high interest rates. The sepoys wanted no part of any anarchy as they will lose high income. Maharajah Jaiiji Rao Scindia of Gwalior sided with British. He only financed his contingent which consisted of sepoys who were recruited on the pattern of Bengal Army.

The sepoys mutinied on June 14 but never marched to Delhi. While A.H. Amin attributes this to clever propaganda by the Maharajah but more important factor was the fact that Maharajah continued to pay their salaries, so they had a more convincing reason to stay at Gwalior. In the early part of the rebellion, most of the rebel sepoys and their leaders fought bravely and with tenacity. As the sieges prolonged, the inner conflicts emerged and initial euphoria dissipated, the sepoys started to waver. In Delhi, due to the laxity of discipline and avoidance of many sepoys to fight, Bakht Khan issued an order that no man who left in the morning to fight could return within the walls until 4 p.m. He also decreed that no man would qualify for the day's pay until he had done battle with British. Several sepoys quietly left for their homes. 17th BNI at Azamgarh, after mutiny plundered the treasury. When they reached Faizabad, they were relieved of their loot by the rebels from Jaunpur and Benaras. The rebels out of control were a larger threat than the British. The rapid deterioration of discipline among sepoys dismayed many. In Oudh, Subedar Teeka Singh of 2nd Cavalry became general while Jemadar Durga Singh of 53rd BNI became colonel. His angry Muslim troopers who accused him of amassing private wealth summarily arrested the newly promoted General Teeka Singh. One aspect of the rebellion which has not been studied and discussed in detail is the murder of British officers and their families.

As it is now clear that there was not a large scale general conspiracy to overthrow Company's rule. Most rebellions in garrisons were local affairs prompted by local causes or excitement generated by the news of successes of rebels in other areas. Even in one regiment, there was not a unanimous decision of all sepoys to mutiny. Many sepoys did not condone the behaviour of the rebel comrades but were caught in the eye of the storm. The ringleaders of the rebellion aware of this clear and present danger probably executed officers and their families as a first act to make sure that there was no going back. This act assured that all sepoys who may not be agreeing with the plans of the rebels have now to throw their lot as after the murder of the officers it was clear to everyone that there will be no pardon or mercy.

In several places British officers were shot or cut to pieces on parade grounds or in their homes. Ironically, the same was to be done more than a century later in East Pakistan (now Bangladesh). East Bengal Regiments which mutinied in 1971, took a page from the history of 1857 rebellion. Although there was a general resentment among the Bengali sepoys but it was the action of junior Bengali officer to execute West Pakistani senior officers in front of the sepoys to assure mutiny of the whole regiment. In Jhansi, 12th BNI and 14th Irregular Cavalry was stationed. On June 5, 1857, only one company of 12th led by one native sergeant marched to Star Fort and became rebellious. The remaining four companies of 12th and 14th Cavalry remained loyal and on parade professed their loyalty and were angry at the conduct of rebellious company.

It was after the murder of commander of the troops, Captain Dunlop that the remaining sepoys joined the rebels. Other officers like Ensign Taylor, Lt. Turnbull and Sergeant Major Newton were killed in the early part of the rebellion. The remaining garrison along with women and children was put to sword by the orders of the Risaldar. Similarly the detachment of 12th BNI at Naogaon commanded by Major Kirk, volunteered to serve against the rebels. A portion of them rebelled after the news of murder of whole garrison of Jhansi arrived in Naogaon.

Only A.H. Amin has discussed in detail the role of Enfield rifle in the conflict and its impact on the results of war. There is no doubt that superior weapons are a key factor in the outcome of wars but the issue has to be evaluated more carefully. In early nineteenth century, the romance of all armies including India army 'lay in its assaults: glorious, audacious, headlong rushes on the enemy' all despite their effectiveness against assault disdained trenches and foxholes. Whenever this technique was used such as by Wheeler's entrenchment in Cawnpur and by rebels in Lucknow, it was successful. Enfield played a significant role but not in all battles of the rebellion. His statement that, 'it was above all the "Enfield" Rifle which was the real victor of 1857'30 seems to be a very general and we need to look more carefully at the role of Enfield.

The effectiveness of Enfield played a significant role in some battles of the mutiny like the battle of Trimu Ghat on July 12 31 and also in the battle of Fatehgurh. Enfield rifle was issued to only British troops and according to Amin in 1857 there were only eight infantry and two cavalry regiments and thirteen batteries of artillery consisting of British troops. No native troops loyal to British and irregular cavalry was issued Enfield. In addition, even the British soldiers were not well acquainted with the new rifle. Havelock left about three thousand Enfield rifles in Allahabad as his soldiers were not accustomed to these rifles. In addition, in the early models of Enfield, bullets jammed so tightly the armourers were forced to bore them out. The high numbers on back sights were taken to indicate velocity instead of range. The result was an elevation that made fire ineffective. In many fiercely fought battles like the ones for capture of Delhi, and many strongholds of Lucknow (Kaiserbagh, Sikandarbagh and Shah Najaf) were frontal charges. Bayonets and close range fighting played a more significant role in these battles. Small fortifications in the cities, blocked streets and loophole walls and houses were taken from rebels by close fight.

At the onset of rebellion at one garrison showed some organization and discipline but it quickly dissipated. Mutiny, confusion, looting, murder and further confusion were a sequence which was tragically repeated in almost all areas with few exceptions. Even in one location there was no unified and organized effort by rebels to plan their actions. In Delhi, the troops, princes, court and commander-in-chief were all collecting funds from the people independently from one another. Only in areas, where a strong leader was able to exert some influence did an organized effort emerge but that was also transient. There were too many mutually exclusive sometimes hostile forces were at play in the rebel camp to allow for a large scale centralized effort against more organized British forces.

Social Aspect

The rebellion has to carefully evaluate as any generalization would lead to wrong conclusions. Overall, the rebellion did not have a clearly defined course and it differed markedly from region to region. Various overlapping factors were at play at same time thus making the task of well organized analysis very difficult. India of 1857 was not one country in modern sense but a collection of various areas inhabited by diverse groups. The rebellion was limited to certain areas and a large segment of the population remained loyal. A.H. Amin had discussed very eloquently this diversity and the reasons for rebellion or loyalty of various groups. As in any conflict, socio-economic factors play an important role but it is important to see them in proper perspective. Some authors have treated the subject appropriately while others have gone to the extreme to portray the whole event as an economic struggle launched by peasants on Marxist lines which is not true.

The rebellion was essentially by the previously dominant classes in the North-Western Provinces (North Western provinces consisted of eight divisions—Meerut, Delhi, Agra, Rohilkhand, Jhansi, Jabalpur, Allahabad and Banaras. Not to be confused with North West Frontier Province which was separated from Punjab in 1901), including both Hindus and Muslims. There is no doubt that a large number of people of India had grievances against the company government. In the early part of rebellion, many preferred to wait and watch rather than throw their lot with one side or another. They expected an aggressive and overwhelming response from the company army. The fact that 'the government had been caught off balance with its military resources stretched to breaking point', resulted in a slow or no response thus encouraging many to side with the rebels thinking that the company rule is coming to an end. This explains the second wave of mutinies in Lucknow, Cawnpur and Azamgurh, which occurred almost one month later than the Meerut uprising.

Several legislative measures of the company challenging centuries old traditions caused many apprehensions. Sutte (burning of widows on the pyres of their husbands) was abolished in 1829. James Ramsay, the 10th Earl of Dilhousie became Governor-General of India in 1847 and embarked on ambitious administrative reforms which will shake the foundations of centuries old customs of the ancient land. The thirty five years old workaholic Dilhousie reformed almost every aspect of the Company's rule in India. Several measures taken by the British in annexed areas raised the caste and religious feelings. These measures roused the suspicions of Hindus and Muslims alike. New legislative measures in 1856, allowing Hindu widows to re-marry raised Hindu suspicions. Enaction of laws allowing converts to inherit property caused doubts in both Hindu and Muslim minds. In early nineteenth century there was increasing missionary activity in India which was seen as an organized attempt of an alien group to let the natives stray away from their religions. British attempts to discourage early marriages and joint messing of convicts in jails and compulsory shaving were seen as intrusion into the traditional ways and an attempt of proselytizing. In 1855, Mr. Edmond issued a circular letter from Calcutta stating that in railway train no caste distinction will be made in the seating arrangements. Even in military, sepoys resented the efforts of some officers with missionary zeal.

These religious activities of Lt. Colonel G.S. Wheler of 34th BNI in Barrackpore and Major Mackenzie in Bolarum were directly responsible for the disaffection among the sepoys. The famous Mangal Pandey who fired at his officers on March 29 was from 34th BNI. In 1837, Persian was abolished as a language of the court thus making a large number of Muslims unemployed in Bengal. English magistrates replaced Muslims who were attached to courts as Qazis, Muftis. In Bengal, even under Muslim rulers, Hindus were employed as revenue officers. Hindus going ahead in education retained the jobs in newly anglicized revenue system. In early part of nineteenth century, the law barring appointment of any Indian to a post carrying an annual salary of 500 sterling pounds effectively curtailed any future prospects of a native under new government.

It should be remembered that east India Company was a commercial entity with the primary objective of increasing its revenue. Social and political fallout from their decisions and long-term negative effects were a low priority on the minds of the agents of the company. The annexation of Oudh in 1856 was the single act which thoroughly alienated almost all classes of that region, including rulers of native states, landed aristocracy, courtiers, sepoys and peasants. In north western provinces, British adopted the policy of not resuming the Jagirs after the death of the holder to its descendants. Instead, they gave the heirs fixed pension. From 1847 to 1856, the company in this way acquired Nagpur, Jhansi, Satara and Sambalpur.

In Bengal and northern India, landholders became fearful of their future under British. Similarly, the revenue free land holders in Bengal and North-Western Provinces came under scrutiny as the company wanted to increase its revenue base. In North Western Provinces a large number of resumptions of revenue-free lands occurred between 1850 and 1856, causing a surge of anti-government sentiment. In contrast, in Sindh, Napier made the landlords as the aristocracy of the land thus attaching their interest with the British, hence no unrest in Sindh during 1857. Talukdar (owners of large groups of villages) were powerful feudal barons and a recognized institution of nineteenth century Central India. They have been the intermediaries between the rulers and village proprietors for centuries. The land policies of British in North Western province removed the intermediary Talukdars. In Rohilkhand (This division consisted of Bareilly, Badaun, Bijnor, Muradabad and Shahjahanpur), many landed elites were Muslims. The new revenue policy disposed many of them. This powerful lot of landed aristocracy became hostile to British and British would pay with blood for this nearly fatal mistake.

The new set of village landowners though removed from the rapaciousness of the talukdars had their own grievances. The mix of specific complaints about revenue and taxes, cumbersome and lengthy new British judicial system and sharing of general anxieties of the public at large resulted in such an equation that the potential beneficiaries of new British policies ended up rallying around the old guard of landed elite. British courts gave legal protection to the money lenders (Mahajans) who were able to acquire landed interests which were confiscated. This was one of the reasons that everywhere, the rebels burned government revenue records, account books of money lenders and destroyed their property. In contrast to Delhi, where soldiers were in the forefront of resistance, in Lucknow it was the levies of talukdars rather than regular sepoys who gave the British tough fight. In 1852, an act was passed for scrutiny of rent-free tenures.

The tribunal called Inam Commission aggressively went after rent-free tenures. From 1852-57, in Southern Marhatta country alone about 35 thousand estates were called for and in 21 thousand cases sentences of confiscation were pronounced. In Bengal similar measures brought extra income of 5, 000, 000 sterling pounds per year while in Bombay it was 370, 000 sterling pounds per year. After the annexation of Oudh in 1856, a vigorous settlement policy was pursued which resulted in enormous social upheaval. In Cawnpur area, boats between Calcutta and Cawnpur transported most of goods. These boats were owned and operated by Hindus living in the vicinity of Sati Chowra Ghat. Their fortunes had been declining with the arrival of British as British-owned steamers, railways and Grand Trunk Road were taking away all their business. The middle of nineteenth century saw the end of the era of military adventurers, most of who were Muslims from northern India. After the Marhatta and Pindari wars, although good number of soldiers was enlisted in the Company army but still a large number became unemployed. In 1854, the number of these angry out of job soldiers was estimated to be 100, 000 in Rohilkhand and surrounding areas. When Wajid Ali Shah was deposed in February 1856, 200, 000 strong royal army was dispersed. Apart from soldiers, many others who depended on the army such as 12, 000 armourers became jobless. Later government ordered talukdars to dismiss their armed retainers thus resulting in swelling of number of unemployed who gradually drifted to large cities. These disgruntled ex-soldiers were now scattered all over Oudh.

Adding insult to injury, British dropped any pretense of respect to previous ruling class. In 1803, Shah Alam was a British pensioner with eleven and a half lakh rupees and ruling powers limited to the Red Fort area. This was a fact but for illiterate native, the King in Delhi still represented a mythical past of glory. Senior officers of East India Company omitted gradually all normal courtesies to a king. In 1844, nazar to King was abolished. In fact, in 1851, Bahadur Shah Zafar was receiving 833 rupees per month in lieu of his nazars. In 1820s, Heber wrote about the possibility of Muslims rising against the British but the reasons he argued will be political and not religious. One of the reasons which he mentioned was 'the conduct of Lord Hastings to the old emperor of Delhi'. The jewels of family of raja of Nagpur were sold in an auction in Calcutta. After annexation of Oudh, chief Commissioner used Umbrella Palace as stable for his horses. Similar measures at local levels in dealings with local elites caused resentment.

The role of Hindus and Muslims and their relationship with each other was also a complex phenomenon and varied from region to region. Hindus mostly led the civil risings in Oudh, Bihar, Gorakhpur and Central India. Many leaders of the uprising such as Nana Sahib, Tantia Topi and Rani of Jhansi were Hindus. After the rebellion was suppressed, land from Hindus was confiscated in large scale in Meerut, Jhansi, Etawa, Jabalpur which were the centres of Hindu dissatisfaction. In Patna and Bijnor, Muslims helped British to regain the control. In Rohilkhand,

Fatehpur and Bulandshahar, the sites of Muslim discontent, confiscations were predominantly Muslim. Nawabs of Karnal, Muradabad, Dacca and Rampur and Nizam of Hyderabad remained loyal to British. Some confiscated land was awarded to the loyal subjects, both Hindu and Muslim and remainder auctioned off.

The relationships between Hindus and Muslims during the rebellion were complex and depended on local scene and the conduct of the local rebel leaders. In Rohilkhand, the rebels were almost exclusively Muslims (In Bijnor their leader was Nawab of Najibabad, Muhammad Khan and in Bareilly Khan Bahadur Khan). The rebels raised the green flag and used religious symbols. When the rebels robbed rich Hindu merchants and bankers, the cleavage lines between two communities widened. The worsening law and order situation in the area with bands of marauding gangs of Gujars, Maiwatis, Jats, Chauhans and Banjaras creating havoc culminated in a sanguine battle between Hindus and Muslims at Haldaur on September 18.44 In Malawa, Firuz Shah headed the rebellion.

The religious zeal attracted many Muslim tribes but alienated Hindus. In Cawnpur, the leadership by Nana Sahib roused the suspicion of influential Muslims. Initially, he arrested Nunne Nawab, an influential Muslim noble of Lucknow who had settled in Cawnpur. Later, under pressure, Nunne Nawab was not also released but made commander of a section of the force with artillery batteries. A crisis situation occurred when two Muslim butchers convicted of killing a cow died from bleeding when their hands were amputated. The sowars of 2nd Cavalry along with a large Muslim crowd confronted Nana and threatened to displace him. The showdown between Hindus and Muslims was averted by an apology from Nana and hectic efforts by his Muslim counsel, Azeemullah. Ironically, the last rebel stand against British was by a former government lawyer, a Hindu chief Ramnarayan at a place named Islamnagar.

The British rule in Punjab and Frontier had effectively ended the anarchy in Punjab and north western borders of India. The populace in general especially Muslims saw British rule as benign and peaceful. That is why, Muslims of these areas sided with

British in 1857. Sikhs, Pathans and Muslims from Punjab rushed to India to fight side by side with British. The famous march of Guides from Mardan to Delhi is now a legend. William Hodson commanded a regiment of irregular horse of 300 Punjabi and Pathan troopers who were known as 'Plungers'. In areas, where the general population sentiment was not hostile to the British, the regiments which rebelled didn't succeed to damage the British. This was the case in Ferozpur, Ambala, Layyah, Mianwali and Peshawar. Ironically, the revolt of 1857 which is seen as a first organized attempt against colonial hegemony, 'established the Punjab as the bastion of colonialism and strengthened the basis of an authoritarian structure'. The results were far reaching as 'political institutions in the Punjab lagged behind their counterparts in the rest of the subcontinent'.

Native Players

Several authors had written a lot about the motives of different leaders of the rebellion. The opinion ranges from 'hatred' to 'some supreme national cause'. As related to other aspects of the rebellion any generalization in this particular area will lead to wrong conclusions. A. H. Amin had discussed this subject more rationally without much rhetoric but he seems to distribute the titles of 'patriot' and 'opportunist' a bit more casually. Each individual local leader of the rebellion had his or her particular reasons for joining the revolt. This was equally applicable to various groups who sided with the rebels. 'The sepoys fighting for fear of castes, the chiefs for their kingdoms, the landlords for their estates, the mass for fear of conversion and agrarian grievances, and the Muslims especially for restoring their old sway, yet all in their own way against the common enemy, the English'. Several tribal communities (Gujar, Jats, Palwars, Bhogtas, Maiwatis) joined simply due to the ample opportunity of plunder in a situation of a general breakdown of law and order.

India of 1857 was not a nation state in modern sense but a collection of various groups with autonomous local chiefs. Rebellion provided to many ambitious men an opportunity to act on their dreams of grandeur. Many rebel leaders invoked the name of old Mughal king of Delhi, but 'that was a pseudolegalistic ploy more than a real act of loyalty'. It is clear from several writings of British and natives that even the rebel sepoys in Delhi actually in contact with the king did not show any respect and talked to him rudely. They probably knew the real worth of the opium addicted statue of a dying era. Petty leaders set themselves up as rajas and even kings.

In Banawar, Qalandar Khan set himself as raja while Kadam Singh of Prachitgarh proclaimed himself king. Umrao Singh declared himself a raja after getting hold of one village of Manakpur while Fatua of Buddhakheri proclaimed himself king of the Gujars. Rao Bhopal Singh at the head of his Chauhan followers declared a Rajput government but poor fellow was surprised at his place and promptly executed. Others like rajas of Kutra and Mainpuri, Apa Sahib, Shahamal and his grandson Lujjram (Jat) of Baraut, Narpat Singh (Rajput) of Akulpur enjoyed the power and fame for few months.

We will probably never know the real motive of a particular local chief to join the rebels or British. Probably several factors may be at play in each case when the critical hour of decision came to choose one's bet. Most of local chiefs which sided with rebels were in the vicinity of Delhi. Abdurrahman of Jhajjar, Hassan Ali Khan of Dojana, Nahar Singh of Ballabgarh, Tularam of Rewari, Walidad Khan of Malagarh and Ahmad Ali Khan of Farrukh Nagar. The Rajput chiefs of Jaipur, Bikanir and Alwar were not much interested in re-surrecting the decaying Mughal rule. The political rivals of local chiefs who sided with British decided to take a chance and sided with rebels. The Maharajah of Jodhpur, Takht Singh sided with British offering his troops. His rival Thakur Kushai Singh worked on Jodhpur Legion which deserted to the mutineers. Mohammad Hassan took control of Gorakhpur rallying disgruntled landed elites although he had no mutinous troops. He was the former governor of Gorakhpur and had lost his position after the annexation of Oudh. Similarly, the Chief of Nargund, Baba Sahib in Southern Marhatta country, who was denied the right of adoption declared war in May 1858 when British were re-asserting themselves after initial setbacks. It was mainly civil uprising as no mutinous troops were involved in the conflict.

In Rohilkhand, Mahmud Khan of Najibabad waited till all areas including Bareilly, Muradabad, Mandawar had rebelled and almost all British officers were killed or had fled to safety. Seeing the changed winds, many locals gathered around Mahmud Khan as he seemed to be poised to take control of the area. When Mahmud arrived in Bijnor on June 7, he had about 200-250 Pathan musketeers with him.

There is no detailed account of the exploits of several local leaders of the rebellion like Mehdi Hassan of Sultanpur, Fazal Azim of Rae Bareli, Banda Hussain a Lt. of Mehdi Hassan, Rao Sahib, Moulvi Sarfaraz Ali of Gorakhpur, Moulvi Sikander Shah of Faizabad, Ghaus Mohammad Khan of Sikandra Rao and Kunwar Singh.

Tantia Topi though with no military experience, learned the art of war on the field. Tantia was six years older than Nana Sahib and his playmate. He arranged for the defence of Bithur, the toughest challenge to Havelock's force. He repelled Windham's assault on Cawnpur. He later made unsuccessful attempt to relieve the siege of Jhansi. Even after the setbacks, he was one of the few who appreciated the opponent's weakness. This resulted in a fast moving guerrilla warfare in Nagpur and Gwalior in the summer of 1858. Unfortunately, this 'display of tactical brilliance was too late to influence the outcome of a war which had already been decided by British victories at Delhi and Oudh'. He was betrayed by Raja of Nawar (Raja rebelled against British but when the pendulum swung in their favour, he betrayed Tantia to re-habilitate himself) and hanged.

Nana Sahib was born as Govind Dhondu Pant and was the adopted son of Peshwa Baji Rao. When Baji Rao died in 1851, the company according to an earlier ruling of not recognizing the adopted sons of a deceased ruler stopped Baji Rao's pension. Nana Sahib was deprived of not only his pension but also hollow titles, his seal and yearly allocation of even blank cartridges for his guards. Next few years Nana kept sending petitions to the Company for resumption of his pension while entertaining British officers at his palace in Bithur without any success. The ideas of Azimullah Khan to attempt to recover his throne and predictions of his guru, Dassa Bawa that one day he will be victorious and his own dreams of grandeur may have effected him to take a bold course of siding with the rebels.

Azimullah Khan was another figure which appeared on the scene of rebellion and had a very interesting background. During the famine of 1837, as a starving boy along with his mother, he was given shelter at the mission at Cawnpur. He attended the free school and became fluent in English and French. After working with several Englishmen, he was hired as translator by Brigadier John Scott. After the death of Baji Rao, he was in the court of Nana Sahib. When Nana chose Azimullah to go to England to plead his case, a search started for an experience guide to accompany him. An educated Rohilkhand noble Muhammad Ali Khan had visited England in the employ of King of Nepal. Muhammd Ali had no love for the British. He was a bright young man and passed the Calcutta Civil Service examinations with flying colours.

Being a native, he was hired as a foreman where his arrogant superior insulted and humiliated him. He resigned the service in 1851 and ended up accompanying King of Nepal on a three month tour of England. In England, the intelligent Azimullah dressed in western outfit impressed many luminaries of the time. He met John Stuart Mill and the wife of Prime Minister's cousin who was gentleman Usher to the Queen, Lucie Gordon. He met Dickens, Carlyle, Macaulay, Tennyson and Thackery and had seen the Queen. He was probably the only Indian of his time who with the intelligence and the opportunity to visit the land of his masters was able to evaluate British. The awe of the British which was maintained in India was to be shaken. The splendid city of London was actually smothered with industrial smoke. He was unable to convince the authorities to resume his master's pension but on his journey back, he stopped in Constantinople and visited the battlefield of Crimea and brought with him a French printing press. Although his mission failed but he had come back with a more dangerous idea. He presented a more ambitious agenda for Nana, telling him 'why worry about his measly stipend when he might annihilate the English and recover his throne?'

The former dancing girl and later the Queen Hazrat Mahal's behaviour was more praiseworthy than her debauch husband, Wajid Ali Shah. Wajid when told about his exile was 'weeping, pleading, baring his head to the appalled and embarrassed Colonel Outram. On the contrary, in November when a shell hit the palace gate, the garrison panicked and soldiers fled away. The indomitable

Hazrat Mahal remained staunch and when told chiefs to cut her head before running away, they stayed feeling the shame and humiliation. On another occasion, she sent a pair of women's trousers to a faint-hearted chief with a note stating that better he should put them on and to retire to his proper place — a harem. She spent 50, 000 sterling pounds of her own money to build a wall around the city. She had the rare leadership qualities to gain the confidence of both Hindus and Muslims. She was able to prevent the division between two communities due to the activities of religious zealots like Moulvi Massih-us-Zaman and Babar Ali. In this effort, she was helped by Moulvi Ahmadullah Shah, who not only worked for cooperation between Hindus and Muslims but between Shias and Sunnis of Lucknow. She was able to rally the soldiers, landed nobility and city population to her cause. In middle of 1859, when the rebel cause seemed to be doomed, Hazarat Mahal and her two staunch Hindu allies, Beni Mado and Hanumant Singh refused to surrender to British.

Lakshmibai, the Rani of Jhansi's role is somewhat controversial. Although she along with several local chiefs had grievances against British, it has not been proven that she had any role in the mutiny of 12th BNI and 13th Irregular cavalry stationed at Jhansi on June 5th. She had to pay ransom to the rebels before they left Jhansi. In fact on June 12 and 14, she wrote letters to Erskine, the commissioner of Sagar division assuring him that she would hold Jhansi on behalf of the British. Erskine in a formal letter authorized her to collect the revenue.

She led her troops against the Dewan of Orchha, an old rival. This suggests that in the early part of the rebellion when she was quite vulnerable to both British and rival chieftain's attack, she favoured siding with British but later the ambiguous British diplomacy and declining of her protestations of loyalty that she decided to fight the British. She personally commanded the defence of Jhansi working with the defenders who consisted of mutineers, levies and mercenaries. She not only showed her superior administrative and military skills but also personal bravery in combat. She only trusted the five hundred Kabuli Pathans of her army, who escorted her after her defeat at Jhansi. She earned the respect and praise of even her enemies when she died on the battlefield at Gwalior.

In Bareilly, the garrison rebelled on May 31, 1857. After the routine of initial confusion, disorder, looting and killing, Khan Bahadar Khan was proclaimed leader. He was the grandson of a revered Rohilla chief. Interestingly, the army in and around Bareilly was the largest, about 57 regiments with gunners and sappers. Despite that there does not seem to be a close cooperation among military and civil leadership of the rebellion to take advantage of this huge difference in balance of power. There were tensions between the civil leader Khan Bahadar and military leader Bakht Khan. Bakht Khan was smart and had taken control of the Bareilly treasury. He calculated his odds and with the treasury and the strength of a brigade under his command, he had a better chance at Delhi. Once in Delhi, with both the money and sepoys, the confidant Bakht Khan approached Bahadur Shah Zafar and asked the old king to appoint him commander-in-chief which the king obliged. Unfortunately, in Delhi, he found his nemesis. The commander of Nimach rebels, Muhammad Ghaus Khan became his bitter rival thus preventing a unified stand of the rebels.

Conclusion

1857 was the watershed in the history of subcontinent. It was such a confusing catalogue of events that to decipher them individually would be an impossible task. On one hand, the rebels were destroying everything attached to the British rule like bungalows, telegraph, official records while on the other the rebel troops fought in their red uniforms under their regimental colours, kept their muster roll update and wore the medals awarded by British. In one instance at Cawnpur, Havelock encountered a rebel unit whose band was playing Auld Lang Syne. The immediate effect after the rebellion was the change of colonial thought process. Prior to 1857, 'The British viewed India as a social laboratory for transformation in the former's image—a social revolution which would change backward India into a modern society along the lines of an intrinsically western model'.

The blend of 'nationalism and evangelism' of British had convinced them that it was God's will which they were fulfilling. They sincerely believed that with the marvels of modernism, railways and telegraph, they will 'bring or drag reluctant India into the modern world'. The great revolt was a kind of rude awakening for the British. British officials saw the revolt as a consequence of upsetting of the social status quo of India by British policies. In post-1857 period, 'enlightment was no longer a priority and maintenance of law and order became the essence of future British policy in India'. In British mind, the native Indian population was divided into two groups. The groups which ignited the revolt (Brahmins and Muslims of Oudh) were seen as cunning and untrustworthy and were awarded the punishment they deserved.

The groups (Sikhs, Muslims of Punjab and Frontier, Princely states) which sided with British were considered loyal and appropriately rewarded. It is clear now that if the loyal natives had not helped John Lawrence in Punjab, Edwards and Davidson in Hyderabad, Gubbins in Benaras, Robert Ellis in Nagpur and Osborne in Rewa, the Indian history would be different. The lessons of rebellion of 1857 are not interesting for historians only but leaders of post-colonial states have to ponder over the blunders made hundred and fifty years ago. The reason for this advice is the fact that both civil and military leadership especially in Pakistan has more of a colonial mind set rather than the thought process of an independent nation.

2

The Causes of the Rebellion

In response to the revolt of Hindustan, the essay about the real causes of the rebellion of Hindustan that I had written— although my heart now wanted to erase them from the page of the times, or rather erase them even from my heart, since the proclamation that Her Excellency the Exalted Ruler, Queen Victoria (long may she reign!) has issued, is a complete cure for every single real cause of that rebellion—the truth is that having seen the matter of that proclamation, the pen would fall from the hand of the writers of the causes of the rebellion. There has remained no necessity for anyone now to analyze them, because now their cure has become complete.

But to reflect on the real causes of those agitations, and with one's best sincerity to describe the true causes, I consider to be an excellent piece of well-wishing toward my Government. Thus it is incumbent upon me that although their cure has been very well accomplished— nevertheless, the causes that are in my heart, I should make them too manifest. It's true that many very wise men and experienced people have written on the causes of this rebellion. But I believe that perhaps no Hindustani man has written anything about it. It's better that the opinion of such a person too should remain. —Sayyid Ahmad Khan [1859]

What was the Cause of the Revolt of Hindustan?

The meaning of "revolt," and examples of it.

Before answering this question, we ought to tell the meaning of "revolt." Know that to confront one's Government; or to join with its opponents; or with an oppositional intention to disregard its command and not to obey it; or brazenly to break the Government's laws and rules; is "revolt." For example:

1. For a servant, or subject, to fight with or confront his Government.
2. Or with an oppositional intention, to disregard and not to obey its command.
3. Or to aid its opponents, and to join with them.
4. Or for subjects to brazenly fight among themselves, and to transgress the limits decreed by Government.
5. Or not to keep in the heart love and well-wishing of one's Government, and not to take its part in time of trouble.

In the complicated time that occurred in 1857, there was none among these types of revolt that did not take place; in fact, very few wise men among us would turn out to be free of the last type. Although this last type, which seems to be a small thing, is of extremely great weight.

Why does the intention of revolt come into the heart?

The intention of revolt that is born in the heart— it has only one cause. That is, things presenting themselves that are opposed to the temperament, and intention, and will, and custom and practice, and nature, and quality, of those who revolt.

From this account it is proved that no particular thing can be the cause of a general revolt. Indeed, the cause of a general revolt can be either something that is opposed to everyone's temperament, or numerous things that people have spread among the temperaments of a group, and gradually it would become a general revolt.

The revolt of 1857 did not arise from any one thing; rather, it was an accumulation of many things.

This happened in the revolt of 1857 too: for a long time many things had kept accumulating in people's hearts, and a very large [powder-]magazine had accumulated. To set it off, there remained only to apply the fire: and the army's rebellion the year before touched the fire to it.

The distribution of chapattis had nothing to do with any conspiracy.

In 1856, in a number of districts of Hindustan, chapattis were passed on from hand to hand, and almost at the same time the revolt took place. Although at that time cholera was raging in all Hindustan, and the thought occurs that this might have been done to remove it, as a charm, because ignorant Hindustanis make constant use of such charms.

But the truth is that to this day, the true reason for it has not come to light. But there can be no doubt that those chapattis cannot have been the basis of any conspiracy. The practice does indeed exist that this kind of thing can be used as a token, to prove the truth of an oral message. And it's apparent that with this chapatti, there was no oral message. If there had been, it's impossible that despite its being widespread and circulating among men of every community and every temperament, it would have remained secret. The way in which the revolt spread in Hindustan, and moved from here to there and there to here, is clear proof that there was no prior conspiracy.

There was no conspiracy between Russa and Persia.

To think that revolt in India arose from a conspiracy of Russia and Persia is an entirely groundless idea. The Hindustanis— no telling what kind of creatures they might consider the Russians to be!— how could they join with them in a conspiracy? The Hindus could not form any conspiracy with the Persians. For the Muslims of India and the Iranians to be in accord, is as impossible as for the Protestants and the Roman Catholics. If it's possible for day and night to join in a single time, then indeed such a conspiracy is possible. It's surprising that when Russia and Persia fought, then nothing happened in Hindustan; and when agitation happened in India, then nothing there; and yet conspiracy is thought of.

An account of the proclamation that emerged from the tent of a Persian Prince.

The proclamation that emerged from the tent of a Persian Prince is well-known. Not a word of it gives any proof of a conspiracy involving Hindustan. Its theme is clearly the incitement of the people of his own country; the mention of the wretchedness of Hindustan is made by way of encouraging the Persians to support the war, not by way of having established a conspiracy with Hindustan.

The writing of a farman to Persia by the ex-King of Delhi is not surprising, but was not the basis of the revolt.

We consider it nothing surprising if the ex-King of Delhi wrote a farman to Persia. The state of the ex-King of Delhi was such that if he had been told that the King of the Jinns in Pari-land was in his service, he would have considered it true, and would have written half a dozen farmans to him. The ex-King of Delhi used always to say, "I turn into a fly or a mosquito, and fly off, and return with news of people and lands." And he considered this to be true, and he wanted the courtiers to confirm it, and they all used to confirm it. If such a deluded man, at someone's behest, wrote a farman, then it's not surprising. But it's impossible that it would have been the basis for any kind of conspiracy whatsoever. Is it not surprising that such a major conspiracy should last for such a time, and our rulers remain entirely unaware? Even after the revolt, not to speak of any soldier or civilian, not even any rebel ever once made mention of any mutual conspiracy, although after the revolt, why would they have any fear?

The seizure of Avadh was not the cause of this general agitation.

Nor do we consider the seizure of Avadh to be the cause of this revolt. There's no doubt that the seizure of Avadh angered everybody, and everybody believed that the Honorable East India Company had acted contrary to its pledges and promises. In general, the people felt as much anger at the seizure of Avadh as has always been felt when the Company has conquered some land; this will be discussed later. Mostly, the fear and fright and anger were felt by the highly-placed nobles and the independent rulers of Hindustan. They all believed that everybody's lands and everybody's dominions and powers would be snatched away. But we see that not one of these rulers and nobles became a rebel. In this agitation the majority were people whose territories were not in their hands. Don't say in reply to this that the Nawab of Jhajjar and the Rajah of Ballabgarh and so-and-so became rebels.

This was not a conspiracy by a 'community' [qaum] to overthrow the rule of a 'foreign community' [ghair-qaum].

Nor ought it to be thought that this agitation came about because of a feeling of longing and regret that foreigners had taken control of the Hindustanis' ancient land— that the whole 'community' [qaum] united in revolt. It must be understood that the dominion of our Government did not come into Hindustan all at once. Rather, this took place gradually, and its beginning is dated from 1757, with the defeat of Siraj ud-Daulah at Plassey. Since that time, until some days previously, the hearts of the whole people and the nobles were drawn toward our Government; and repeatedly hearing of the morality and virtues and mercy and consideration and pledge-honouring and care for the people and peace and indulgence of our Government and its governors, the flag-bearers of the Hindus and Muslims who were neighbours [shade-sharers] of our Government used to wish to be under its protection [shade].

Even the kings of other lands placed perfect reliance upon our Government, and whatever promise or agreement they made with our Government, they considered it to be extremely fixed and graven in stone.

Despite the fact that our Government now has, compared with former times, much more power as compared to the Hindustanis; the nobles and subahdars and great ones of Hindustan now have only the smallest fraction of the strength and authority they once had. Although in those times our Government faced many wars with every 'community' [qaum] of Hindustan, with Hindus and Muslims, and our Government was constantly victorious. And all Hindustanis believed that one day our Government would hold dominion over the whole of Hindustan, and that all these peoples of Hindustan, whether Hindu or Muslim, one day would come within the grasp and power of our Government. Despite these beliefs, in that time there was no sort of revolt and confrontation with the Government: all the histories are devoid of the mention of it.

If the agitation were because of this, then it's certain that instances of these agitations would be found in those times too. Especially since in those times there was more scope for such agitations. During the time of conflict that began in 1839, when in Hindustan there wasn't any kind of revolt, despite the fact that for hundreds of years Hindustan had been under the rule of princes of those very regions, with whom the conflict was taking place. And because of those very kings, Muslims had received dignity and elevation in Hindustan. So now the thought absolutely can't be entertained, that the Muslims have created the present agitation out of grief for the vanishing of their kingship.

The ex-King of Delhi received no esteem among the people of Delhi, or in those cities that were near Delhi, but only among outsiders; Lord Amherst's saying that the Timurid dynasty was not the ruler of Delhi.

Absolutely no one longed for the rule of the ex-King of Delhi. The frivolous and foolish behaviour of this dynasty had lowered them in the sight of everyone. Indeed, outsiders who were not aware of the King's circumstances and behaviour, and [low] degree of esteem and authority, undoubtedly respected the King greatly, and considered him to be the King of Hindustan and the Honorable East India Company to be his agent. In particular, Delhi people and people who lived in neighbouring areas had no regard for him whatsoever. Despite all this, no Hindustanis felt any sorrow at the deposition of the King.

It will be remembered that when in 1827 Lord Amherst Sahib Bahadur made an announcement that 'now our Government is in no way subordinate to the Timurid dynasty, but rather it is itself the ruler of Hindustan', then at that time the common people and lords of Hindustan paid no attention; although the royal family especially might have felt some sorrow.

There was no previous conspiracy among the Muslims for 'Jihad'.

That the Muslims had been for a long time conspiring and plotting among themselves with the intention that 'we would join together and do Jihad against the people of another religion, and become free of their dominion', is an extremely groundless idea. Since Muslims were under the protection of our Government, they could not in any way perform 'Jihad' in the Government's dominion.

Mention of the preaching and Jihad of Maulvi Muhammad Ismail.

Twenty or thirty years earlier a very well known Maulvi, Muhammad Ismail, preached the practice of Jihad in Hindustan, and incited men toward Jihad. At that time he said flatly that those residents of Hindustan who live under the protection of the English Government cannot perform Jihad in Hindustan. For this reason, thousands of jihadis gathered in every district in Hindustan, and didn't create any agitation in the Government's dominion. And they went to the western border, and went and attacked the Panjab. And the way contemptible and ignorant men in every district invoked the name of 'Jihad'— if we consider them jihadis, even then this absolutely no preparation for this conspiractook place before the tenth of May, 1857.

In that turmoil nothing was done according to the Muslims' religion.

One ought to consider carefully that in that time the people who raised the banner of Jihad were such wretched and ill-conducted and badly-behaved men that besides drinking wine and watching spectacles and seeing dances and shows, they had no other profession. What the hell— how could they be counted as leaders and initiators of Jihad? In that turmoil nothing at all took place according to religion. Everyone knows that to plunder Governmental treasure and wealth which was a trust, and for servants not to be 'true to their salt', was not, with respect to religion, proper. It's entirely clear that the murder of innocents, especially women and children and the aged, was, according to religion, a very major sin. Then how could this turmoil have been a war of Jihad? Though indeed, some ill-born wretches, out of worldly greed, and to fulfil their wishes and deceive the ignorant and add to their own ranks, did invoke the name of Jihad. Then this action too was one more bastardly act among the bastardly acts of these agitators; it was not, in reality, Jihad.

The fatwa of Jihad that the rebels printed in Delhi is in reality a fake.

The fatwa of Jihad printed in Delhi is considered to be an excellent proof of Jihad, but I've heard an analysis— and there are many proofs of its reliability— that it is only a fake. I've heard that when the traitorous army went from Meerut into Delhi, someone wanted a fatwa with regard to Jihad. Everyone gave the fatwa that Jihad cannot take place. Although I've seen a copy of this previous fatwa, since the original fatwa does not exist, I can't say to what extent this copy is worthy of credence. But when the army of Bareilly arrived in Delhi, and a second fatwa was given— the one that's well-known, in which it's written that Jihad is necessary— that one is undoubtedly not genuine. The publisher of this fatwa, who was an agitator and a longtime extreme scoundrel, in order to deceive and mislead the ignorant, wrote people's names on it and thus gave it extra circulation when he published it. Rather, he applied to it the seals of several people who had died before the sedition. But it's well known that some men had also applied their seals because of the force and violence of the rebel army of Bareilly and their agitator companions.

In Delhi, a large group of maulvis who considered the ex-King an 'innovator' and didn't perform namaz in mosques controlled by him.

In Delhi, a large group of maulvis and their followers were such that with regard to religion they considered the ex-King of Delhi very bad, and a 'innovator'. Their belief was that in the mosques of Delhi in which the King had power and access and control, namaz was not proper. Accordingly, those people didn't even perform the namaz even in the Jumma Masjid, and published fatwas on this matter from long before the sedition are available. Then the intelligence can never accept that such people would have given fatwas that Jihad was proper and that the King should be made the leader.

Among those whose seals have been affixed to the fatwa, a number of them protected the lives and honour of Christians.

Among the people whose seals had been affixed to that fatwa, some of them gave shelter to Christians, and protected their lives and honour. Not one of them joined the fight and came forth into the battle. If in reality they had thought the way they are believed to have thought, then why would they have done these things? In short, in my opinion it never entered the Muslims' heads to unite together to do Jihad against the Christian rulers.

And the ignorant and the agitators who raised a clamour of 'Jihad! Jihad!' and went around calling out 'Haidari!'— they're not worthy of belief. Although indeed, the causes for the Muslims to be dissatisfied with regard to religion, and the reason for this— that we will describe clearly below. There's no doubt but that compared to the Hindus, the Muslims were largely dissatisfied with practically everything. And this is the reason that compared to the Hindus, in a number of districts the Muslims former a larger proportion of the agitators. Although the districts in which Hindus agitated are also not few in number.

There was no prior counsel for rebellion in the army.

In the army, there was absolutely no consultation and prior

planning for a rebellion. It's an established fact that the rebels of the army, even after the rebellion, never mentioned such a thing, even among themselves. Indeed, after the event at Barrackpore, and especially during the period when men of many platoons had been brought together for the teaching of the new rules [=drill?], there used to be mutual agreement, and unanimity, that 'we will never use the modern cartridges'. Even at that time, there was no other kind of intention and resolve. Rather, they considered it certain that the Government would withdraw the order. Although it was withdrawn, still after the tenth of May 1857 there was no benefit toward repairing the agitation that had occurred. That fire was not capable of being extinguished by such means.

There was no prior conspiracy between the rebel army and the King of Delhi.

The idea that the rebel army previously formed a conspiracy with the ex-King of Delhi is entirely without foundation. No one considered the King of Delhi to be a saint and a sanctified being. People used to flatter him to his face, and laugh at him behind his back. People used to become his disciples with some advantage in view, not by way of true belief. It's not strange if some soldier or Subahdar from some platoon would have become his disciple. But that has no connection with a conspiracy for rebellion. Undoubtedly, the rebel army gathered at Delhi. But when it had fallen out with the Government, then besides the King of Delhi what individual was there around whom the army could rally? For this, there was no need for prior conspiracy. Without a doubt the Government's maintaining the figure of the King of Delhi was always improper and objectionable. And the scheme devised by Janab Lord Ellenborough Sahib Bahadur was unquestionably worthy of acceptance; rather, it was necessary to do even more than that. Unquestionably the King of Delhi was a spark among the embers— one that, being borne aloft by the power of the wind, set fire to the whole of Hindustan.

The non-participation of the Hindustanis in the Legislative Council was the true cause of the agitation.

The true cause of this agitation I consider to be only one. As for the rest, however many causes there are, they are all branches of this one. And this understanding of mine is not illusory and merely speculative; rather, the opinions of many wise men of former times have already been in agreement with it, and all the essays on the "principle of government" [=English phrase] support me in this matter. And all the histories of Europe and Africa offer firm testimony to the justice of my opinion.

This matter was very necessary.

Everyone has long agreed that in connection with the principledness and excellence and stability of Government, access of the people is among the necessities of governance. The rulers learn the goodness or badness of their plan only from the people, before evils would reach such a level that then their cure would not be possible. [A Persian verse by Sa'adi:]

The fountainhead may be blocked by a stone
The full torrent may not be crossed even on an elephant

And this is not achieved until the people have access to the government of the land— our Government, especially, which was a resident of a foreign country and had a religion, and customs, and a temperament, and habits, different from those of this country. It was necessary to keep in mind that the structure of Government, and its excellence and principledness and stability, is dependent upon acquaintance with local ways and habits, and then upon the people.

Because from looking at former histories, which are in reality a chronicle of the habits and opinions and ways of various kinds of people, it can be learned that these habits and opinions and ways were not obtained through any intellectual rule; rather in every land and community [qaum] they have come about by happenstance. Thus the rules of the Government are based on those manners and ways, not those manners and ways and habits on the rules of the Government. And in this is the stability and basis of Government, because as long as those habits and morals are firm and have become human nature in the hearts of the people, to act contrary to them is to act contrary to human nature, and to keep everyone aggrieved. Will we forget that chaotic condition of Bengal that occurred when in 1758 the English Company Bahadur accepted the Divani, due to that very ignorance? On this subject John Clark Marshman Sahib's history refreshes our memory. And won't we remember the excellence there was in

Bengal, through Lord Hastings Sahib Bahadur's acquaintance with the language and the country's customs and habits?

Undoubtedly, the entry of the people of Hindustan into Parliament was impossible and quite without benefit. But there was no reason for their not having entry into the Legislative Council. Thus it's this one thing that is the root of the agitation of all Hindustan; and however many additional matters became collected together, they are all branches of it.

We don't say that our Government made no attempt to inquire about the country's situations and ways. Rather, we are heartily convinced that it did, and we consider a number of the laws of Government, and the advisories of the Board of Revenue, and the Honorable Thomason Sahib's advisories about revenue, to bear witness to this. But undoubtedly the Government didn't devote attention to ascertaining the circumstances and habits and thoughts and manners and ways and temperament and disposition and capabilities of the people. Without a doubt, our Government didn't know what each passing day brings to the people, and what nights of difficulty befall them— and what sorrows go on collecting in their hearts from day to day, that gradually had accumulated in great numbers, and from a single small movement suddenly rained down.

From this cause the people's attitude toward the Government did not become revealed, and the virtuous intention of the Government did not become apparent to the Hindustanis; rather, the opposite was believed.

From the non-participation of Hindustanis in the Legislative Council not only this much harm occurred, that the Government was not able well to know the real damage of the laws and requirements that had been put in place; and the wishes of the common people, to respect which was necessary for the Government, did not remain respected; and the people did not obtain the opportunity and power to remedy this damage and present their own wishes. Rather, the very great harm was that the people didn't learn the intention and true purpose and inner desire of the Government; the people misunderstood every scheme of the Government. Whatever scheme of the Government there was, because the people were not participants in it and thus were not aware of the nature of this scheme, and did not know its basis, the Hindustanis always considered that 'this thing too is for the ruination and destruction and debasement and irreligiosity of us and our fellow-countrymen'. And those various things that were issued by the Government that were in reality contrary to custom and against the temperament and disposition of the Hindustanis—regardless of whether in their own right they were good or bad, generally they gave credibility to these erroneous views. By degrees a state of affairs came about that the people of Hindustan always gave for our Government the similes of sweet poison and a honeyed dagger and a cold flame. And then in their hearts they believed to be true, and considered, that 'if today we have escaped from the Government's hands, then tomorrow it will not be so; and if tomorrow it is so, then the day after tomorrow it will not be so'. And no one was there to inquire about their situation, and there was no means for removing this erroneous opinion of theirs.

If the position of the people toward the Government would be that which ought to exist toward a mortal enemy, then from such a people, toward such a Government, what expection of faithfulness can there be? Since our Government was in reality not such as that, then such erroneous opinions' becoming settled in the Hindustanis' hearts, and the grief that filled their hearts— for it not to be remedied was due only to the fact that Hindustanis were not participants in the Legislative Council. If they had been, then all these things would have been remedied. Now careful attention be given, then it is only this one single thing which, having given rise to many branches, created an inappropriate agitation in all Hindustan.

Don't say that our Government had given to the presses permission to publish all other matters except abuse and mischiefs and such things as would bring about mischief and revolt; and that before a law went into effect it was first made public, and every individual had the right to present objections to it. Because these actions were simply insufficient— or rather, entirely without advantage— for the remedy of those great, impressive matters of which we speak.

And we don't wish on this occasion to be addressed about how it would be for the Hindustanis, who are extremely ignorant and untrained, to participate in the Legislative Council, and what benefit would emerge from the Hindustanis' participation; and if the people of Hindustan were given entry into the Legislative Council as in the case of Parliament, then would be the method of their selection. There would be many difficulties in this, because on this occasion we have only to prove this much: that it would be very good and necessary for the Government, and for this very reason these agitations arose. And with regard to the people's means of entry, we have a separate opinion; it ought to be looked at, and whatever discussion there would be, ought to be held there.

The occurrence of the revolt is based on five causes.

The defect that was in our Government spread itself in all Hindustan. And to whatever extent causes of revolt accumulated, although they are dependent upon this one action, if they are all brought under careful consideration, then they are based on five causes.

First: The misunderstanding of the people; that is, considering measures to be opposite to what they were.

Second: The putting into effect of such laws and regulations and methods of governance as were not suitable to the governance of Hindustan and to the habits of the Hindustanis, or were injurious.

Third: Government's remaining unacquainted with the true conditions and manners and habits of the people, and with those difficulties that affected them and through which the people's hearts gradually became torn away from the Government.

Fourth: The abandonment on the part of our Government of such actions as were incumbent and necessary for the governance of Hindustan.

Fifth: Ill-arrangement and non-supervision of the army.

Now we will consider separately these five causes and every one of their branches, if God so pleases.

The First Cause

First, the misunderstanding of the people; that is, considering measures of Government to be opposite to what they were.

At this point however many matters we discuss, our meaning

through them is not that in reality these things were in our Government. Rather, the meaning is that people erroneously considered this, and it became a cause of the revolt. If a Hindustani too had entry into the Legislative Council, then this misunderstanding would not have been present.

Their considering that there was religious intrusion.

Religious intrusion— there's no doubt that all the people, ignorant and capable, and high and low, considered it certain that our Government's secret intention was to intervene in religion and custom and tradition; and to bring everybody, whether Hindu or Muslim, around to the Christian religion and the customs and traditions of their [=the Government's] land. And the biggest cause of this revolt was exactly this.

Every individual deeply believed that the orders of Government come into existence gradually, and that which they have to do, they always do by slow degrees. Along these lines they will not suddenly and forcibly tell Muslims to change the style of their religion, but as they get more of a grip, to that extent they will keep on intruding; and those matters that had manifested themselves, which will be discussed below, kept reinforcing and proving that erroneous doubt. Everybody believed that our Government would not use open force for the change of religion. Rather, by hidden schemes they would render the knowledge of Arabic and Sanskrit virtually extinct, and the land impoverished and needy. And by causing people to be unacquainted with the aspects of their [own] religion, and spreading books and teachings and instruction in their [=the Government's] faith and religion, by arousing a greed for positions they would deprive people of religion.

Mention of the orphans of Sikandra.

In the drought-year of 1837, those orphaned boys who were made Christian— in all the zilas and regions, western and eastern, that was counted as one example of the intention of Government: that making Hindustan impoverished and needy like this, they would bring them into their own religion. I say truly that when the government of the Hon'ble East India Company used to conquer some region, the people of Hindustan never used to feel any grief— except for people's knowing that to the extent that the authority of our Government increased, confrontation with any enemy and neighbouring ruler, and concern about agitation, would no longer remain, and to that extent they [=the Government] would make more intrusion into their religion and custom and tradition.

A great deal of religious discussion took place.

In the beginning of the rule of our Government in Hindustan, there was very little discussion of religion. It went on increasing day by day, and in this age has reached its limit. Undoubtedly our Government had no entry into these actions, but every person considered that all these matters are with the order and the hint and the wish of Government. Everyone believed that the Government has appointed the Padri Sahibs in Hindustan, and that the Padri Sahibs receive a salary from the Government. And that the English governors who come from abroad who are employees in this country give the Padri Sahibs a good deal of money, and books to distribute, and in every way are their helpers and assistants.

The covenanted officers' adoption of missionary behaviour.

Many covenanted officers and army officers had begun to talk to their subordinates about religion. Some sahibs ordered their servants, 'come to our house and listen to the teaching of the Padri Sahib', and it used to happen just so. In short, this practice became so widespread that no one knew whether under management of the Government his religion would remain secure for himself or for his children.

The teaching of the Padri Sahibs.

The teaching of the Padri Sahibs took on a new aspect. Books of religious insistence, in the form of question and answer, began to be printed and distributed. In those books, with regard to other people's holy personages, sorrow-causing words and themes appeared. In Hindustan, the custom of teaching and narrative is that they sit in their own religious places or homes and speak; whoever's heart might wish, and whoever might be attracted, he would go there and listen. The method of the Padri Sahibs was the reverse of this: they themselves went to the gatherings and holy places [tirth] and fairs of other religious, and preached. And only through fear of the rulers, no one forbade them. In some districts the custom developed that an escort [chaprasi] from the police station began to go with the Padri Sahib. In their preaching the Padri Sahibs did not content themselves with simply discussing the Holy Bible. Rather, they referred to the holy personages and holy places of other religions very abusively and disdainfully, from which the listeners felt extreme sorrow and inner trouble, and the seed of disaffection toward our Government was sown in people's hearts.

Missionary schools.

Many missionary schools were started, and in them religious education began. The people all said that these were sponsored by the Government. In some districts very highly placed and highly respected covenanted officers used to go to those schools, and encouraged people to join them and participate in them. Examinations based on religious books were held, and young boys among the students were asked 'who is your Lord, who is your Saviour?'; and they answered according to the Christian religion, and for this they were given a prize. Due to all these things, the people's hearts kept moving away from our Government.

Here an important objection arises, that if people were unhappy with this education, why did they enrol their boys? We ought not to consider this a sign of non-unhappiness; rather, it is a great proof of Hindustan's condition having become entirely wretched and impoverished and extremely straitened and ruined. The cause was only the neediness and poverty of Hindustan: people thought that, 'having been enrolled in those schools, our children will obtain some means of livelihood and living'. Such a harsh necessity, which no doubt caused inner sorrow and spiritual grief, they neither approved of nor accepted.

Village schools.

From the establishment of village ['rural'] schools, all the people considered it certain that these schools had been set in motion only to make them Christians. The Parganah Visitors and Deputy Inspectors who used to move around in every village and town giving people the advice, 'enrol your boys in the schools'— in every village the name for them was 'Black Padris'. In whichever village the Parganah Visitor or Deputy Inspector arrived, the villagers spread the word among themselves that the Black Padri had come. The common people thought that, 'these are Christian schools, and they take students in order to make them Christians'. And intelligent people, though they didn't think this, nevertheless considered that 'in those schools there's only Urdu education; having studied in them, our boys will become entirely unacquainted with the commands and views and beliefs and customs of our own religion, and will become Christians'. And they likewise considered that, 'this is the very intention of the Government— that it would obliterate Hindustan's religious knowledges, so that in the future the Christian religion would spread'. In a number of the eastern districts of Hindustan the establishment of these schools, and the enrollment of boys in them, took place by outright coercion, and they said that it was the Government's order that boys should be enrolled.

The establishment of girls' schools.

In Hindustan there was much discussion of the education of girls, and everyone considered it certain that the Government's purpose was that girls should come to the schools, and obtain education, and become unveiled [be-pardah]— which was utterly unacceptable to the Hindustanis. In quite a number of districts examples of this were established. The Parganah Visitors and Deputy Inspectors considered, 'if we make an effort and establish girls' schools, then we will obtain very favourable notice in the Government'. For this reason, they used every method, permissible and non-permissible, to induce people to establish girls' schools. And for this reason in people's hearts there commonly grew feelings of discontent, and their erroneous opinions were confirmed.

The change in the method of instruction in the large colleges.

The various large colleges that had been established in the cities— it was as if people had been more or less suspicious of them from the first. In that era, Shah 'Abd ul-'Aziz, who was a maulvi renowned in all Hindustan, was alive. The Muslims asked him for a fatwa. He gave a clear answer: 'To enter into the English college and study, and to learn the English language— according to religion, it is all proper'. Upon this, hundreds of Muslims entered the colleges. But at that time the state of the colleges was not such [as it is today]; on the contrary, the curriculum was very good. Every sort of learning— Persian and Arabic and Sanskrit and English— was taught. There was permission to teach Fiqh, and Hadith, and poetics. There was a [regular] examination in Fiqh; certificates were obtained. There was no kind of religious encouragement. Instructors were appointed who were honoured and respected and well-known and learned and abstemious.

But finally this situation did not remain. The esteem for Arabic became very little, and training in Fiqh and Hadith all at once started vanishing. Nor did Persian remain especially esteemed. The aspect of education and the customary books became entirely transformed. Urdu and English became the customary thing— as a result of which the suspicion that 'Government seeks to wipe out Hindustan's religious knowledges' became established. The instructors were no longer respected and learned. Those very students of the colleges, who had not as yet earned respect in people's eyes, began to be instructors. Thus these colleges too came to be in the very same state.

The Government's proclamation with regard to eligibility for employment.

While the village schools and the colleges were in such a state that the suspicion of their promoting the Christian religion was universal, then suddenly a proclamation was issued by the Government that whoever will be educated by a school [madrasah], and will have passed an exam in the English language and in such-and-such fields ['ulum] and received a degree, will be considered to be ahead of everyone for employment. Even petty positions became dependent on certificates from the Deputy Inspectors— whom as yet all the people considered to be "Black Padris." And these erroneous opinions added a burden of grief to everyone's hearts, and in everyone's hearts displeasure with our Government was born, and people considered that in every way Hindustan was being deprived of livelihood and impoverished, so that when these people were desperate, gradually a change and alteration in their religious views would come about.

The arrangements for food and drink in jails.

At this very time in a number of districts the scheme was made that the prisoners in the jails would eat food cooked by the hands of a single individual, from which the religion [mazhab] of the

Hindus was entirely destroyed. Although in the Muslims' religion there was no harm in this, everyone felt grieved at heart that the Government had set out to take away everyone's religion, and in every way was scheming to that end.

The matter of the letters of Rev. E. Edmond.

All these evils were happening in people's hearts, when suddenly in 1855 Rev. [Padri] E. Edmond sent from the seat of government, Calcutta, to all the official Government servants, low and high, letters of which the purport was that now in Hindustan there has come to be one rule, through use of the telegraph information about all places had become unified, through railways and roads travel to and from all places had become unified— religion too should be one. Therefore it is proper that you people too should become religiously unified as Christians. I say truly that after the arrival of these letters, because of fear, darkness appeared before everyone's eyes. The ground beneath their feet receded. Everyone became convinced that the time the Hindustanis had been expecting had now come. Now however many Government servants there were, first they would be compelled to become Christians, and then the whole mass of the people. Everyone undoubtedly considered that these letters had come through the order of the Government.

Among themselves the Hindustanis asked the Government office-holders, 'Have you gotten a letter?' The intent of this was, 'you too, through greed for a job, have become a Christian'. These letters caused such blame to be placed on Hindustani office-holders that those to whom the letters had come used to reply, out of shame and in order to hide their disgrace, 'it has not come to us'. People used to answer, 'now it will come— aren't you a Government servant?'

If you want to know the truth, these letters were what made the erroneous suspicions of the Hindustanis solid and firm— thus they did so, and no device succeeded in erasing them. It's not at all strange that at this very time, some disorder and a certain amount of agitation broke out in the country— as, from the circumstances of that time, is manifest. But Janab of Lofty Title the Nawab Lieutenant Governor Bahadur of Bengal quickly learned of it, and issued a proclamation that, for a time, brought comfort to people's hearts, and that restlessness that had come about, became calm. But it did not create the firm subduing and suppression that was necessary. People considered that this matter was absent only for the present, sometime when control had been gained, at an opportune time, it would again be brought forth. Rev. E. Edmond's letter and the proclamation of the Nawab of Lofty Title, the Lieutenant Governor Bahadur of Bengal are entered at the end of the book; you can see them there.

The Muslims' having more sorrow at intrusion into religious affairs, and the reason for it.

With all these things the Muslims, as compared to the Hindus, were very much more dissatisfied. The reason is that the Hindus fulfil their religious injunctions [mazhab ke ahkam] in the form of custom and habit, not in the form of religious injunctions [ahkam mazhab ke]. The injunctions and rules of their religion, and those inner matters of belief on which ultimate salvation, according to their religion, depends— to them these are absolutely unknown, nor do these form part of their practice. For this reason they are exceedingly ignorant and lax in their religion. Apart from customary matters and avoidances [of certain foods] in eating and drinking, they are not firm and zealous in any religious principle. If in their presence matters contrary to this creed of theirs, which ought to be believed in the heart, would constantly happen, they feel no anger or sorrow. By contrast, Muslims know very well which things, according to their creed, will give them Paradise, and which will place them in Hell; and considering these injunctions to be religious injunctions, and injunctions sent by the Lord, they carry them out. For this reason, they are firm and zealous in their religion. For these reasons, the Muslims were mostly dissatisfied, and in comparison to the Hindus their taking a larger part in the agitation seemed likely— and accordingly, exactly this happened. Without a doubt, to whatever extent the Government's intervention into religion is contrary to the principles of statesmanship, similarly to put a stop to the education of any religion— especially that religion that its adherents (?) consider true— is improper and inappropriate. But our meaning is only this: that although our Government is such [as it is(?)], things were so carried on that the people's erroneous suspicions were not dispelled.

The Second Cause

The putting into effect of improper laws and rules: the issuing of such laws and rules and forms of government as were not suited to the governance of Hindustan and the habits of the Hindustanis.

Act 21 of 1850.

From the Legislative Council too there came intervention into religious matters; Act 21 of 1850 was a clear case of the disturbance of religious rules. Then, because of this Act, for one thing people suspected that the Act had been issued especially to encourage people to accept the Christian religion. Because it was clear that no person from another religion can be admitted among the Hindus, the Hindus were deprived of any benefit from this law. If some man from another religion would become a Muslim, then from the practice of the religion that he has adopted, he is forbidden to take any inheritance from his bequeathers who were of another religion. Thus neither could any new Muslim obtain any advantage from this Act. But indeed, whoever accepted the Christian religion, he could obtain advantage. For this reason, people thought that in addition to religious intervention, this Act was a clear enticement.

Act 15 of 1856.

Act 15 of 1856 interfered with the religious customs of the Hindus with regard to widows. Although a great many discussions took place about this, and judgments in Hindu law [baivaste] too were obtained, still the Hindus, who are more devoted to customs and traditions than to religion, disliked this Act extremely. In fact, they considered it a couse of dishonour, and of family ruin, to them; and they suspected that this Act had been issued so that the Hindus' widows would become autonomous, and whatever they might want, thus they would begin to do.

The autonomy of women.

The rule of women's autonomy that was observed in the criminal courts— how much harm it caused to the Hindustanis' honour and pride and custom and tradition! Even married women became autonomous in criminal court. The guardianship of guardians was removed from over women, and these things manifestly caused harm to religion. The confiding of reparation for this to the civil court was undoubtedly insufficient and without benefit. And a thing for which the reparation was urgently needed, according to religion and custom and tradition, was subjected to such delay and complexities that a great deal of agitation arose from this. The civil court decrees with regard to the giving back of wives were probably very rarely acted upon. Many judgments will turn out to be such that the woman gave birth to two or three children in the house of the abductor, and still the plaintiff is eagerly seeking a means for finding a trace of her.

Some laws contrary to religion despite both parties' being of the same religion.

Some Acts and laws are such that through their effect, despite both parties being of the same religion, decisions in civil court were made that were contrary to their religion. Our meaning is not that our Government should show partisanship toward any religion. In the situation of being of different religions, undoubtedly justice must be respected, on condition that justice not be contrary to both religions or the creeds of both parties. When the two parties are of the same religion, then it's necessary that the judgments of the court in connection with their rights be according to their religion alone, or their custom and tradition alone.

The seizure of revenue-free lands.

The laws of the seiaure of revenue-free lands, of which the last was Law 2 of 1819, were extremely harmful to the realm of Hindustan. The extent to which the seizure of lands made the common people of Hindustan disaffected and ill-wishing toward our Government — no other thing had made them more so.

The saying of Lord Munro and the Duke of Wellington.

Lord Munro and the Duke of Wellington Sahib Bahadur had said truly that to seize the revenue-free lands was to engender enmity with the Hindustanis and to make them impoverished. I cannot express the extent to which the Hindustanis felt dissatisfaction and inward sorrow and ill-wishing toward our Government, and the extent of difficulty and straitened circumstances they experienced for this reason. Many revenue-free lands had come down as such for centuries, and with the most trivial excuses they were seized. The Hindustanis definitely thought that, 'the government itself did not take care of us; rather, those estates that previous kings had given to us and to our ancestors— the Government took them too; then what hope is there from the Government?'

With regard to the seizure of lands, even if this excuse from our Government be considered true and genuine, that if the seizure of revenue-free lands had not taken place then in connection with fulfilling the expenses of Government, which we ought to consider extremely prudent economics, it would have been compelled to make a scheme for taking some other revenue from the people of Hindustan. But the common people are not in any way comforted by this, and the difficulty that befell them cannot be eliminated by this. Just look— in that time, wherever the rebels issued proclamations in order to mislead and inveigle the common people, in all of them there's no mention of anything else except two things: that is, religious intervention and seizure of revenue-free lands. From this it is well established that these two things were the true sources and very major causes of the dissatisfaction of the people of Hind— especially of the Muslims, who experienced very much more harm in comparison to the Hindus.

The auction of estates.

In previous regimes, no doubt the custom existed of [transfer of] landholding rights through private foreclosure and mortgage and inheritance/gift, but it happened very rarely, and to whatever extent it took place, it used to be voluntarily and willingly. There was never a custom of forced auction of landholding rights, by order, because of unpaid taxes or of debt. In Hindustan, landholders consider their ancestral landholding to be very precious, and from its loss they feel complete sorrow. If the matter be reflected upon, then in Hindustan every single landholding appears as a small kingdom. From ancient times, through everyone's consent one individual used to be the headman. He controlled the discourse, and every landholder used to have, in proportion to his share of landholding, the right to speak and to intervene. The peasants, the local residents, and the Chaudharis used to be in respectful attendance, and said their pieces. If some case took an unduly long time, then it was decided by order of the chief and headman of some large village. In every single village in Hindustan the very particular aspect of a small kingdom and a parliament was present.

Beyond question, to the extent that a king feels sorrow at the loss of his kingdom, to that very same extent a landholder felt sorrow at the loss of his landholding. Our Government disregarded this entirely.

From the beginning of its rule to this day, there will be hardly a single village left in which there would not have been a certain amount of such transfer. At the very beginning these auctions had become so uncontrollably numerous that the whole land was turned upside down. Then our Government, to remedy this, issued Regulation 1 of 1821, and a Commission was appointed. From this, hundreds of other types of evils arose— to the extent that this task was not able to be brought to a conclusion as desired, and finally this commission was ended.

At this point we don't want to discuss what the government would then do, if it didn't maintain this practice for the receipt of revenue; or why an auction should not take place, since the hand is mortgaged to the government for revenue payment and is considered to be its responsibility. Because at this point we say only this: that they became causes of the revolt, whether the reason for their existence was compulsion or ignorance, And if discussion about this matter is desired, then look at our account [in another work] of the methods of the governance of Hindustan. But here we only write this much: that to consider land to be pledged for revenue payment is very dubious: in truth, the government's claim is on the produce, not on the land.

The custom of auction of land right for the payment of debt gave rise to a great deal of agitation. Moneylenders and the wealthy, having given cash loans to the landlords, have practiced much trickery in order to snatch away their land rights. And in the courts they have brought every kind of case, some with and some without merit, and have shut out the old landlords and themselves become the masters. These disasters have shaken all the landlords in the whole country.

The harshness of the system.

The system of revenue collection that our Government created is extremely worthy of praise. But in comparison with previous systems, it is heavy. In previous regimes, a portion of the harvest used to be taken by way of revenue collection. Sher Shah had fixed for the Government a share of one-third of the harvest; unquestionably there were many difficulties with this method, and harm to the Government was possible, but the cultivators all remained settled and no one was forced to pay for losses. Akbar at first adopted this very system— that is, he chose to take one-third of the harvest, and put this system into practice. But he refined the system, as is recounted in Lord Elphinstone Sahib's excellent history, and is also described in the A'in-e Akbari.

Akbar fixed different kinds of land. For the first kind of land, of which the name was 'pulich' and which was sowed every year, a regular share of revenue was taken. The second kind of land, of which the name was 'paroti', was not always cultivated, but rather was sometimes left lying, in order to increase its strength; revenue was taken for this land for those years in which it was cultivated. The third kind of land, of which the name was 'chachar', gave no return for three or four years, and also required expenditure to fix it up. In the first year of use, two-fifths was taken, and then the amount increased until in the fifth year it was complete. The fourth kind of land, of which the name was 'banjar', gave no return for more than five years; for it there were even gentler terms.

The conversion of the in-kind settlement into cash was in this way: the harvest of every bigah, and every kind of land, was taken according to the average weight of its grain. For example, from a bigah were previously taken nine maunds of grain, and to take from the farmer three maunds of grain from that bigah was fixed as the Government's share. Then the value of the grain was fixed according to the average current price, and that was fixed as the cash value of that bigah. Then a great advantage in this was that if the farmer considered the cash value to be greater, he had the right to give three maunds of grain. Within the governmental settlement, many matters had not been taken into account. To land lying fallow the same assessment was attached. Lands that had to remain fallow for some time in order to increase their fertility were not exempted.

From being farmed continually every year, the fertility lessened, the harvest began to decrease. The account that was made at the time of the settlement no longer remained. In a number of districts every single settlement became harsh, the landlord and farmers suffered harm; gradually they became impoverished. Their implements became very few, and for this reason from the land they farmed they didn't earn what they ought to have. From this reason too, a reduction in the harvest occurred. In order to pay the revenue, they incurred debt. The interest and the debt began to increase; many wealthy landlords, who used to have very good property and made prudent expenditures, became poor. Those villages in which there was an unusual amcunt of land lying uncultivated became even more wretched. The Honorable Thomason Sahib Bahadur in his instruction-letter, section 64, writes that in the settlement of Regulation 9 of 1833, on the whole it could be seen that the collection for good villages was devised to be somewhat mild, and the collection for poor villages became harsh.

The landlords' illegal extortions gradually ended; although this was a very good thing, at the time of the arrangement they should have received indulgence, which didn't happen. In short, for these reasons poverty had *144* overtaken landlords and farmers, for which reason, despite the security and ease that the landlords had, the memory of previous regimes was not erased.

The crushing of the Taluqdars, especially in Avadh.

The crushing of the Taluqdari system, although we don't say that there was any injustice in it, nevertheless became a prime cause of the agitation, especially in the Avadh region. These Taluqdars had become Rajas, in their territory they exercised full powers. They collected revenue. That kingship and income of theirs suddenly vanished. In this matter too, if the government had not done this, then how would the actual landlords have emerged from the hands of these tyrants— on this occasion we will not discuss this. Rather, discussion of it is contined in another [expression of] opinion of ours. Here, it's necessary to say only that the defeat of the Taluqdari system too was a cause of the agitation.

Stamps.

The use of stamps is entirely a European creation. It is the practice of a land where it's as if the income [from land] is not taken. Its introduction into Hindustan, and then the gradual increasing of its price, of which the extreme limit is in Regulation

X of 1829, were without a doubt contrary to the temperaments of the people of Hind. Rather, with regard to the state of poverty of the people of Hindustan, earlier people have had much discussion about the introduction of stamps, and many items of evidence have been presented. The actual case is the opposite of this [pro-stamp case].

But on this occasion we want to ignore all these discussions, and we consider it sufficient to write only this much: that the need for these discussions is in countries where the people are educated and affluent and perceptive and quick of understanding. The people of Hindustan, who grow day by day more impoverished, are absolutely not fit to bear this burden. All wise men have disapproved of this form of taxation; their view is that however blameworthy and merely unreasonable to levy a tax on title-deeds, a tax on that paperwork which is done for the sake of justice is even worse. Besides the burden of expense, in many circumstances it circumvents the dispensing of justice. Accordingly, Mill Sahib's book "Political Economy" and Lord Brougham's "Political Philosophy" are on the undesirableness of this. And to whatever extent it is to be avoided in Europe, its adoption in Hindustan is very much more blameworthy.

The Civil Court system [in Bengal and Agra] is better than in the Punjab, but is in need of revision.

The system of civil courts that is in the Presidencies of Bengal and Agra is extremely creditable; it has no involvement in this sedition. I know that the opinion of a number of government officers will be contrary to this, and they will prefer the system of the Punjab. But this topic requires a good deal of discussion. The 'law of the Punjab' is an overview term for those laws that are in force in that region. Rulebooks have not been established for their application and scope. Every official is himself in authority over them; it's not necessary that the officials' opinions would be in accordance. Then, to what an extent flaws in it are bound to result, can only be imagined!

The civil court is the best of all the courts, to which the greatest trust should be given. On this court depend the security of the land and the transport of merchandise and the increase of commerce and the establishment of rights. In the Punjab, this court is coming to be held in extremely little respect. The officers pay it absolutely no attention— rather, we say that they have no time to pay attention. To the extent that cases in governmental courts in these regions are scrutiny-requiring because of deaths and many matters and the passage of long periods of time— as yet these are not there in the Punjab. And when they will be there, then beyond all doubt the laws of the Punjab are not sufficient to decide them properly.

In this sedition the effect of the civil courts that is found, it is only this much: first, the transfer of rights upon a death; and second, the affairs of debtors and indebtedness. Both these matters became the cause of mutual agitation, not of confrontation with the government. From these matters there was inward grievance. And it's a rule that when governance is slack, then mutual tension gives rise to agitation.

Then, of those two matters because of which people had grievances against each other, the greatest cause of this was that unwarranted death transfers, and unjust debt judgments, had come down on people's heads, and they became indebted through false decrees, and for this reason blame is placed on the civil courts. It's necessary to reflect that to the extent that inattentiveness and inadequacy and superficial investigation and arbitrariness by the officers of the civil court courts exists in the Punjab, will create even more evils than these.

The effect of the civil courts does not become apparent in ten years; after fifty years, rather than now, the court system and the effects of the civil courts in Punjab ought to be compared with those in the Northwest. We acknowledge that the law of the civil courts of the Bengal and Agra Presidencies is capable of being improved.

In the decision of cases there is much delay. Because stamps are costly, because many levels of appeal have been established in every court, people are burdened. Because the court officers had not been given some kinds of authority, there was damage to the decisions of the cases. Thus Act 19 of 1853 made some improvement, and to the extent that [the problem] remains, it is in need of correction. If anyone would care to see more discussion of this, look at our other opinions that are in our work on the government of Hindustan.

The Third Cause

The ignorance of Government of the true circumstances and ways and habits of the people; and of the difficulties which befell them, and because of which the hearts of the people went on becoming torn away from our Government.

The ignorance of Government of the state of the people.

Beyond all question, our Government had no awareness of the circumstances and ways of the people, and of their sorrows. And what cause was there for them to be aware? Because awareness of circumstances and ways comes from affection and connection and informal mutual coming and going; and when one community [qaum] mingles into the other, and creates love and goodwill in the way of fellow-countrymen, and adopts [the country as] a homeland, the way the Musalmans, belonging to another religion and dwellers in another country, adopted Hindustan as their homeland, and created [such affection], and created brotherly interactions with those from the other country. But in truth our Government was not able to obtain awareness in this way, which is the true cause of knowing the circumstances of the people, nor does our Government seek to settle down here and intermingle.

Now there remains this: if the people themselves would have announced their difficulties, then the people had no power to do it. Because the people of Hindustan had not the slightest means of access to the government. And if someone spontaneously sent some petition or letter, or presented it to Huzur the Governor General, then it was considered as a form of complaint, not as a form of rightful access to the Government, and for this reason it brought no benefit. Now it was necessary that some other person would make the Government aware of the condition of the people; that awareness was dependent upon the reports of the local officers.

The local officers were absolutely unacquainted with the conditions of the people.

They themselves were unacquainted with it, and there was no way for them to obtain information. And their non-attentiveness in this matter and their temperamentalness is a well-known fact. Everyone was afraid of their oppressiveness. No one had the nerve to tell them the truth about anything— especially something contrary to the officers' wishes and desires. Everyone, both subordinates and elite courtiers, flattered them out of fear.

And our Government, which in reality is a [genuine] (?) kind of Government, from those matters created the aspect of an authoritarian (?) Government. Then, this form of information about the conditions of the people through the local officials was not merely insufficient, but rather in reality was nonexistent. For this reason the conditions of the people always remained concealed from our Government.

The new law that was promulgated by the Government, the damage it did to the situation of the people and their welfare and prosperity— there was no one to rectify it and to convey information about it. In actions of this kind there was no sympathizer for the people. Except for their tears of blood, which remained burning within their bodies, and except for their helplessness, at which they themselves wept, and remained silent.

The poverty of Hindustan, especially of the Musalmans.

Under the rule of our Government, why would there not have been poverty and straitened circumstances in Hindustan? The biggest livelihood of the people of Hindustan was service, and this was considered a special profession. Although the people of every community [qaum] were aggrieved about there being no livelihood, this complaint was especially that of the Musalmans. One ought to reflect that among the Hindus, who are the original dwellers in this land, in former times no one used to take service; rather, everyone was absorbed in traditional work.

The Brahmins had no connection with service; the Vaishya caste, as they were called, were always absorbed in business and money-lending. The Kshatriyas, who at one time had also been the rulers of this land— it is proved from ancient chronicles that they too did not seek service, but rather kept land as an estate, and maintained family control over every single scrap of land.

They had no soldiers among their servants, but in time of need gathered together through family loyalty, and used to fit themselves out as an army, just as, to provide something of an example, used to be found in the lands of Russia. Indeed, the Kayasth community [qaum] can be seen to take service, from ancient days in this land.

The service positions of the Musalmans in particular were very few; the service professionals, who were generally Musalmans, were in very much straitened circumstances.

The Musalmans are not the [original] inhabitants of this land; rather, they came into Hindustan with former kings, in search of livelihood, and settled here.

Thus every one of them was dependent on service; and through the shortage of service they had more complaint, compared to the original inhabitants of the land. Honorable service in the military, at a rank higher than that suitable for the uneducated people of the country, was very scarce under our Government.

Well-born people considered it a defect to take employment in the Government's army, which was largely made up of common soldiers. Indeed, there was still service for the well-born in the cavalry, but the number of posts was so small compared to the cavalry of former times that there was no comparison. In addition to Government service, in former eras the well-born used to take service in the retinues of provincial governors and chieftains and nobles, and we ought not to assume that these posts were few in number.

Now this situation, under our Government, doesn't exist. For this reason there was the most extreme shortage of service posts. The result that came of this was that when the rebels wanted to employ people in their service, thousands of people gathered for employment. And the way in time of famine a hungry man falls on grain, in that very way people fell on the posts in service. A [Persian] verse: [call it 'a hungry heretic in an empty house' / the intellect did not believe that he thought of Ramzan].

Because of this poverty, people's acceptance of posts with the rebels that paid one anna, or one and a half annas, or a seer of grain per day.

Many men took service in posts that paid only an anna or an anna and a half per day. And many men received, instead of a daily salary, a seer or a seer and a half of grain. From this it is clearly proved that to the extent that the common people of Hindustan were eager for service, to that very extent they were in needy and straitened circumstances through poverty and lack of resources.

From the termination of charitable pensions and stipends, Hindustan's becoming poorer

There was one more path under former rulers to the well-being of the people— that is, jagirs, allowances, and other grants and favours.

When Shah Jahan ascended the throne, only in honour of the occasion he gave away four lakh bighas of land and 120 villages as jagirs, and lakhs of rupees as grants. Not only was this practice entirely given up by our Government, but even prior jagirs were seized— through which seizure thousands of men were deprived of their daily bread. We have already described the state of the landlords, and the poverty of the cultivators. The livelihood of the craftsmen, because of the opening up of trade in things from Europe, has been severely declining— so much so that in Hindustan no one any longer even dreams of finding any needle-makers or match-makers in Hindustan. The thread of the weavers has entirely snapped— those wretches who were the most fervent of all in this turmoil. Since it was through the Lord's grace that Hindustan too entered the empire of Great Britain, it was certainly the government's duty to pay attention to this straitened condition of the people, and to attempt to remove their mental grief and inward sorrow.

The indebtedness of the country to the Company's notes.

Through Company notes, the country came under a new kind of indebtedness, which had no parallel under any former government. The amount of rupees that were borrowed, the means for paying the interest on the debt, even the means for paying interest and costs, and the profit— in short, in every way the country became poor and needy.

Only because of poverty did the people want a change in government.

Old families, who used to receive thousands, were in dire straits even for their livelihood, and this was a real cause of the disaffection of the people with the Government. People wanted a change in government, and were eager for a new government, and were pleased about it from the heart; I say truly that it was for this very reason. We say truly— and again, we say truly— that when the Government conquered Afghanistan, people were very much grieved. What was the reason? Only because now religion would be openly taken in hand. When Gwalior was conquered, the Punjab was conquered, Avadh was taken, people were utterly sorrowful. Why so? Because from these nearby Hindustani states, the Hindustanis received great comfort. Positions in service were usually available; every kind of Hindustani merchandise was saleable. When these governments were ruined, then the Hindustanis grew steadily poorer and more needy.

In the rule of our Government there were also extreme excellences and virtues. I don't point out everything as a flaw. As some [Persian] poet says, [you've spoken of all the faults, now speak of the virtues too / don't deny wisdom for the sake of a few common hearts]. Peace and tranquillity and freedom; the clearing of the highways; the wiping out of dacoits and highway robbers; the fixing-up of the roads; the convenience for travellers; the way merchants' goods are sent for long distances; the chance for poor and rich alike to send letters to remote lands; the ending of blood-spilling and affrays; the lifting of the power of the oppressors from off the oppressed; and many other things like this, are so good that they have never existed in any government, nor will they. But reflect that because of these things the difficulty about which we are speaking does not go away.

Consider another point: that this gain from the government that has been mentioned— for which people was it greatest? First of all, for women, who were benefited in every way: to have their children killed in affrays; to be looted at the hands of 'thugs' [thag]; to have their husbands and children not safe from the hands of the administrators— from thousands of such difficulties they were protected. So look at what well-wishers and admirers of the Government they were! The merchants and traders were greatly benefited— so among them not one was an ill-wisher. The conclusion is that the people who had not been harmed by the Government, not one of them became an ill-wisher.

The Fourth Cause

Not doing those things that it was incumbent upon the Government to do

The abandonment on the part of our Government of tasks that it was incumbent upon our Government to do, for the rule of

Hindustan, and that were necessary. Although the matters about which we write at this point may be distasteful to some rulers, it's necessary for us to write the truth and open our heart. The thing we speak of is something that ensnares wild animals of the jungle, and tames beasts of prey— not to speak of human beings. Are Lord Bacon's 'Essays' not enough, that we would here speak of the laws of friendship and affection and connection and unity? But indeed, we must at least say this much: that through mutual affection and neighbourly friendship the amity between the government and the people is greatly increased. A friend is obliged to be friends with a single individual; and a government, with the whole of its people. The lover and the beloved are only two individuals, and through heartfelt connection they are counted as one. The government is obliged to create with the whole people such a connection that the people and the government would all come together and become a single body.

Want of cordiality towards the Indians.

A Persian verse: [the peasant is a seed, the sultan a tree / my son, the tree is stronger than the seed]. Was this situation impossible for our Government to create in Hindustan? Why could it not have existed? Because night and day we find heartfelt agreement between two men from different countries and different religions, in cases where they wanted to agree. And we also see in two men of the same group [qaum] and the same religion and the same homeland [vatan], completely enmity and hostility. This proves that for affection and agreement and friendship, it's not necessary for people to be of the same religion and the same homeland and the same group [qaum].

Is not this advice of Saint Paul full of wisdom, that "And the Lord make you increase, and abound in love one toward another, and toward all men, even as we do toward you." (1st Epistle of Paul to the Thessalonians Ch. III, Verse 12)? The result of which is that we ought to feel true affection not only for our fellow-countrymen and those of the same community [qaum], but rather for everyone, even for enemies. And that affection and kindness should keep increasing. And is not this saying of the sainted Messiah comforting to the heart, that "Therefore all things whatsoever ye would that men should do to you, do ye even so to them, for this is the law and the Prophets" (Matthew VII, 12)? The point of the sainted Messiah in this advice was affection. In short, no wise person can deny that affection and agreement are an excellent thing, and give many very good results, and prevent many evils. To this day, our Government has now created this affection with the people of Hindustan. It is also a common rule of affection that naturally grows up among people and even beasts, that affection flows from the high toward the low.

The father's love first flows toward his son, not the son's toward the father. In the same way, a man's love toward his woman is prior to the woman's love toward the man. On this basis, if a lowly man would begin to show affection toward a lofty one, it is counted as flattery, not affection. The result of this is that our Government ought to have first shown affection toward the people, and first taken a step toward agreement. Then this rule of affection that has been acquired from thousands of experiences, that willy-nilly the affection has an effect on the other's heart, and draws the other toward itself, would have had an effect on the people's heart, and the people would have felt even more affection toward our Government— in fact, they would have been infatuated with it. A Persian verse: [love is that destruction of households/that brought you to our house]. But alas, that our Government didn't do any such thing. If our Government would claim that this statement is incorrect, that 'we have not acted in such a way— rather, in return for affection and goodwill we have found evil', then we will appeal to the Government itself: if this were so, then undoubtedly the people would feel even more affection than the Government did.

Beyond question, affection is a thing of the heart, that doesn't come into being from words or contrivances. Although its effects are outwardly manifest, the truth is that it itself can neither be described, nor can any token of it be pointed out. But the heart knows it very well; rather, in its hand is a true balance-scale, and it recognizes deficiency and excess. A Persian verse: [a heart has a path to a heart, through the dome of the heavens / hatred from hatred, and kindness from kindness]. To this day, our Government has kept itself as separate from the Hindustanis, as unmingling, as fire and dry grass. Our Government and the Hindustanis are two fragments of rock, one white and one black, that are recognized as separate. And then, between the two there's a distance that day by day keeps growing. Although with our Government and the Hindustani people it ought to have been like a mottled stone, that is one despite having two colours. In a white color black dots look very beautiful; and in blackness, whiteness shows an extraordinary verdancy. We don't speak unjustly. Undoubtedly our Government ought to have a special religious affection toward the Christians. But we want from our Government toward the people of Hindustan that brotherly affection, and on top of it that brotherly love, that has been advised by Saint Peter: "And to godliness, brotherly kindness and to brotherly kindness, charity" (II Peter 1,7). Now reflect: our rulers and the Hindustanis were not one in blood; they were not one in religion; they were not one in customs and habits. The people felt no inward acceptance, there was no affection and agreement between them. So on what grounds did our rulers expect faithfulness from Hindustan?

In previous regimes, until affection was established with the Hindustanis, there was no tranquillity.

Look at the situation under Hindustan's former sultanates: first the Musalmans were victorious. In the sultanate of the Turks and Pathans, affection and mingling with the people of Hindustan did not take place until the sultanate had taken on an aspect of confidence and ease. In the sultanate of the Mughals, excellent mingling began from the era of Akbar I, and it continued until the time of Shah Jahan. Although in that time too troubles came to the people through the irregularity of the system of the sultanate, that wound used to be eased by this brotherly affection that existed between them. In 1779— that is, in the time of Alamgir— this affection broke off; and because of the rivalry and revolt of the Hindu community [qaum]— for example, the Maratha Shivaji, etc.— Aurangzeb became angry with the whole community of Hindus and sent orders to his Subahdars that they should treat the whole community of Hindus with harshness, and take jizyah from every single one. Then, the injury and disaffection felt by the people are clear. In short, even in a hundred years of rule our Government has not created affection and love with the people.

Contempt toward the Hindustanis.

No one can deny that to treat the people with honour and

conciliate them— that is, to hold their hearts in your hand— is a very great cause of stability of a government. If a man would receive little but would be honoured, then he is very much happier than if he would receive much but would be little honoured. To dishonour a man is a kind of thing that causes sorrow at heart; it's a thing that, without any outward harm occuring, creates enmity; and it causes such a deep wound that it never heals. Verse [in Arabic]: [the tongue's own wounds have a remedy / but what the tongue wounds cannot be cured]. The quality of conciliation is contrary to this: it's a thing from which an enemy becomes a friend, and friends' affection increases, and a stranger becomes one with you. It's this thing through which wild beasts of the jungle become obedient domestic animals. Then if it would be used with the people, to what an extent they will become docile and obedient to orders! In the beginning of the [Company's] rule this thing was there, and it drew everyone's hearts toward our Government. It created a heartfelt obedience. Beyond question, our Government has forgotten these things; undoubtedly the whole of the people of Hindustan maintain that our Government has treated them with great disrespect and contempt. A man of the gentry of Hindustan has not even as much worth before a petty European, as a petty European has before a very great duke. Thus it used to be imagined that in Hindustan there's no such thing as a gentleman.

The harsh temper and rude speech of local officials.

All these things— that is, affection and love and honour and conciliation— toward the people on the part of the Government are manifest. Except by means of those local officials, through whom our Government in Hindustan functions and maintains relationships and connections with the people, no matter how virtuous the Government's intention may be, it will never be expressed— not until these people would set themselves to express it. The habits and ways and manners of the rulers of the earlier time were very much the contrary of those of the present rulers. Those former people used to show great respect; they used to look out for the Hindustanis in every way; they used to hold their hearts in their hands. In a friendly way they shared in their grief and joy, although they held very great lordship and rule in Hindustan, and although they didn't let slip from their hands the grandeur and imposingness and pomp proper to the rulership. Then, they showed such love and honour to Hindustanis that every single person used to become infatuated with their courtesy and their love, and used to say with surprise, 'What good people these are, that despite grandeur and loftiness and rulership, they are without pride; and with what courtesy they meet with us!' In Hindustan those people who were counted among the venerable elders [buzurg] used to behave toward them in exactly this way.

Undoubtedly those people were among the followers of St. Peter, and to brotherly affection they added love as well: "And to Godliness, brotherly kindness; to brotherly kindness, charity." (II Peter V, 7). Among the rulers of the present, the temperaments of a number of them are the opposite of this. Has not their pride and arrogance made all Hindustanis nothing in their eyes? Has not their ill-temper and indifference placed in the hearts of the Hindustanis an inappropriate dread? Does our Government not know that the greatest, most honorable Hindustanis trembled before the rulers, and were intimidated by the fear of dishonour? And is it a hidden thing that when a nobly-born secretary is reading out a case before a Sahib, and is speaking with hands joined [in humility], he is is suffering at heart over the Sahib's ill-temper and harshness of speech and even abuse? And he says [to himself], 'Alas, what a pity that I can't earn my bread somewhere else— to earn a living by cutting grass would be better than this!' I don't accuse all rulers of this defect. Undoubtedly there are also some rulers that are known to everybody for their affection and courtesy and good qualities, and all Hindustanis recognize them as 'the moon and sun', and consider them a replica of the former rulers.

And in truth, they are guided by the advice that the holy Messiah gave to the sainted Simon [Peter] and Andrew, when they cast their net into the sea for fish: "Follow me and I will make you fishers of men." (Matthew, IV, 4). They, through their good character, have drawn the people into the net of their affection. These rulers have both retained the dignity of their rulership, and have also not shown inappropriate pride toward the people. And they have earned that blessing that the holy Messiah had spoken of: "Blessed are the poor in spirit, for theirs is the kingdom of heaven" (Matthew, V, 3). These rulers have treated the people with fair-minded forbearance, and have ruled the land the way the holy Messiah had said: "Blessed are the meek for they shall inherit the earth" (Matthew, V, 5). These rulers have also, according to the saying of Jesus the Messiah, shown their light to the people: "Let your light so shine before men that they may see your good works and glorify your father which is in heaven" (Matthew V, 16). Rulers of this kind, although they were few, wherever they were, were cherished.

These things were more displeasing to the Musalmans; and the reason for it.

There is also no doubt that these things were displeasing to people of every single community [qaum], but seemed more oppressive to the Musalmans. But the reason for this is very clear: for centuries the Musalmans have been coming into to Hindustan too with honour. In their temperament and disposition there is a sense of honour. In their hearts is very little greed for money; they don't want to lose their honour through some greed. There must have been a great deal of experience that those things that other communities will do without sorrow, even less lowly things [than those] are extremely difficult for Musalmans to endure. We acknowledge that this disposition in Musalmans may indeed be very bad, but there's no choice: the temperament that the Lord has created cannot be changed. This may indeed be the Musalmans' ill fortune, but it's not a sin. These were the sorrows because of which the heart wanted a change in the government, the heart became happy on hearing news against the government. But it's a pity— for our Government was not neglectful of the welfare of the Musalmans; their capability and education, their culture, everything was before its gaze. But these people were not aware of it, and the intention of our Government and its inner purpose were not made clear by the rulers.

Hindustanis' not making progress; and the progress that Lord Bentinck made was not sufficient.

A major cause of the dissatisfaction of the people of Hind, and especially the Musalmans, was that there was very little progress in the high positions. Very little time had passed since these people were respected in all Hindustan, and they obtained lofty positions. Their resolve and intention now too was exactly the same; thus they wanted positions according to their worth, and apparently no prospect could be seen. At the beginning of government rule, people who were of fine family and honorable rank used to be selected, and they received positions. Gradually, this practice ended. Undoubtedly, some among these people did not have capability. Thus the practice of examinations, in our opinion, is not in any way deserving of blame, nor in truth is anybody [entitled to feel] aggrieved by it. Beyond doubt, through examinations excellent officers would come to hand. But such people were appointed to those honorable posts who were, in the eyes of the Hindustanis, extremely unworthy. In receiving a certificate very little consideration was given to the person's being of fine family and honorable rank. The extent to which Lord Bentinck Bahadur arranged for the progress of the Hindustanis has never since been exceeded. Unquestionably that progress was extremely inadequate, because of the insufficiency of positions. Many highly-placed rulers affirm that the kind of progress by the Hindustanis that was needed, did not take place.

The nonexistence of regal durbars.

It was the ancient practice of the people of Hind that they used to be in attendance in their kings' durbars; having seen the glory and grandeur and pomp and circumstance of the king, they were happy. There is a natural rule innate within a human, that having met with his king and master he is inwardly happy: he knows that 'this is our king and our master, we are his servants and people'. Especially the people of Hind have had from ancient times this practice— which had now for some time been unavailable. Although the Nawab Governor General Bahadur held durbars while on tour, this was not sufficient to fulfil the wishes of the Hindustanis.

Although Lord Auckland and Lord Ellenborough Sahib Bahadur held regal durbars, perhaps this behaviour was somewhat displeasing in England, but the truth is that it was extremely appropriate to the conditions in Hindustan. Or rather, even with those, there were not as many as their ought to have been. The Lord is always the protector of our exalted Queen Victoria; the Lord is always the protector of the Ruler of the Land of Hind, the Ruler of Rulers the exalted Queen, and the Governor General

Bahadur of Hindustan. We hope that now no longing of the people of Hind will remain unfulfilled.

The durbars held by Lord Auckland and Lord Ellenborough Sahib Bahadur were extremely proper.

It is true that the real kingship belongs to the Lord Most High, who created the whole world. But God the Most High has created kings as an illustration of His true kingship, so that His servants would recognize from this illustration their True King, and render thanks to Him.

Thus many great learned ones and wise men have declared that the qualities and bounty and generosity and graciousness of the True King ought to be illustrated in those merely human kings as well. It's for this reason that many wise men have declared the king to be the 'Shadow of God'. From this the conclusion emerges that the way the Lord Most High shows limitless generosity toward all of his servants, in the same way kings' generosity and bounty ought to be shown toward their whole people.

Although at first the thought comes to mind that to give rewards and benefits for very little things is to empty the treasury for no gain, but it's not like this. Rather, the great advantage of rewards and benefits is that the people's affection for their king increases. It's a universal rule that 'man is a slave of benefits'; thus the whole people, having seen their king's rewards and favours, willy-nilly come to have heartfelt affection, and are eager to do him many good services and be his well-wishers.

It is clear from books of history that it was very customary under previous governments for every kind of reward and favour to be given to the people and the chieftains. Very expensive robes of honour and excellent gifts and money in cash and land in jagirs used to be bestowed.

Men of fine family obtained titles, and these created honour for them among their peers, and made them very zealous at heart. And the people of Hindustan were very pleased with this practice; in fact, they had been accustomed to it for centuries. Our Government put a complete stop to this tradition: no one among the people any longer had any expectation of this kind of outward rewards and favours. And for this reason their hearts wanted a change in the government— so much so that when they heard the news that the contract of the Honorable East India Company was ended, and about the rule of the exalted Queen, they were happy. Under the rule of former kings, rewards and favours used to be of two kinds.

One was what the king used to spend in caring for his debauched companions and those of undesirable character. In truth, this was undesirable, and the Hindustanis too disliked it; in fact they used to be angry at rewards given to immoral people and those with no claims.

The second kind of reward was what the king gave to his well-wishing servants and victorious chieftains, to the learned ['ulama] among his people and to the virtuous and to ascetics [faqir] and poets and recluses and the poor. All the people long for this type of reward, and are displeased at its nonexistence. Although from these things people become spiritless and ease-seeking, and don't remain industrious and able to earn their bread with the strength of their arms.

Thus it's better for the king to ignore this kind of rewards, and give another kind of reward— that is, freedom, so that he [the recipient] himself would have the scope to earn his bread. This is true, but this reward can only be in force as long as the people would be comfortable and educated, not that one would remove the bit from animals' mouths and drive them into the jungle without food and water and tell them to search for their own food and water. What will be the result of that, except that they will either die, or act like those same wild animals? The result of which intention of ours is this revolt in Hindustan.

The extent to which the real revolt happened in Hindustan was shown as greater than it was.

Anger is a thing such that it hides from the eyes the truth of affairs. The temperament turns its attention toward vengeance and punishment. It's true that the events that took place in Hindustan in 1857 were such that to whatever extent our rulers became angry, and to whatever extent they would avenge and punish, it is all appropriate. But we ought to reflect on the condition of Hindustan: to what extent there was in reality a genuine revolt in Hindustan, and why it increased to such an extent, and why it appeared to such an extent, and why the ill-fortuned Musalmans appeared in some districts to be more rebellious.

It's a cause for reflection that for centuries the governance of Hindustan had been unstable. For the people of Hindustan it was a customary habit that when some leader or chieftain or king became more powerful, thousands of men rallied to him. To take service with him, to act on his behalf, to administer on his behalf, they didn't consider a sin on their part in any way.

It's proverbial in Hindustan that there's no sin in taking service. Whoever retained a man as a servant and gave him a salary, that's whom he served. Although when a chieftain would be displaced, and another would be established in his place, not to obey him [=the new chieftain] they considered a sin. The leaders and chieftains of Hindustan— and especially those who ruled Hindustan before the regime of the Government, and because of whom Hindustan was becoming a crossroads of the nations— never placed any blame on those who served with the sword or pen. That custom had taken hold among all ~~the~~ people of Hindustan.

When in Hindustan the agitators raised their heads and wanted to take people into service, thousands of men who were in need of bread and desirous of employment went and took service. Everyone said, 'What sin is it of ours? We are professional servants.' From among the common people many persons became retainers of the rebels, according to this ancient custom that they would obey whoever was now the ruler, that they were the people and would obey whoever had the power.

Many government servants considered that they would make a show of obeying the rebels and save their lives, and when the Government would return, they would again be obedient to the Government. They too became criminals, although there's no cause at all to doubt that they were at heart followers of the Government. A number of people and government servants, on some occasion, whether out of compulsion or stupidity or because they were merely human, got involved in something. They thought, 'Now we have committed this sin by chance, or under compulsion, or from ignorance; the Government is not one to overlook it, and will punish us'. Helpless through this fear and dread, they went and joined the rebels. Many men had in reality done nothing, but through fear and other thoughts gradually went and joined the rebels. Many people at that time did this, who in their own mind and their own understanding didn't consider it the crime of opposition to the Government.

If the circumstances of the whole of Hindustan with regard to the rebellion will be looked at, then we believe that both communities [qaum] that live in Hindustan will be seen in this agitation, each one more than the other. And for proof of this, all the circumstances of Hindustan are present in witness. But as for those districts in which Musalmans were seen to be mostly agitators, we ought not to think that the cause of this was only that a Musalman king had made a claim to the sultanate of Delhi, and that in truth the Musalmans had become agitators as would appear to be the case.

The temperament of the rulers sometimes became angry over those things that seemingly the Musalmans had done. Their enemies came to have great scope— in order to present self-interested concerns, they greatly magnified small things and told about them. On the one hand the rulers became more angry, on the other hand the Musalmans mostly felt fear and despair; and through their destiny, they appeared more as agitators than they were. No doubt among Musalmans there was much rebellion of the 'fifth kind', and they were happy at the thought of a change in government— the reason for which we have been recounting in every section.

Nevertheless the knowledge will not be hidden from our Government, despite all this, of who in this turmoil show rised their lives and showed the most loyalty. Before the Lord, Whose is the true kingship, and before the kings of the world whose contingent rulership the Lord has bestowed, all are sinners. Saint David, may peace be upon him, truly said, "Enter not into judgement with thy servant, for in thy sight shall no man living be justified" (Psalm cxliii, 2). "Have mercy upon me, O God, according to Thy loving kindness; according unto the multitude of Thy tender mercies, blot out my transgressions. Wash me thoroughly from mine iniquity, and cleanse me from my sins" (Psalms li, 1 and 2). The Lord is always the protector of our exalted

Queen Victoria; I cannot express the excellence of that merciful proclamation that our exalted Queen issued.

The exalted Queen's proclamation is extremely praiseworthy; rather, it has been issued through the Lord's inspiration.

Undoubtedly the Lord's hand is on the head of our exalted Queen; undoubtedly this merciful proclamation has been issued through inspiration. A very ancient custom has come down in Hindustan that when a new king is established on the throne, whether by right or without right, all the regional chieftains used to submit to him, In this turmoil too this happened: when the King of Delhi seated himself on the throne, and news reached the regions that the King of Delhi had taken control of the throne, they all submitted themselves to the king.

Since the King of Delhi has been seized, and the kingship has come into the grip of our Government, everyone has believed that all the agitators who had raised their heads high, will obey. Perhaps the people of the rebel army would not do so, but we don't consider it necessary, in our view, to discuss the reason for their not having done so.

The Fifth Cause

The poor arrangement and neglectedness of the army.

The paucity of the English forces.

Our Government's arrangement of the army was always deserving of criticism: the shortage of English troops was always an occasion for criticism. Ever since Nadir Shah conquered Khurasan, and the two different lands of Iran and Afghanistan came within his grip, he organized two equal armies: one Persian and Qizlbash, the other Afghan. When the Persian army sought some change in government, then the Afghan army was there to subdue it; and when the Afghan army grew arrogant, then the Qizlbash one was there to put it down.

Our Government did not do this in Hindustan. We considered that the Hindustani army was the government's great supporter and well-wisher and life-sacrificer. But where had any vow been taken, that there will never be any order contrary to the wish of this army, and that this army will not be dismayed at some order?

Then, in the case of this army's becoming disaffected, as happened, what means had our Government retained, through which this refractoriness could at once have been resolved?

Taking into service Musalmans and Hindus in mingled platoons.

It's true that our Government took into service Hindus and Musalmans, both communities [qaum], which are opposed [mukhalif] to each other. But because of both those communities' becoming mingled in every platoon, this division [tafriqah] didn't remain. It's obvious that in a single platoon however many are serving, because of their living in a single place and being arranged in a single line, among them unity and brotherly connection used to develop. The sepoys of a single platoon used to consider themselves a single brotherhood [biradari], and for this reason there was no distinction of Hindu and Musalman. Both communities considered themselves brothers; whatever the men of that platoon did, they all participated in it; they used to become each other's supporters and helpers.

If there had been a separate platoon of Musalmans, then perhaps the Musalmans would not have objected to biting the cartridges.

If the platoons of those very two communities [qaum] had been arranged in such a way that one platoon had been only of Hindus, in which there had been no Muslim, and one platoon had been only of Musalmans, in which there had been no Hindu, then this mutual unity and brotherhood would not have managed to exist, and the same division [tafriqah] would have remained established. And I think that perhaps the Musalman platoon wouldn't have had any objection even to biting the modern cartridges.

The Hindustani army's becoming extremely arrogant, and its causes.

Because of the English army's paucity, whatever fear the people as well felt was only of the Hindustani army. In addition to this, the Hindustani army too was extremely arrogant: they had no regard for anyone except themselves. They considered that the English army was worthless; they believed that the victories in the whole of Hindustan were due only to the power of their own swords. It was their dictum that 'from Burma to Kabul, we've given the government victory'.

Especially after the conquest of the Punjab, the arrogance of the Hindustani army had become greatly increased. Now their arrogance reached such a degree that they were ready to object to the smallest things. I believe that the arrogance and haughtiness of the army had reached such a degree that it wasn't strange that they would have objected to both setting out and halting.

At such a time— when the army was in this state, and their heads were full of arrogance and haughtiness, and in their hearts they believed that whatever whatever they set their minds on and demanded the government would be forced willy-nilly to grant— the new cartridges were given to them, about which they confidently believed that there was an admixture of fat, and from the use of which their religion [dharm] would cease to exist. They refused to bite them.

When the platoon at Barrackpore was disbanded for this offense, and the order was read out, then the whole army became extremely grieved. Because they considered that by reason of the harm to religion [mazhab], the Barrackpore platoon had committed no crime, and had only been disbanded without cause through the government's injustice.

The whole army was very grieved: 'we were loyal to the government, got our heads cut off conquering land after land for the government, and the government is out to take away our religion, and for an obligatory thing has disbanded them!' At that time there was no agitation, because other than disbandment no other violence had been done to the army. But in the hearts of the whole army, partly because of the belief of there being fat in the cartridges, partly because of grief at the disbandment of the platoon at Barrackpore, and most of all because of pride and self-regard, and with the thought that 'whatever we are, we are our own selves', a fixed resolve developed, that 'among us no one at all will bite the cartridges, no matter what may come of it'.

After January 1857, the army's taking counsel and sending messages that 'we will not bite the cartridges'.

Without a doubt, after the events at Barrackpore, the army began to write and correspond among themselves. Messages arrived that no one would bite the modern cartridges. Up to this point there was no doubt dissatisfaction and anger in the hearts of the whole army, but in my opinion there was no intent of agitation.

In Meerut, the existence of inappropriate punishment, and because of grief and arrogance the army's taking to revolt.

In the course of destiny the wretched month of May 1857 came. In Meerut the army was given harsh punishment, which every single wise person considers to be very bad and displeasing. The grief that this punishment caused to the hearts of the army is beyond expression. They remembered their medals, and seeing themselves instead wearing leg irons and handcuffs, they wept. They thought of their acts of faithfulness, and looked at what reward had been given them in recompense. And in addition to this, in their heads was limitless arrogance, because of which they considered themselves extremely great, and which gave them more grief. Then the whole army stationed at Meerut became convinced that either they would be compelled to bite the cartridges, or this very day [of punishment] would be allotted to them. In this state of grief and anger, on the 10th of May that misdeed was undertaken by the army, of which the equal is perhaps not to be found in any history. What recourse did this army have, after this misdeed, except as far as possible to complete the agitation?

After the agitation, the Meerut army's no longer trusting the Government.

Wherever in the army this news reached, the whole army became more aggrieved. Because of the misdeed done by the Meerut troops, the whole Hindustani army confidently believed that now the government no longer had trust in the Hindustani army, that the government would find an opportunity and punish them all. And for this reason the whole army had no trust or belief in the words or deeds of their officers. They all said among themselves, 'at this time there are such words; when the time comes, they'll change their tune'.

I say on very trustworthy grounds that in the rebel army that had gathered in Delhi, thousands of men felt grief over this inappropriate misdeed and profitless rebellion. They used to weep and say, 'Our destiny caused us to do this deed'; then with much regret they used to say 'If we had not done it, then what would we have done? One day or another the government would have destroyed us. Because now the government no longer trusts the Hindustani army.

When they found the chance to seize us, they would have destroyed us.' In the beginning of the rebellion when there was an intention of sending an army to the Hindan, but the army had still not as yet set out, it was the clear opinion of some men that at the time when an attack by the army on Delhi would begin, then undoubtedly the whole Hindustani army would prove disaffected.

Accordingly, exactly this happened. The reason for this was that after the army began the fighting, it was not possible that the rest of the army would remain confident in the government. They certainly considered that 'when they/we kill our brothers and comrades, then they will turn their attention to us'. For this reason they all girded their loins for agitation, and became disaffected; those too in whose hearts there was no agitation, because of being part of the army, could not separate themselves from the majority. The Hindustani people considered that all that the government had was the Hindustani army. When it became widely known that the whole army had become disaffected, all lifted their heads [in arrogance], the fear of the government left their hearts, and agitation arose everywhere.

The reasons for there being no revolt in the Punjab.

Now apply my opinion to the situation of the Punjab. The Musalmans of the Punjab handed endured great tyranny at the hands of the Sikhs; from the rule of the government they had received no harm. In the beginning of the government's rule in the Punjab it had practiced great severity, and now day by day it gradually relaxed this— in contrast to Hindustan, where the situation was just the opposite.

In the beginning of its rule the weapons of the whole land had been taken; no one had the power for agitation. Although that wealth that formerly existed was no longer possessed by the Sikhs, the earned money that they had saved had still not been spent; and that poverty that there was in Hindustan had not as yet come there.

In addition, three other reasons that the Punjab did not become disaffected were very powerful. First, that an English army was present there. Second, through the intelligence of the rulers there, the weapons of the Hindustani army were suddenly, without warning, taken away. Because of the turbulence and numerousness of the rivers, and the shutting up of the crossing-points, the Hindustani army became powerless. Third, all the Sikhs and Punjabis and Pathans who were capable of agitation had entered government [military] service, and they had a great greed for loot. That which the people of Hindustan obtained with difficulty and humiliation from the rebels, was vouchsafed to the people of the Punjab obtained honourably and without trouble. Thus the circumstances of the Punjab were entirely different from the circumstances of Hindustan.

3

Results of the Revolt

End of Company's Rule

The British Parliament passed an "Act for the Better Government of India" in 1858, whereby the administration responsibility was passed into the hands of the British Queen and her Parliament. With this, the rule of the Company came to an end. The Board of Control was abolished and the Board of Directors had no power left. A secretary of State for India was to take the place of the President of the Board of Control. He was advised by a board of fifteen members. The designation of the Governor-General was changed. While he remained Governor-General for the provinces under his rule, he came to be known as Viceroy while dealing with Nawabs, Rajas and native princes.

Change in The British Policy towards Indian States

To appease native princes, the British declared that they would honour all treaties and the agreement entered into by the East India Company with the native rulers. Further, Doctrine of Lapse was abandoned and the right to adoption recognized. The Indian princes were assured that their territories would never be annexed. Henceforth, the continual existence of Native States was guaranteed. However, there were clearly defined restrictions and limitations to them. The military prowess was greatly reduced.

End of Peshwaship and The Mughal Rule

Nana Sahib escaped after the Revolt as he had actively taken part in it. He could not be traced after that. With his escape the Peshwaship came to an end. The title of Mughal emperor was also abolished as the last Mughal emperor, Bahadur Shah Zafar died in 1862 and he also took part in the Revolt. Thus came the end of the glorious Mughal dynasty founded by Babur in 1526 in the first battle of Panipat.

Reorganization of The Army

The British soldiers realized that the numerical inferiority of the British Indian army was one of the causes of the Revolt. The British soldiers were increased in number which means, the expenditure also increased. Artillery and other advanced means of warfare were in the care of British hands. In order to break down the unity of the Indian soldiers, they were divided and separated

Economic Exploitation of India

Economic exploitation of the country was an inevitable situation after the Revolt. In words of Majumdar, "the extinction of the East India Company's Rule brought in grave economic perils to India. India now became a dumping ground of British manufacturers and an almost inexhaustible field for investment of capital for it offered unlimited scope for commercial and industrial enterprises like railways, steamers, tea, and coffee plantations etc.". The British henceforth started abusing political power for the enhancement of their commercial and economic interest.

Rise of Nationalism

The sacrifices of some great Indian rulers during the Revolt of 1857 aroused feelings of Nationalism among men. Nana Sahib, Rani of Jhansi and Bahadur Shah became National heroes. People celebrated their heroism and their attempts to fight for freedom. The revolt became a symbol of challenge to the mighty British power in India.

According to Tara Chand, "the memory of 1857 substantiated the later movement, infused courage into the hearts of the fighters furnished a historical basis for the grim struggle and gave it a moral stimulus-(its) memory distorted but hallowed with the sanctity, perhaps did more damage to the cause of the British rule in India than the revolt itself".

Policy of Divide and Rule

During the Revolt of 1857 the Hindus and Muslims had unity and fought together for the welfare of the country. The British government realized that the unity of the Hindus and Muslims was posing a serious threat and therefore the best thing would be to create a wall between the two communities. Thus, they adopted the "Divide and Rule" that completely destroyed the relationship. So much so that the unrest between the two communities has still not been resolved. As the Muslims had taken a prominent role in the Revolt, they were deprived of patronage in education, business and services and Hindus were given preferential treatment. At a later stage the Policy was reversed. The British used this disharmony to their advantage and widened the gulf between the two major communities. It was on this ground that India had to be partitioned on the event of her independence in 1947

The Causes of The Rebellion

Maj (Retd) Agha Humayun Amin from Washington DC Gives a Brilliant Analysis of The 1857 War of Independence

The events of 1857 were unique both in terms of historical precedence and in terms of the socio-political sphere as far as India was concerned. India as a region has known foreign invaders more frequently than any other region in world history. The reason for it does not lie in the docility or weakness of the Indo-Pak people but in the peculiar geographical position of India by virtue of being bounded in the north by a vast inhospitable and unproductive region which starts from beyond the Indus valley and stretches far north into the steppes of central and eastern Asia.

It is an irony of history that the east Asian tribes and races forced the west Asian nomads of Mongol and Turk origin to seek their barbaric design for plunder westwards and these central Asian people repeatedly invaded India. In the process these central and north east Asian nomadic people conquered and colonized China also but also extended their sway in South Asia as well as West Asia.

The first important aspect of the whole affair is to broadly analyze the conduct of the races who conquered India. This is a relatively simple exercise. Starting from the Aryans, Huns, Greeks etc. the invaders of India can be classified into two broad categories *i.e.* 'Settlers' or 'Plunderers'. The settlers were the ones who came to the country, conquered it and settled here. They can be compared with Normans or Saxons who went to Britain and gradually got assimilated in the country which they had initially conquered. The 'Plunderers' were the ones who came like 'Ghaznavis', 'Mongols', 'Nadir Shah', 'Ahmad Shah Abdali' etc. looted the country and went back to their country of origin.

For those who do not know Indian history it is important to specify that the first Muslim invaders of India *i.e.*, the 'Arabs' were settlers and not plunderers. They conquered and annexed a part of India and made it a province of their empire. Mahmud of Ghaznavi was both a plunderer and a settler. Initially his concentration was on simply acquiring the material wealth which during that age was done by 'Plunder'. Subsequently geographical and logistical factors forced him to also act as a part settler and thus he made present 'Punjab' and 'Frontier' a province of his empire. But even then area east of west Punjab remained his area to be plundered. The 'Ghauri' Turks who were 'Muslims' by religion were the first Muslim settlers in India east of Indus valley region. They made Delhi their capital and gradually got assimilated in India. They were followed by various Muslim dynasties of Central Asian or Afghan/Pathan origin who may be classified as usurpers.

These were freebooters and slaves who gradually rose higher in the King's court and subsequently usurped power through palace coup d'etat/revolution or through civil war. The only exception to these settlers was Tamerlane who sacked and destroyed Delhi in 1398 and did not establish a dynasty in India.The relevance of discussing only the Muslim invaders of India prior to the British while omitting pre-Muslim invaders is simple. In 1857 people belonging to three religions or three broad groups who were fighting with certain objectives. These were the British, the Hindus and the Muslims. It is in this context that an endeavour is made in these paragraphs to acquaint only the layman reader about the broad mechanics of Indo-Pak history

The last settler-invaders of India prior to the British were the Mughals. They came to India in 1526. They defeated the then Pathan Muslim King of Delhi at Panipat and established the Mughal dynasty. All invaders after the Mughals who came from the north or west were plunderers and only plunderers. These include 'Nadir Shah' and 'Ahmad Shah Abdali'. In justice to Ahmad Shah Abdali it must be stated that Ahmad Shah Abdali in 1761 did want to become a settler and establish his dynasty in India but he failed to do so because his soldiers had rebelled and demanded a return back to Afghanistan. All Muslim invaders who attacked India from the north did not distinguish the Hindus from Muslims and subjected all Indians to indiscriminate looting.

For a casual reader of history in this light the British may also appear as just one of the earlier invaders of India. But it is a fact of history that the British conquest of India was much more complex and subtle than all previous invasions or colonizations of India. Four features make it different: (1) The Third Religion Factor. (2) The Communication Factor. (3) The Economic Factor. (4) The Organizational Factor. India's history prior to Plassey was relatively simple. Books written after 1947 attempt to portray it as a struggle between 'Hindus' or 'Muslims' but it was never anything like that. But then historians are prisoners of time and the society they live in at least in the vast majority of cases. Those who endeavour to write history as it happened do so at the risk of their life or loss of social approval or just because they are not bothered or pushed about pleasing the majority. The struggle in India prior to 1757 and even after 1757 was between individuals who were 'Muslims' or 'Hindus' by pure chance and who manipulated their followers or subjects in a certain direction guided and propelled not by any religious convictions but by personal whims and subjective designs. 'Religion' was just one of their tools, a political expedient, a wartime slogan, a matter of policy.

Muslims killed Muslims and Hindus killed Hindus for simple power or for patronage or economic benefit. Hindus killed Hindus for Muslim Kings and Muslims killed Muslims for Hindu Kings. Everything was mixed, diverse and complex. Rajput Hindu Generals fought for Aurangzeb against the Hindu rebel Shivaji. Aurangzeb preferred to ennoble Mahratta Hindus who formed 16.7% of his nobles in the period (1679-1707) than lets say 'Punjabi Muslims' who were not even 2%. Thus Hindu Rajputs and Hindu Mahrattas were the bulk of Aurangzeb's nobility and their number in the period (1679-1707) stood at 31.6 %32.

Thus we see that in the period between 1526 and 1707 the India of the Mughals was a state which had opened its doors to the 'Natives' as the British later degradingly referred to the Indians. The British who became a force to reckon within India after 1757 brought a totally new phenomena to India *i.e.*, 'slavery' and 'subjugation'. An 'Indian' could be a common soldier or a non-commissioned officer or a junior commissioned officer but remained junior or subservient to the junior most British officer who may have been a cook or son of a cook in Britain! The civil servants, the governors, all ranks and appointments of any consequence were open to only the white man.

This was a new experience for the Indians. They had been colonized by the Aryans, the Greeks, the Arabs, the Turks, the Pathans. But all these people had either plundered them and left or if they had stayed, they always allowed the native Indians to be a part of the dominant classes. The problem with the British was that they thought that they were very special whereas India had been conquered even by 'Horse Thieves' and central Asian adventurers who could not fight with the Uzbeks! The Indians were surprised and disillusioned and there grew a feeling in north India that these new invaders were different. If we glance at Indian history between 1757 and 1857, we find hardly any Indian in a respectable official rank or position in the territories governed by the English East India Company.

Whereas if we compare this with lets say the Mughals we find that the third Mughal Emperor Akbar just about three decades after his grandfather Babar had established the Mughal Empire in India was freely employing Indians both Hindus and Muslims in all the ranks and appointments of his army and civil service. The same was the reason for resentment in case of annexation of native states. It closed all doors of advancement to an Indian in any profession/service.

The British were different not because they were racists or fascists but because of the circumstances in which history had placed them. We will take the first of these *i.e.*, 'The Religion Factor'. Before 1757 all contenders in Indian politics were either Hindus or Muslims. But this was irrelevant because both the parties used religion just as one of the means to a personal or political end. Shivaji later eulogized as a Hindu freedom fighter was in service of a Muslim state. Aurangzeb's most famous general Jai Singh was a Hindu Rajput. Ahmad Shah Abdali later on portrayed as a purely Muslim hero could find no better governor of Muslim majority Lahore than 'Kabuli Mal' a Hindu! Ranjit Singh's (the Sikh hero) most trusted advisors were the Muslim Fakir brothers of Lahore. Now suddenly after 1757 a third religion 'Christianity' appears on the Indian scenario.

The British were 'Christians' by accident and religion was an insignificant factor in their list of priorities. But the very fact that there was a third religion made the scenario complex. New probabilities and possibilities opened for political leaders, religious thinkers and all those who held positions of power or patronage. Had the British assimilated like the earlier conquerors their religion would not have been given much importance. But since their conduct was discriminatory and biased 'Christianity' also became an issue. The new possibility that the Hindus and Muslims could combine against a common enemy provided a good propaganda theme for manipulators (politicians) for purpose of political propaganda. This is ironic since 'Islam and Christianity' have many things in common. But even then between 1757 and 1857 most of the conflicts were between states and groups in which Muslims frequently allied with the British and the British frequently allied with the Hindus or Muslims against other Muslim states or other European powers.

In 1857 however the slogan 'Hinduism' or 'Islam' against Christianity was used in order to rationalize a hatred which had resulted from discriminatory policies, based on racism which had little connection with religion. Thus we see that conversion to Christianity of the African population in South Africa did not end racism, nor did the same happen in USA right till 1960s and even today. 'Religion' was not an issue in itself but the EEIC policy of discrimination made it an issue and 'Religion' in a symbolic sense was used as a slogan by the freedom fighters' leaders in 1857.

The second factor which made the British different from all other previous invaders was the communication factor. England was many months journey by sea or overland from India but the 'sea communications' which the British used were guaranteed and reliable by virtue of British naval mastery established after 1588 and consolidated as a result of a series of naval victories in the 17th, 18th and 19th centuries. Thus reliable/guaranteed communications kept the British in touch with the home country. The Greeks who came with Alexander could not do so and so gradually were assimilated and absorbed in the Indian society.

The Mughals also could not maintain direct contact with their home country since they themselves had been expelled from their home country by the Uzbeks. The Mughals did employ many men of Turko-Mongol origin but political expediency and the demand and supply gap both necessitated a nobility drawn from a diverse array of Persian Afghan/Pathan and selected Indian background. In the British case the communication factor made it different. Had the Mughals reached India by sea from a far off island and had good naval commanders like Drake, Rodney and Nelson they may also have behaved differently! Thus reliable overseas communications ensured a constant supply of manpower for lower intermediate and higher military civil and political jobs. Britain at this time was experiencing a population boom and India was an opportunity for many Britons who may have ended unemployed or in debtor jails had they stayed in Britain.

The third factor was the economic factor created because of trading objectives and the industrial revolution. The English East India Company's presence was based on trade between India and Britain and pure business or economic activity confined to India only was not their sole objective. India was a base for raw material which had to be transported to Britain. This necessitated economic exploitation and discriminatory taxation and commercial regulation. The English East India Company in this aspect was a prisoner of circumstances and its consequent unpopularity in the Indian populace was regarded by its British Directors sitting in London as a necessary evil. In this aspect, the East India Company was a sophisticated version of Mahmud Ghaznavi or Nadir Shah or Shivaji or Ahmad Shah Abdali. These honourable gentlemen graced the scene for a short duration and then left. The East India Company was there to stay.

The fourth and the most crucial factor which made the British racist and discriminatory and thus different from all previous invaders of India was the 'Organizational Factor'. The Mughals who came to India from Central Asia were exiles or political refugees. Their first founder King Babar could not hold his ancestral state 'Ferghana' in Central Asia. He crossed the Oxus and went southward into present day Afghanistan where he established a new Kingdom. Subsequently he came to India, defeated the reigning Pathan Muslim King of Delhi, and then decided to stay on in India although he detested India's hot weather just like the English East India Company's officials later on. Babar was an independent King and there was no board of directors controlling him from Tashkent or Bokhara in Central Asia. He had decided to stay in India and his descendants never thought like an Englishman of 19th century that one day they would go back and live in a palace or cottage in Central Asia. This was so not because they disliked Central Asia but because it was not economically viable or safe to go and live there. Babar, the founder of the Mughal Empire despised native Indians just as much as many arrogant officials of the English East India Company. But Babar's descendants had no option but to employ Indians in their army and civil service keeping in view the dictates of their situation by virtue of logistical political and social necessity.

The Britisher who came to India in 1757 or in 1847 was not always a racist. Many of them married here, intimately mingled with Indians, took a deep interest in Indian history and made very positive contributions in the literary, social, educational and economic spheres. But all said and done these Britishers were servants of a company which had its headquarters in London, where all policies pertaining to general operations, legislation, recruitment etc. were made. Even if they wanted to, they could not follow a policy which was fair and just for the Indian natives.

The British parliament had many Indian lovers in its ranks but these legislators could not directly interfere with the government of the East India Company. Lord Dalhousie, one of the Governor Generals in India wanted for example to include Indians in the higher government of India but his wish was overruled by the court of Directors of the English East India Company. During the discussions while drafting the India Act of 1853 in the British Parliament a proposal was made to have Indian members in the viceroy's legislative council. This proposal was defeated due to opposition on part of Sir Charles Wood who stated that 'No two Indians could be found to represent adequately the diversity of Hindu and Muslim society'. There was an element of truth in Charles Wood's argument but it was just a minute fraction of the truth against the whole argument in favour of having Indian members. Later on after 1857, the British by and large accepted it as one of the principal causes of the rebellion of 1857. Sir Syed writing in the post-1857 era declared 'Exclusion' as the principle cause of the rebellion.

Lord Macaulay a man who is very often grossly misunderstood and unjustly criticized in India and Pakistan was a matter of fact a great advocate of inclusion of Indians in the higher ranks by virtue of allowing them to compete in the open competitive examinations. Macaulay had been trying to promote the Indian cause since 1833-36. He laid the foundation of modern education in India.

However, in sum total the 'organizational' factor was the principal cause of the deep British-Indian divide which led to the events which erupted like a volcano in 1857. This 'Discrimination' was a major underlying cause of the rebellion of 1857. It was this 'Discrimination' which compelled Indians to think of the British as alien exploiters. It led to exclusion of Indians from the higher legislative and political forums and thus contributed to evolution of laws which were perceived by Indians as an attack on caste and religion.

The Policy of Annexation

The policy of annexation and conquest has also been widely pointed out as one of the principal causes of the rebellion of 1857. This aspect is not as simple as it appears at first sight. The standpoint from which it is mostly condemned is morality or moral grounds but there is no morality in empire building or politics. The policy of annexation on part of the English East India Company was nothing but a logical outcome of superior military strength. The British victory at Plassey had made the English East India Company de facto master of Bengal, Bihar and Orissa. The abolition of the Nawabi in Bengal made them the de jure master also in 1765 or in 1773 technically speaking. By 1764 after having won at Buxar from the political and military point of view the English East India

Company (EEIC) was the master of north India at least as far as all territory of the Oudh state extended.

The EEIC could have annexed Oudh in 1765 but they did not do so in 1765 because they assessed that it was practically not possible for them to manage this vast territory. But they started the process of annexation in 1775 when the Nawab of Oudh agreed to cede to the EEIC territories comprising Benaras, Jaunpore, Mirzapur etc. held by Chait Singh as a subsidiary of the Nawab. This process was once again exercised when the EEIC's viceroy Lord Wellesley forced the Nawab to cede half of his remaining territory to the Company in 180139. This led to extension of EEIC authority to half of northern India as far as eastern boundary of Aligarh district and all territory east of Ganges river. As a matter of fact, Lord Wellesley was planning to annex whole of Oudh state in September, 1801 when for this purpose he had sent his brother Henry Wellesley to the state's Capital Lucknow However long negotiations followed in which the viceroy's brother agreed to cession of only half the territory to the EEIC's domains.

This annexation rendered Oudh politically geographically and militarily little more than a petty vassal state of the East India Company. The probable reason why the viceroy's brother agreed to only half the territory appears to have been partly a fear that complete annexation may be perceived as politically inexpedient being a violation of 1798 between Sir John Shore and Oudh. The EEIC had guaranteed in this treaty that it would protect Oudh in perpetuity. There are two aspects of this annexation. From the strict legal point it can be criticized as unjust. However from the political military or economic point of view it strengthened the EEIC's position in northern India. It brought a vast increase in land revenue since the land revenue was approximately 13,523,474 rupees. Militarily it rendered Oudh incapable of concluding an effective alliance with the Mahrattas or another power since now Oudh was surrounded on all three sides by EEIC's territory whereas previously the EEIC territories were only on its eastern borders.

An interesting fact to be noted here is that the EEICs acquisitions from Oudh in 1801 comprised almost half territory which had initially been assigned by the Mughal Emperor Shah Alam to EEIC in 1765 *i.e.* the Kora and Allahabad areas. This also included Rohilkhand which had been conquered by the Nawab of Oudh by employment of EEIC's Bengal Army brigade which the Nawab had hired in 1774. But this is not the appropriate place to go into any further details. Our aim is to debate the influence of the EEIC's policy of annexation as a subsequent cause of the outbreak of the 1857 rebellion.

We see that the EEIC annexed half of Oudh state whereas they were initially planning to annex the whole of it. It was the viceroy Lord Wellesley's decision and was approved by the Board of Directors. Oudh's army also as per this agreement was to be reduced to less than one tenth of its previous size. Viewed from the political and strategic expediency point of view this treaty was a masterstroke.

In the long term, it laid the foundations for future war against the Mahrattas in the North and against Sikhs and Afghanistan subsequently. How should we view this action today? Keeping in view the origins of the Oudh Nawab we see that his ancestors were the governors of the Mughal Emperor in Oudh. Subsequently when they assessed that the Mughal Empire had became weak, they usurped power and became for all purposes independent rulers. Militarily they were convincingly defeated by the EEIC at Buxar in 1764. But after Buxar the EEIC did not annex Oudh because Lord Clive felt that it was too big to be practically controlled or managed by the EEIC, keeping in view the EEIC's organization and potential at that time. The EEIC resident was not far from the truth once he explained to Nawab Saadat that 'These countries did not belong to your ancestors but were added to the family possessions by the power of the British arms'.

There was however one subtle contradiction in all this. All things said and done Oudh remained an independent and comparatively peaceful region at a time when, most of other parts of India including Delhi, Punjab and Central India witnessed considerable bloodshed, anarchy and destruction. Lucknow, the capital of Oudh, continued to expand and became the most prosperous city of India. New palaces continued to be built, roads were constructed and widened and the people of Oudh had a pride which was much more than inhabitants of any part of India except the Hyderabad state, another British lackey in the south.

Here comes in the contradiction, men of vision like Sir Syed even in 1840s knew that the English East India Company was there in India to stay, but the man with average perception and these constitute the vast majority in all historical situations, always naively thought that Oudh still was a great power and the EEIC will not swallow what remained of Oudh after 1801.

The military lessons of Buxar figured nowhere in the minds of the large majority of the population of Oudh. We see exactly the same phenomena in Germany after 1918 once the German populace mistakenly believed that they had never been militarily defeated but had been stabbed in the back. Myths in themselves are nothing but once whole nations believe in them, the consequences can be disastrous. The Pakistani public was at a loss once they learnt from the terms of the peace agreement of Tashkent that the impression that Pakistan had won the war of 1965 was false.

We are discussing Oudh in considerably greater detail because it was in this region that the rebellion of 1857 came closest to what we call a 'Peoples War'. Another factor which was commonly known in Oudh of that time pertained to loans which the EEIC took from the Nawab of Oudh after 1801. These were less loans and more of a forced exaction since the Nawab clearly knew that in case he refused a loan the EEIC may use force in order to make him pay. There are three aspects about the loans. From the strict pragmatic and expediency standpoint the EEIC was squeezing a docile vassal who they had militarily defeated and who was under their political bondage. Secondly, from the strictly moral or emotional point of view the conduct of the EEIC was regarded by the people, the nobles and the king as blackmail. This added to the prevailing hatred against the EEIC.

The third aspect is the Nawab's behaviour. The Nawab's sole interest was to stay in power. Had he taken a resolute stand and resisted the EEIC's unjust or unfair demands we could have said that he was a hero. But the Nawab's sole interest was in his personal comfort, his concubines and in his debauchery. Here a sharp distinction has to be drawn. The ruling house led by the Nawab had little to do with patriotism or any other lofty moral ideals. Their sole motivation was self-interest. Militarily they had lost the contest in 1764. EEIC's agreement to let them rule stemmed not from any fear of the Nawab's military might but from a simple pragmatic assessment in 1765 and even in 1801 that Oudh was too large a morsel to be swallowed in one go. The EEIC was above all a commercial organization and thoughtless, unplanned impulsive expansion figured nowhere in the principles which guided its foreign policy in India. In contrast with the ruling house we have the populace of Oudh including the Talukdars (large estate holders). This group was a better lot as compared to the Nawab.

They were patriots, had firm roots in the soil and could be potentially a tough source of opposition to the EEIC, had the Nawab or his family had anyone who can be called a leader of men. But alas! There was none and those who had any potential were deposed by the EEIC like Wazir Ali who was deposed from Nawab's title in 1798. It is important to note that the vast majority of Oudh's Talukdars were Hindu Rajputs. Wazir Ali unlike most of Indian rulers after 1757 was surprisingly a true patriot. He succeeded his father Asif-ud-Daula who ruled Oudh from 1775 to 1797 in September, 1797.

The Wazir Ali episode is not directly connected with the events of 1857 but my purpose in relating it here is to acquaint those readers who are not aware of this incident about the self seeking and ulterior motives of majority of Indian rulers in the period 1757-1857. Wazir Ali was claimed to be his son by Asif-ud-Daula and was generally acknowledged to be so by the vast majority in Oudh at least till 1797 when he succeeded his father Asif-ud-Daula as Nawab of Oudh in September 1797. Whether he was or not is a minor issue once we view Wazir Ali as a true patriot. But there is one thing we know with certainty, that once the EEIC discovered that Wazir Ali was anti-EEIC and wanted to strengthen his army they immediately started digging facts to prove that Wazir Ali was a bastard, since the late Asif-ud-Daula was impotent! Wazir Ali immediately after his assumption of power had annoyed his nobles by declaring his intention to reduce their power. He also wanted to reduce the influence of the EEIC's Resident at Lucknow who were performing the same role as Ambassadors of some so-called super powers perform in today's third world countries.

The nobles immediately started their intrigues and urged the EEIC Resident to depose Wazir Ali. Sir John Shore, the Governor General received a divine revelation that Wazir Ali was an illegitimate son! EEIC lackey Saadat Ali Khan who was half brother of Wazir Ali's father and had been fed on crumbs thrown by the EEIC for some 20 years in form of a pension also played an instrumental role in this affair. Saadat Ali Khan had attempted to overthrow his half brother, Asif-ud-Daula in 1776 and once his attempted coup failed he sought asylum in EEIC territory. The EEIC gave him asylum and assigned him a handsome pension. Saadat Ali Khan intrigued with the EEIC in late 1797 and a bargain was struck. Initially the EEIC demanded cession of more territory in return for placing Saadat Ali as Nawab. Subsequently this was changed to financial exactions and handing over of the impregnable and strategic Allahabad fort to the EEIC. Saadat Ali's elevation to the rulership of Oudh was the result of acceptance of a humiliating treaty consisting of 23 articles which further weakened Oudh. The Company was now solely incharge of the external defence of Oudh.

The annual subsidy which Oudh had to pay was increased to 76 lakh rupees. The Oudh army for internal security was now not to exceed 35,000 men. Oudh could no longer have any contact with any other foreign country and was barred from allowing any European to either serve in its army or even to settle in Oudh without the EEIC's permission. Thus we see Saadat Ali, a pensioner of EEIC residing at Banaras being informed about his elevation to the Nawabi of Oudh. Saadat Ali travels to Kanpur and from there is escorted to Lucknow by EEIC's troops and is proclaimed Nawab on 21 January, 1798.

But this is not the end, it is the same Saadat Ali who again yields to the EEIC half more of Oudh in 1801. Wazir Ali was exiled to Banaras from where Saadat Ali came to assume Nawabship. The EEIC however was not happy to allow Wazir Ali to stay so close to Oudh's border. They, therefore, resolved in end of 1798 to transfer him to Calcutta. Wazir Ali resisted this attempt and in this connection visited the British Resident a certain Mr. Cherry on 14th January 1799. Mr. Cherry reportedly raised his voice during the course of discussion upon which Wazir Ali lost his temper and struck Mr. Cherry with his sword. This was a signal for Wazir Ali's armed retainers to attack which they did killing the Resident Mr. Cherry and four other Englishmen.

The fifth Englishman in that room managed to escape 49. Wazir Ali fled from the scene, raised an army of 6,000 but was defeated. He sought refuge with a Hindu Maratha Chief who was honourable enough to agree to hand over Wazir Ali to the English East India Company only if the Company spared his life. The Company kept its promise. Wazir Ali was shifted to Calcutta from Banaras in 1800 and died a natural death in March 181750. The English Company was more honourable than some third world armies of the post-1947 who first swored on the Holy Quran to do the same as in Wazir Ali's case and later handed some insurgents to the EEIC. The Wazir Ali affair was used by the new EEIC Viceroy Lord Wellesley to pressurize Saadat Ali to disband his army and to replace it by a pure EEIC force.

The writing that the EEIC wanted to annex whole of Oudh was on the wall right from 1775 when they took Banaras from Oudh. It became clearer in 1797 during the Wazir Ali affair and by 1801 it was crystal clear. The Oudh Nawabs made the EEIC designs easier by gross mismanagement and debauchery. From 1798 to 1856 their guiding principle of conduct was to somehow stay in power, however much Oudh is reduced in sovereignty or territory or in financial terms. The EEIC did not end the matter of exactions in 1801.

In 1814 they again interfered with succession to Nawabship on Saadat Ali Khan's death and placed the candidate of their choice Ghaziuddin Haider on the throne. The price of this succession was forced loans to the EEIC by Oudh on extremely low interest rates. Thus Ghaziuddin Haider loaned the EEIC some 3.085 million Pound Sterlings during his reign from 1814-2753. Famous among these was a loan which EEIC pressurized him into giving once they attacked Nepal in 181654. Ghaziuddin was also influenced by the EEIC viceroy Lord Hastings into declaring himself King in 1819 and thus theoretically setting aside his political subservience to the Mughal Emperor at Delhi.

Practically the Mughal Emperor was also an EEIC pensioner56 from 1803 once the EEIC captured Delhi but theoretically EEIC was his subject and servant. Here it is interesting to note that Tipu

Sultan had also declared himself King repudiating the Mughals and had acknowledged the Sultan of Ottoman Turkey as the Caliph of Islam. Similarly Shivaji had declared himself a King, independent of the Mughal empire in second half of 17th century. It is interesting to analyze EEIC's subsequent excuse in 1856 of citing mismanagement in the final annexation of Oudh.

As a matter of fact it was the policy of forced loans which destroyed the economy of Oudh. These loans were exorted from Oudh at 5% to 6% rate of interest which at that time was considered very low since from 1793 the EEIC had been paying its shareholders 10.5% per annum. The first loan of 1.85 million pounds was taken in 1814. The second of 1.00 million Pound Sterlings in 1815 and the third of 1.00 million Pound Sterlings in 1825. The second loan was never repaid and instead a worthless part of Terai forest territory taken from Nepal was given to Oudh. The same territory was returned to Nepal in 1858 59 as a reward for sending a force to assist the EEIC in the final capture of Lucknow in March 1858.

In 1837, the Governor General Lord Auckland forced on Oudh a treaty by which it asserted its right to take over what remained of Oudh if the Company felt that the country was being mismanaged. The treaty also imposed on Oudh an annual payment of 1,600,000 Rupees. This last clause was in violation of treaty of 1801 by which the Company had agreed to defend Oudh in return for cession of half of its territory. Even the Board of Directors of the EEIC viewed this treaty as unjust and unfair and declared it null and void. The Governor General however never informed the King of Oudh that the treaty was entirely annulled. He only informed him that he would not have to pay for his defence. King Muhammad Ali Shah (1837-42) continued to appease the EEIC. In around 1839 he granted them a loan of 3,240,800 Rs. at 4% interest. In 1842 he again loaned the EEIC 1,400,000 or 140,000 Pounds at 5% interest.

These two loans were exorted to make up for the disastrous First Afghan War. It is significant to note that all interest which the EEIC paid back to Oudh was used for pensions and allowances of the Oudh Royal Family. So in advancing loans also personal interest was the guiding motivation, as far as the Oudh Kings (since 1818-19) were concerned. Muhammad Ali Shah's successor

Amjad Ali Shah (1842-47) was also forced to grant the EEIC a loan of Rs.3,200,000 on his accession in 184262. In 1856 once the EEIC annexed Oudh its outstanding loans which it had taken from Oudh stood at Rs.35,000,000 or 3.5 million Pounds. The purpose of this considerable attention devoted to the EEIC conduct in Oudh may seem a little too detailed. It is however important since it illustrates bad faith and greed on both sides and the sufferers in this case were the common people.

The year 1848 was an important year for India. It was in this year that the 36 years old Lord Dalhousie came to India. Dalhousie was a utilitarian and progressive man. He rightly viewed the princely states of India as an unnecessary anachronism. On 18th September 1848 he in a letter said, 'I have got two other kingdoms on hand to dispose of, Oudh and Hyderabad'. But this was not all, Dalhousie went further and he made another profound observation which convincingly proves that Dalhousie had a remarkable insight about the character of the Indo-Pak rulers of that time. This observation was true not only for the king of Oudh but for almost all Indo-Pak rulers of that time and to a certain extent even those of today in many third world countries. Dalhousie thus wrote about the king of Oudh 'The king won't offend or quarrel with us, and will take any amount of kicking without being rebellious!'. Thus Dalhousie made a firm resolve to annex Oudh.

In 1849, Dalhousie appointed Sleeman as Resident of Oudh. Sleeman was instructed by Dalhousie to prepare a report on the existing affairs of Oudh. Sleeman by his deep knowledge of India and its languages was ideally suited for this task. Born in 1788, Sleeman joined the East India Company's Bengal Army as an ensign in 1810 at Allahabad Fort. He fought in the Anglo-Nepalese War of 1814-16. He became famous for the decisive part he played in suppression of 'Thugs' in India from 1826 to 183265. Sleeman's report was published in 1851. He agreed to the fact that Oudh was mismanaged but also expressed his opinion against annexing it. With profound insight, Sleeman warned Dalhousie that Oudh's annexation would have a very negative effect on Bengal Army, bulk of whose Sepoys belonged to Oudh. Sleeman actually warned Dalhousie that annexation of Oudh would lead to a mutiny in the Bengal Army. The next Resident James Outram who succeeded in

1854 also prepared another report largely based on Sleeman's report. Outram also agreed with the 'mismanagement' concept but was not in favour of outright annexation. Outram favoured a regency council led by the EEIC who would reform Oudh's state of affairs. Dalhousie prepared a minute on the 'Oudh' question in which he recommended that entire administration should be taken over by the EEIC while the king of Oudh should be allowed to retain his title.

The viceregal council of Dalhousie was however against violating the 1801 treaty which guaranteed the sovereignty of Oudh. The difference of opinion however was resolved by the EEIC court of Directors and the British government's decision to annex Oudh. Wajid Ali Shah resisted the decision but was forced to abdicate and Dalhousie issued a proclamation dated 13th February 1856 through the medium of which he declared annexation of Oudh to the territories of the EEIC. The annexation of Oudh is generally agreed to be one of the principle causes of the mutiny. This was not true. As we shall see later that the rebellion began from Meerut and Oudh followed the lead given by the Meerut Troopers only after two months! What was true was the fact that the rebellion lasted for a far longer time because bulk of the Bengal Army was recruited from the Hindu Rajput and Hindu Jat population of Oudh. This was why the struggle in Oudh did come closest to the modern conception of people's war in 1857. It did take the EEIC almost one year to recapture Oudh. The reason for this protracted affair was concentration of some 80% sepoy regiments in Oudh and the immense pride of Rajput Talukdars.

The foremost cause of resentment in the people of Oudh against the EEIC was its extortionist policy from 1775 onwards. The EEIC to a considerable extent rightly accused the Oudh Nawabs and subsequently its kings of misgovernment and mal-administration. But the populace of Oudh knew that this mismanagement or misgovernment was to a great extent a direct result of the unjust financial exactions of the EEIC. And yet the EEIC annexed the state in 1856. Inwardly or militarily Oudh may have been very weak but culturally or symbolically Lucknow of 1820s or 1830s had outshone Delhi. It was a modern city of palaces spacious gardens and paved road. The nobles and a large part of populace were prosperous and owed their prosperity to Oudh being an independent state. The king had an army and a host of other officials numbering more than 1,60,000. On annexation most of these were rendered jobless. Heavy tax was imposed on opium which was a very frequently used drug.

This enraged a considerable part of the populace. Land deeds and titles of ownership were subjected to scrutiny and zealous young civil servants of the EEIC in a bid to emancipate the peasants annoyed the Talukdars (Jagirdars or big landlords). This phenomenon was paradoxical, since the British intention in this case was positive but the landlord of that day had a much greater influence and, this the British agreed to accept at the cost of enlightenment of the people of the subcontinent after 1857.

Thus, though 1857 which in itself was a positive affair resulted in retarding growth of progressive ideas in India which men like Dalhousie wanted to advance. Thus after 1857 the British Government which assumed the Government of India decided to ally with the feudals whereas before 1857 their predecessor the EEIC were following an excellent policy of destroying feudalism in India. There were cases where estates were rightfully held but the proofs of ownership were missing. Confiscation of these estates also alienated a large number of landowners in Oudh. Even if the annexation of Oudh itself was not a negative step, the conduct of many officials of the EEIC alienated a vast majority of the populace. Sir James Outram the Resident at Oudh who had been appointed the Chief Commissioner on annexation of Oudh was a reasonable man.

He was however forced to leave for England due to illness. His successor a certain Mr. Coverly Jackson who was only the officiating Chief Commissioner was a very short-tempered and irrational man. His arrogant and racist behaviour immediately alienated all those people who came into contact with him. The conduct of the EEIC officials was careless and irresponsible and in the process made the EEIC administration more unpopular. For more than an year through sheer carelessness and negligence the allowances were not paid to pensioners which was part of the EEIC settlement terms. Covertly Jackson occupied the palace which had been earmarked for the Oudh Royal family.

The EEIC committed yet another significant tactical blunder. Dalhousie had given detailed instructions to Outram regarding disarming the populace of Oudh who at the time of annexation were well armed since in those days security of the common citizen or village was their own affair. Outram however did not carry out this order since he felt that it could be done after the summer. Dalhousie in a demi official letter addressed to Outram in 1856 had thus written, 'It is my intention that not a single fortified place should be left in Oudh with the exception of those that belong to Government. It is further my intention that the whole population should be disarmed... as was done with such excellent effect in the Punjab in 1849'. This disarming was as a matter of fact not carried out and thus prolonged the war of independence in Oudh till almost 1859. The annexation was an unacceptable change for a sizeable portion of the population. Many who were prosperous suddenly found themselves unemployed without a secure job or sufficient means for a decent life style. The Bengal Sepoys who belonged to Oudh were a privileged class in Oudh since they were EEIC employees. They were given a preferential treatment in their private dealings with Oudh state officials once they visited their houses and villages on long leave. Now they were just like any other common man living in Oudh. Thus a sepoy noted that 'I used to be a great man when I went home, a servant would carry my bags, the rest of the village rose when I approached. Now the lowest puffs their pipes in my face'. In sum total the net situation in 1856 was explosive in Oudh in particular and Northern India in general.

The Attack on Social and Religious Beliefs

The EEIC was different in another way from all other conquerors of India. Apart from being a commercial entity many of its officials took a deep interest in emancipation of the population and eradication of many genuine social evils and outmoded practices. In this regard, they sharply differed from their predecessors the Mughals who were not really bothered about social or religious enlightenment. There were definitely some Mughal Kings and Governors who at least tried to ensure that no woman was forced to commit Satti (Self-immolation on her husband's death) against her own free will, but there was no definite policy and varied from ruler to ruler. This perceived attack on caste and religion was generally more relevant to the Hindus, but the bulk of Bengal Army soldiers were Hindus, some 80%, and these were either Brahman or Rajput both the highest Hindu castes and very fussy and fastidious about matters pertaining to religious beliefs and rituals.

Lord William Bentinck who was Governor General from 1828 to 1835 abolished Satti (widow burning) in 1829 vide Regulation No.XVII of 04 December. It is of interest to note that Akbar the Mughal Emperor had also made an attempt to restrict this practice. The Mahrattas were also against it and it was a practice mostly found in High Caste Hindus or Rajput landlords. Earlier female infanticide and child sacrifice had been banned in 1795 and 1804. Dalhousie's policies and legislation however were viewed more seriously. His religious disabilities Act of 1856 gave protection to Hindus all over India who had converted to Christianity. In the year 1832 a similar law was passed giving protection to Christian converts in inheriting property, but this law was confined only to the Bengal presidency area, notably in the case of inheriting property. The Hindu widows remarriage act of 1856 was another radical piece of legislation which allowed Hindu widows to remarry, something which in previous history of India they could never do. All these were highly progressive and radical pieces of legislation.

The activities of Christian missionaries were also very critically perceived by both Hindus and Muslims. But in this case also the Hindus were more seriously affected since the most lucrative target of the Christian missionaries were low caste Hindus who were more prone to become Christians since conversion to Christianity improved their degraded and oppressed position in the caste conscious Hindu society. In 1855 Mr. Edward a Christian missionary of Calcutta published a leaflet distributed all over India in which he urged all Indians to convert to Christianity. The Government schools held Bible classes which was again perceived as an attack on religion.

Before we proceed further it is important for the sake of posterity to examine various EEIC attitudes about missionary activity in India. It would be unfair to brand all EEIC officials as

Christian fanatics. The following excerpt from the EEIC Board of Directors Despatch to Lord Minto proves that the EEIC was not following an organized policy aimed at religious conversion; 'On the other hand, wrote the court (Court of Directors) it will be your bounded duty vigilantly to guard the public tranquillity from interruption, and to impress upon the minds of all inhabitants of India, that the British faith, upon which they rely for the free exercise, of their religion, will be inviolably maintained.'

But by and large, the common man perceived that his religion was in danger and thought that the EEIC aimed at converting all Indians to Christianity. This belief was reinforced by the presence of many missionary minded people in the ranks of the EEIC's civil service and the Bengal Army. This feeling that both Hinduism and Islam were in danger played a decisive role in uniting both the Hindu and Muslims. At least till 1857 the British policies in India were more anti-Hindu and this demolishes the myth in Pakistan that the British were more anti-Muslim.

Causes Specifically Relating to The Bengal Army

Today we find historians very confidently asserting that there was no conspiracy in 1857 and it was a spontaneous act. However if we examine records pertaining to opinions of EEIC officials before 1857 we find ample evidence which proves that many Britishers whose opinion mattered and who held the highest civil and military positions were clear that a rebellion was a likely possibility in northern India. Sleeman warned Dalhousie about it in the case of annexation of Oudh as we have already seen. Sir Charles Napier, the Commander-in-Chief prophesied it and Dalhousie was very apprehensive about it and we can see this from following actions of Dalhousie:-(1) He gave detailed instructions to Outram, the Chief Commissioner of Oudh regarding disarming of the population of Oudh and dismantling of fortification. He foresaw that a rebellion was possible. (2) He repeatedly urged the British government to increase the number of European troops in India in ratio to the native troops. Despite repeated reminders Dalhousie's suggestion were not even discussed by the EEIC Board of Directors for two years. (3) Dalhousie also realized that Indians felt excluded from the government and it was necessary to include Indians in higher policy formulation.

Keeping this in mind Dalhousie made various attempts to obtain authorization of the British Government and EEIC Board of Directors to have an Indian as member of his legislative council. This however was not agreed to in the British Parliament. Sir Syed Ahmad Khan, in his famous pamphlet 'Causes of Indian Mutiny' singled this out as one of the salient causes of the events of 185779. Dalhousie was aware that the policy of annexation was creating unrest. However as we have seen that Dalhousie did not want to abolish the King's title in Oudh but was ordered to do so by the Board of Directors of EEIC.

In the case of Hyderabad, Dalhousie refused to interfere soon after he arrived in India despite the fact that he was urged to do so by the Directors of the EEIC. In this case he actually threatened to resign. In the case of Bahawalpur state he refused to interfere. Dalhousie encouraged recruitment of troops from Nepal and Punjab. We will see that these troops played a crucial role in 1857. It was Dalhousie who ordered the raising of the Punjab Frontier Force vide G.G.O. dated 18 May 1849.

Sir Charles Napier, the Commander-in-Chief of Bengal Army was also convinced that the Bengal Army was the most serious threat to EEIC rule. In 1849 he wrote that it was apparent to him and to all officers on the spot who were conversant with Native and Sepoy habits and feelings, that a widely spread and formidable scheme of mutiny was in progress, and great danger impending 82.'

Whatever historians may state now a cursory glance at the situation in 1857 makes one thing very clear that without the Bengal Army there would have been no rebellion, but this is only one aspect. The other aspect is that without the Bengal Army or for that matter the Madras or the Bombay armies there would have been no EEIC's conquest of India. So the 'Bengal Army Factor' works both ways, it was instrumental in EEIC's success in the first place and it was instrumental in the rebellion also. But the Bengal Army's alienation was a slow process. Mutinies started right from 1757 but these were over administrative, financial and caste matters and not to overthrow EEIC's rule. The transition of rebellion or a bid for independence is always a slow and subtle process. It is in this regard that the British argument that 1857 was just a soldier's mutiny is baseless. The Bengal Army did fight for EEIC for hundred years but by 1857 it was no longer the force that it was in 1757. We will examine the salient aspects which brought this change of perception in the Bengal Sepoy:-(1) The prime motivation of the Bengal Army soldiers in joining the army was economic. Just like the Irishmen of 18th, 19th or 20th centuries.

It is true that the British were masters in making other races fight their wars through a subtle system based on regimental pride, motivation, resolute leadership espirit de corps etc. But the essential fact was that the Bengal Sepoy was an Indian and a subject. It is true that the British treated their native soldiers much better than most native soldiers were treated by native rulers. But race is a very rigid barrier and is made more rigid by difference of religion. Man's basic needs are food, water and air, but once these are fulfilled he strives for higher needs and ideals like freedom and independence.

The racial barrier which made it impossible for a native to ever be an officer was a major factor in producing alienation. (2) The Bengal Army was composed of 80% Hindu Brahman and Rajputs. Their daily rituals were complicated and conflicted with demands of military life. Slowly and steadily it increased their hatred of their officers and EEIC not because of any personal reason but simply because they belonged to an alien race who they perceived as bent upon damaging their religious sensitivities. Two aspects were important in this regard *i.e.* travel across sea which was regarded by the high caste Hindus and Rajputs of that time as something which would soil and pollute the purity of their caste. The second was going across the Indus westwards which again in their opinion polluted the purity of their caste.

Thus once the First Afghan War started the Bengal Army was deployed west of Indus. This had a serious effect on the morale of the Hindu Brahmans for the reasons: (1) Once the Brahmans crossed the Indus their caste was rendered impure and on return to India they had to spend heavy sums of money on the rituals through which they had to undergo in order to be readmitted to their high caste. (2) West of Indus they had to eat food which they considered impure and this also soiled their caste. (3) In Afghanistan due to cold climate the Hindus could not carry out the rituals of bathing etc. This was the major reason for the post 1841 rapid decline in the Hindu soldiers morale and not the initial reverses suffered in the First Afghan War. (4) The Muslim troops employed in the First Afghan war were demoralised because they were deployed after a long time against the Muslims. The last time they were deployed against a Muslim state was in 1774 during the Rohilla war. The most intriguing of these incidents, unnoticed by large majority of historians was the refusal of the 4th Bengal Cavalry on 2nd November 1840 during the First Afghan War, to charge a party of Afghan horsemen led by Dost Muhammad Khan at Perwan, north of Kabul. The British historian John Fortescue had no answer for the reason why the 2nd Bengal Light Cavalry fell back and fled from the battle field. Fortescue thus said about this incident that; 'And then followed one of those incidents which after endless explanation remain always mysterious.

The 2nd Light Cavalry was a good corps with good officers; but such misconduct could not be overlooked and the regiment was with ignominy disbanded'. The British did not understand why 2nd Light Cavalry had behaved like that. There was another likely explanation for this behaviour which had a deep connection with 2nd Light Cavalry's history. The 2nd Light Cavalry was raised from Afghans of Kandhari origin settled at Lucknow in 1788 by the Nawab Vizier of Oudh. It became the 2nd Bengal Light Cavalry only in 179685. It is possible that their peculiar Afghan origin may have played a part in their reluctance to charge the Afghans at Perwan!

The EEIC forces retreat from Kabul in January 1842 shook the faith of the Bengal Army native soldiers in the invincibility of EEIC and the Britishers. Although hardly 700 out of total of this force of some 4,500 troops were Europeans, the psychological effect of this debacle on the sepoys was tremendous. The EEIC did subsequently capture Kabul and inflicted such a sharp defeat on the Afghans that they dared not attack India in 1857 once the EEIC position was highly vulnerable. But all this was not registered by the Sepoy. He saw the EEIC retreat from Kabul to Jalalabad of a column in which only one doctor reached Jalalabad. The human mind is not a computer and its mechanism is subject to various biases. Thus while the Afghans were administered a tough lesson, the Indian soldiers drew erroneous conclusions from this single episode of the Afghan war about the fighting potential of the EEIC. Had occupying Afghanistan been worth it the EEIC would have done it. But it was simply not cost effective being a barren, desolate and unproductive country.

The EEIC conquest of Punjab in 1849 created another unique situation. Firstly the EEIC had conquered the whole of India and the Bengal Sepoy feared that now the EEIC may reduce their army. As a matter of fact the EEIC did start reducing their army after 184987. The second fear pertained to the new recruitment policy of the EEIC. The British recruited from Oudh because they regarded the Oudh Rajput or Brahman as suitable fighting material, but they did so because till 1845 the Hindustani was their best available choice. The EEIC officers were fed up with the caste prejudices and hang-ups of the Hindus who formed 75% the of the Bengal Army. But till 1845 the EEIC did not have any other option. After 1845-46 (First Sikh War) and 1848-49 (Second Sikh War) the EEIC found that they could recruit good soldier material from Punjab and trans Indus about whose fighting qualities in case of Sikhs the EEIC was convinced by virtue of the excellent fighting performance in the two Sikh wars. Secondly, Punjab was a Muslim majority province and the Muslim potential soldiers of Punjab had no caste complications. The Muslims were in minority in the Bengal Army before 1845 because in Oudh and North West provinces (later UP) the Muslim were an overall minority in terms of population.

There was yet another military cause which played a far more crucial role than the annexation of Oudh in alienating the Hindus who were the vast majority of the Bengal Army. This was a major change in the terms of service of the Bengal Army which was conceived and planned by Dalhousie but introduced by his successor Lord Canning greatly demoralised the Hindu soldiers.

As per the terms of service prior to 1856 the Bengal Army regiments could not be transported across the sea. This severely restricted the mobility of the Bengal Army. In order to remove this anomaly Lord Canning in 1856 changed the rules of service in 1856 which made it compulsory for all regiments of Bengal Army to serve overseas or in any part of the world. This was again perceived/viewed by High Caste Hindu soldiers as an attack on their religion. This was the General Service Enlistment Act of 1856.

News of British reverses in the Crimean War of 1856 also encouraged Bengal Army sepoys belief that the Britisher was not invincible.

But the introduction of the Greased Cartridges in 1857 was the final and decisive blow. These cartridges which the sepoys thought contained cow or swine's fat was a definite attack on the religion of both Hindus and Muslims. These cartridges gave a simultaneous common ground to both to rationalize their hatred of the EEIC European. The dispersion of British troops and their being outnumbered overwhelmingly in 1857 was the final blow. 'Petty parsimony on part of supreme government in matters of allowances provoked a number of small mutinies in 1843 and 1844.'88 This is the verdict of Sir John Fortescue, the official historian of the British army. Fortescue went further, he noted that 'the same cause amounting to positive injustice brought a number of Bengal Regiments to the verge of revolt in 1849'89. In this case, Sir Charles Napier the Commander-in-Chief of the Company's Bengal Army's confrontation and subsequent resignation was a decisive event. There were two mutinies in the two respective regiments of Bengal Army over stoppage of allowances. Sir Charles Napier disbanded one and restored the allowances for the second. Lord Dalhousie censured him and revoked his orders. Dalhousie was a civilian and a young man. He did not understand the demoralizing effect which this action had on the soldiers of Bengal Army. Sir Charles Napier resigned and went back to Britain in 185090. Sir John Fortescue's opinion on this episode is worth quoting, 'The sepoys thus saw the chief, who had observed equity on their behalf, rewarded by public disgrace'.

Another reason was the successive decline in the quality of officers of the Bengal Army by the process of secondment to civil duties after the annexation of Punjab. Yet another factor was the greater centralization which reduced power of units commanding officers to reward or to punish. This reduced the esteem attached to the Commanding Officer in Sepoy eyes.

In short all the causes though they did contribute towards the mutiny were insignificant compared to the last two *i.e.* the 'Greased Cartridges' and the dispersal of the British or white troops and their overwhelming inferiority in number to the native troops. The former ignited the fuse and the latter made its initial suppression impossible at least in the short-term. This gap in terms of time and space enabled the sepoys to occupy and concentrate at two strategic places *i.e.* Delhi and Lucknow.

Since the 'Greased Cartridges' were the most immediate and specific cause of the rebellion of 1857 we will examine it in a little more detail. Till 1856, the British and EEIC armies used Brown Bess which was a muzzle loading rifle. Meanwhile from early 1850s trials had been carried out at Enfield in England on a new rifle with three grooves. This was called the Enfield or Enfield-Pritchett rifle. 'Enfield' because the trials were carried out at a place called 'Enfield' and 'Pritchett' because 'Pritchett' was the name of the man who invented its bullet.

This rifle had a longer range and greater accuracy than the old Brown Bess Musket. It was again a muzzle loaded rifle. Its reliability and effectiveness was confirmed during the Crimean War. In the old Brown Bess musket lubrication was done with linseed oil and bees wax. Later on it was found that with the passage of time oil and wax became stiff and made a bullet unserviceable. Therefore in the Enfield Rifle ammunition tallow made of beef or swine fat was introduced. The cartridges for Enfield Rifle to be introduced in India were also to be manufactured in India by local contractors. It was evident that since in India mutton was twice as expensive as beef or pork the local contractors would use beef which was cheaper.

The bullet's cap had to be removed before being loaded. This could be done either by hand or by biting with the teeth, which was a quicker way and therefore the one used in loading drill. The EEIC also decided to introduce the Enfield Rifle in its army in late 1856. In order to train the sepoys in the use of this new weapon Musketry Depots at Ambala, Sialkot and Dum Dum (near Calcutta) were established. From later 1856 and early 1857 detachments of five men each were sent from each battalion to these depots in order to train the sepoys in the handling of the new Enfield Rifle. The rumours that the greased cartridges contained pig and cow fat started circulating in the sepoys from January, 1857. It was this rumour which was the immediate and direct cause of the mutinies in the Bengal Army from March 185793.

1857: History vs Myth: Sudhir Sharma—Academician and Scholar of History

No doubt the 1857 uprising was a sepoy mutiny; it was also the last attempt by Muslims to recover their own rule from the British. The role of the Hindu princes was peripheral and the epicentre of the uprising was the erstwhile kingdom of Oudh. So, the argument that any attempt to celebrate 1857 will amount to heaping insult on the sacrifices made by Rajputs, Marathas, Jats and Sikhs to throw out Muslim invaders from India seems tenable. After all, why should one celebrate an episode that aimed at reverting back to medievalism?

Field Marshal Lord Frederick Roberts of Kandahar, who was in India between 1852 and 1893 and had participated in quelling the mutiny at several places, including Delhi, wrote: "The first threatening of coming trouble were heard in the early part of 1857. During the months of February, March and April rumours reached us at Peshwar of mysterious *chapatti*s (unleavened cakes) being sent about the country with the object, it was alleged, of preparing the natives for some forthcoming event. We heard that the 19th Native Infantry at Barhampur, a military station about 100 miles from Calcutta, had broken open the bells-of-arms... that a sepoy named Mangal Pandey at Barrackpore had wounded the Adjutant and Sergant Major of his regiment; and that sepoys at the Schools of Musketry had objected to use the cartridges served out with new rifles."

As the news spread, the native regiments based in Peshwar, Naushera, Umbala, Mian Mir (Lahore), Multan, Ferozpore and other places were disarmed. The happenings at Meerut triggered the revolt elsewhere; and, it is from there that the sepoys marched to Delhi and declared Bahadur Shah as *badshah*.

The participation of Gurkhas and Sikhs to recapture the Imambara in Lucknow on March 14, 1858, proves that there was no national spirit behind the revolt. The British also received cooperation from the Amir of Afghanistan. Commissioner of Lahore Division Sir John Lawrence had strongly advocated the policy of trusting the Maharaja of Patiala and the Rajas of Jind and Nabha.

Lord Frederick Roberts further adds, "The causes which

brought about the mutiny were so various and some of them of such long-standing, that it is difficult to point them out as concisely as I could wish.

Mohammedans looked back to the days of their empire in India... Their *maulvis* taught them it was only lawful for true Musalmans to submit to the rule of an infidel if there was no possibility of successful revolt, and they watched for the chance of again being able to make Islam supreme. The late Sir George Campbell says that the mutiny was a sepoy revolt, not a Hindu rebellion."

But what about the role of 1857 in our national movement? Hasn't it inspired our national leaders to take on the British? Can't we celebrate it just for the reason that it helped us unite against foreign rule?

It was this symbolism that made Veer Savarkar term it India's first war of independence. Even Jawaharlal Nehru insisted on using this expression. He pointed out that while the landmark event was an expression of "deep-seated resentment against the British rule and an attempt to oust it", the "movement was not organised", nor was it "co-ordinated". He also underscored that both "Hindus and Muslims participated in it-in spite of our ingrained habit of intense feuds-and in victory as well as in defeat, they marched shoulder to shoulder".

Nehru, who was born 32 years after the uprising, said "I remember that when I was a child, which was a long time ago, there were still people around who had seen or heard about the incidents of 1857. When I was nine or 10-year-old, I used to listen to the tales of those old people about what happened in 1857-58 in Allahabad, Delhi, Lucknow and other places. They were real stories and the people recounting them had experienced them at first hand. As you know, such things make a deep impression on a child's mind. It made a deep impression on me and filled me with anger."

"Historians now write treaties full of complex arguments which is all right. We must read their works no doubt. But I have often wondered what impact the events of 1857 made on the minds of the common people in India. Later, when I had the opportunity of visiting Oudh and the rural areas of Allahabad district, I often heard tales of 1857 in those parts... So there is no doubt about it that the events of 1857 did make an indelible impression on a very large part of the country," Nehru further added.

Today, we know the 1857 uprising was the last attempt by Muslims to recover their rule from the British. Yet, we need to celebrate it for rekindling the spirit of independence among us.

Sikh Rajahs were Amply Rewarded for Saving the British Empire

Patiala

A tract of land out of the confiscated territories of Nawab of Jhajjar, valued at about two lakhs of rupees a-year, was conferred on the Maharaja and his heirs in perpetuity on condition of good behavior and of service, military and political, at any time or quarrel, danger or disturbance." Also, his family estate of Bhadaur, adjacent to his estate, which had recently been absorbed by the British, was restored to him. "Zeenat Mahal" in (New) Delhi, belonging to Bahadur Shah's favourite wife was also given to the Maharaja of Patiala. A number of additions were made to his titles – now the *Farzand-i-Khas* (Special Son).

Jind

Raja Saroop Singh of Jind was given lands confiscated from Dadree, valued at about a lakh of rupees a-year; several villages from pargannah of Thanesar worth 14, 500 rupees yearly revenue. His titles were also increased, and now he was *Farzand-i-Dilband,* or most cherished son.

Nabha

Raja Bharpoor Singh of Nabha was given two districts, worth a lakh of rupees annual revenue, from the confiscated land of Jhajjar. He was also awarded additional titles, and he was now *Farzand-I-Arjumand,* or Noble son of good faith.

Faridkot

Though no conspicuous services were rendered by the Raja, yet he showed himself loyal and eager in our [British] cause, " and "In acknowledgement of these services, he was delivered from the duty of furnishing his contingent of sowars to the Ferozepore Commissioner, and received an increase of honours and titles.

Kapurthala

In acknowledgement of services of 'Almost Christian' Raja of Kapurthala, Randhir Singh Ahluwalia, Government remitted the entire tribute for the year 1857, and reduced yearly amount in future from yearly 150, 000 rupees to a quarter of a lakh.

Some Side Bars

After peace was proclaimed by Lord Canning, automatic pardon was announced for all rebels who would surrender before January 1, 1859, unless they had been involved in massacres.

Charles Dickens, furious on learning about announcement of Amnesty, wrote on October 4, 1858:

"I wish I were commander-in-chief in India, I should do my utmost to exterminate the Race upon whom the stain of the late cruelties rested" Nothing less than extermination of the Hindus would have satisfied Dickens, who was disgusted by reports that Canning had offered amnesty to mutineers not directly involved in the killings." (Dickens, C., Letters of Charles Dickens, II, 459, 473. (Oxford, 1995); James, Lawrence, *Raj: the Making and Unmaking of British India*, p.283)

Queen Victoria in Defence of Duleep Singh

Maharaja Duleep Singh was in London. Some Englishmen observed that he had not condemned his countrymen's atrocities, during the mutiny. Lord Clarendon was one of those, who were very vocal against Duleep Singh. Queen Victoria came to his defence and justified his reaction, whatever it was.

"Lord Clarendon wrote he was indignant to learn that the boy Maharaja Duleep Singh, who was being educated in England, had shown little or no regret for the atrocities which had been committed. The young Maharaja's father, one of the most harsh and cruel of Indian rulers had been deposed by the British government and his son taken under British protection.

The Queen pointed out that in spite of gentleness and amiability the Maharaja had an Eastern nature, and could hardly be expected as a deposed Eastern sovereign to be very fond of British rule or to like hearing the people of his country called fiends and monsters and that they being brought by hundreds if not thousands to be executed. She advised Lord Clarendon to say nothing on he subject."

British Policy of "Divide and Rule" to Continue

Lord Canning wrote in his letter dated October 9, 1857:

"The men who fought against us in Delhi were of both creeds; probably in equal numbers. If we destroy or desecrate Musalman Mosques or Brahmin Temples we do exactly what is wanting to band the two antagonist races against ourselves ...as we must rule 150 million of people by a handful (more or less small) number of Englishmen, let us do it in the manner best calculated to leave them divided (as in religion and national feeling as they already are) and to inspire them with the greatest possible awe of our power."

State	*Entry*	*Exit*	*Combat Forces*	*Population*	*Losses*
Britain	1857	1858	60000	30000000	2000
India	1857	1858	500000	250000000	8000

Indian Mutiny also called Sepoy Mutiny (1857-58), widespread but unsuccessful rebellion against British rule in India begun by Indian troops (sepoys) in the service of the British East India Company. It began in Meerut and then spread to Delhi, Agra, Kanpur, and Lucknow.

To regard the rebellion merely as a sepoy mutiny is to underestimate the increasing pace of Westernization after the establishment of British paramountcy in India in 1818. Hindu society was being affected by the introduction of Western ideas. Missionaries were challenging the religious beliefs of the Hindus. The humanitarian movement led to reforms that went deeper than the political superstructure.

Lord Dalhousie had made efforts for the emancipation of women and had introduced a bill to remove all legal obstacles to the remarriage of Hindu widows. Converts to Christianity were to share with their Hindu brethren in the property of the family estate. There was a widespread belief that the British aimed at breaking down the caste system. The introduction of western methods of education was a direct challenge to orthodoxy, both Hindu and Muslim. To these problems may be added the growing discontent of the noble Brahmans, many of whom had been dispossessed of their revenues or had lost lucrative positions. Everywhere the old Indian aristocracy was being replaced by British officials.

The mutiny broke out in the Bengal army because it was only in the military sphere that Indians were organized. The pretext for revolt was the introduction of the new Enfield rifle; to load it the sepoys had to bite off the ends of lubricated cartridges. There appears to be some foundation for the sepoys' belief that the grease used to lubricate the cartridges was a mixture of pigs' and cows' lard; thus, to have oral contact with it was an insult to both Muslims and Hindus. Late in April 1857, sepoy troopers at Meerut refused the cartridges; as punishment, they were given long prison terms, fettered, and put in jail. This punishment incensed their comrades, who rose on May 10, shot their British officers, and marched to Delhi, where there were no European troops. There the local sepoy garrison joined the Meerut men, and by nightfall the aged pensionary Mughal emperor Bahadur Shah II had been nominally restored to power by a tumultuous soldiery.

The seizure of Delhi provided a focus and set the pattern for the whole mutiny, which then spread throughout northern India. With the exception of the Mughal emperor and his sons and Nana Sahib, the adopted son of the deposed Maratha peshwa, none of the important Indian princes joined the mutineers.

From the time of the mutineers' seizure of Delhi, the British operations to suppress the mutiny were divided into three parts. First came the desperate struggles at Delhi, Kanpur, and Lucknow during the summer; then the operations around Lucknow in the winter of 1857-58 directed by Sir Colin Campbell; and finally the "mopping up" campaigns of Sir Hugh Rose in early 1858. Peace was officially declared on July 8, 1858.

A grim feature of the mutiny was the ferocity that accompanied it. The mutineers commonly shot their British officers on rising and were responsible for massacres at Delhi, Kanpur, and elsewhere. The murder of women and children enraged the British, but in fact some British officers began to take severe measures before they knew that any such murders had occurred. In the end the reprisals far outweighed the original excesses. Hundreds of sepoys were shot from cannons in a frenzy of British vengeance (though some British officers did protest the bloodshed).

The immediate result of the mutiny was a general housecleaning of the Indian administration. The East India Company was abolished in favour of the direct rule of India by the British government. In concrete terms this did not mean much, but it introduced a more personal note into the government and removed the unimaginative commercialism that had lingered in the Court of Directors.

The financial crisis caused by the mutiny led to a reorganization of the Indian administration's finances on a modern basis. The Indian army was also extensively reorganized.

Another significant result of the mutiny was the beginning of the policy of consultation with Indians. The Legislative Council of 1853 had contained only Europeans and had behaved arrogantly as if it had been a full-fledged parliament.

It was widely felt that lack of communication with Indian opinion had helped to precipitate the crisis. Accordingly, the new council of 1861 was given an Indian-nominated element. The educational and public works programs, roads, railways, telegraphs, and irrigation continued with little interruption; in fact some were stimulated by the thought of their value for the transport of troops in a crisis. But insensitive, British-imposed social measures that affected Hindu society came to an abrupt end.

Finally, there was the effect of the mutiny on the people of India themselves. Traditional society had made its protest against the incoming alien influences, and it had failed; the princes and other natural leaders had either held aloof from the mutiny or had proved for the most part incompetent. From this time all serious hope of a revival of the past or an exclusion of the West diminished. The traditional structure of Indian society began to break down and was eventually superseded by a westernized class system, from which emerged a strong middle class with a heightened sense of Indian nationalism.

Reforms of Dalhousie and the Sepoy Uprising (1848–1858)

The mid nineteenth century India, under the British rule, experienced monumental changes in both its socioeconomic and political scenes that laid the foundation for the Indian National Movement, which became the precursor to the eventual ouster of the British rule and establishment of an independent India. Ninety years before gaining independence from the British by peaceful means-largely due to the tenacity and perseverance of one man, Gandhi – the concerted effort to remove the British had begun by an armed and bloody revolt by the Indian soldiers serving under the British army.

This event of 1857-58 came to be known as the Sepoy Mutiny-implying a failed attempt by armed thugs who were biting the hands of the legitimate overlords that fed them (the term Sepoy-originally *Sipahi* – referred to soldiers of Indian origin who served in the British armed forces). However, the uprising was more a revolt than a mere mutiny against the British. The British had found great success with little bloodshed in amassing substantial acreage of land in India, and were busy with implementation of 'reforms' in order to civilize the 'barbaric natives' at an accelerated pace. The decade between 1848 and 1858 was an event filled one that altered the course of the British history in India.

Hindu widows were allowed to remarry, by decree. Earlier in the century *sati* (the practice of immolation of the wife in the funeral pyre of her dead husband) and *thugi* (ritual murder by strangling and highway robbery in the service of Mother Goddess Kali) had both been abolished by William Bentinck with the assistance of Rajaram Mohan Roy. The princely states, which thus far had been loyal allies of the British, were systematically stripped of their privileged domains, and their lands were annexed under the pretext of "lapse" and "paramountcy." The treaties between princely states and the John Company were ignored especially if there was no natural "heir and successor."

The long standing Hindu practice of adopting a son to succeed the throne, if no natural male heir was available was outlawed with the stroke of a pen and old treaties were torn apart. If the land belonging to princely states could not be acquired by this means, other excuses were invented such as depravity of citizens and inept administration by the princes etc. Another wily tact was also followed when the pensioner's titles and pensions awarded to princes and other land owners as compensation for lands seized from them were also allowed to "lapse" and not renewed.

Dalhousie's Reforms

James Andrew Broun Ramsay, Marquee of Dalhousie (1812 – 1860) had been appointed the governor-general of India by the Company in 1848. He was on a mission to unify India and control it. He earnestly believed that more of India annexed by the British the better it was for the Indians. First order of business was to let the internal feud in Punjab fester and then wage war with the ruler at Lahore. The master mind of Punjabi Empire, Ranjit Singh had died leaving behind weak replacements. After subduing the Sikh army, Dalhousie quickly annexed their lands, including Kashmir that was under their rule. Kashmir was then sold to Gulab Singh, who once was a feudatory of the mighty Ranjit Singh. The kingdom of Kashmir would enjoy relative independence until the next one hundred years and the progeny of Gulab Singh. Only after the Indian independence, would Hari Singh, the last maharaja of Kashmir aligned himself with India, which in turn set the stage for the struggle in Kashmir that even rages today.

Dalhousie started his cunning annexations in the year 1848 and the social reforms were shoved down the throats of Indians. Both Hindu and Muslim orthodoxy had always been viewed as barbaric, and social reforms were passed as laws with little sensitivity towards ancient religious practices of both Hindus and Muslims. It had also not gone unnoticed by the Hindus and Muslims that a slew of missionaries had appeared in India in the early part of 19th century. Conversions of Hindus were carried on without much objection, though there was much discomfiture among the orthodox Hindus. Moreover, a large contingent of young British men eagerly coveted positions in the company, solely for the purpose of infusing "civilization" to the misdirected "heathen natives." By mid century full blown discrimination was practiced by giving preference in civil jobs and other monetary rewards to those who converted to Christianity.

Dalhousie and the company were basking in glory in the aftermath of their success in Punjab, which was now firmly under the control of British after the treaty with the Sikhs. Revenues from the fertile soil of Punjab had exceeded their wildest dreams. The company stockholders in London were very pleased. The English language had been chosen as the language in schools and colleges over few objections. Sanskrit and other common native languages had been relegated to secondary and minority status. This had created a class of Indian intelligentsia which was vying for education in the English language both at home and abroad in England. A new class of Indians was developing that was in little touch with native languages and cultures and consider themselves more English than Indian.

Dalhousie did not confine himself to social reforms. He had visions of unifying the entire country through railroad. His goal was to connect the major British residencies in Madras, Bombay and Calcutta by rail. Construction began in 1850. The first was built in Calcutta, a 150 mile long railroad track connecting Howrah (opposite Calcutta on the right bank of River Hughly) to the coal mines of Raniganj. Another was built in Bombay, a shorter route of only 21 miles between Bombay and Thana. Dalhousie considered railways to be the greatest boon to India ever conferred by England. Two other modes of communication were also considered equally important by Dalhousie in modernizing India. Telegraph and postal services throughout India were both started under his watch. First telegraph lines were laid in 1851 by the brilliant and ingenious Dr. William O'Shaughnessey in Bengal. Soon work was begun to connect Madras, Calcutta, Agra, Lahore and Bombay by wire. As the construction of thousand mile links were completed in 1854, Dalhousie took personal pleasure in receiving telegraphic messages from O'Shaughnessey. 2500 miles of telegraphic wires had been laid out in a single year in 1854.

India's first Post Office Act had been enacted in 1837 but the completion of telegraphic links gave an additional impetus to it. Dalhousie again took personal interest in modernizing the inefficient postal system and soon the half-anna letter was able to reach many remote corners of India. Within three months of its implementation, the number of letters delivered by the postal service increased by 50 percent. Communication within the country was revolutionized. One-anna newspapers, a uniform price throughout the country increased the opinion making potential at all levels. What Dalhousie had explicitly pronounced in his summary minutes to the directors of the company on the eve of his departure to India had come to fruition. "Three great engines of social improvement, which the sagacity and science of recent times had previously given to the Western nations – I mean Railways, uniform Postage and the Electric Telegraph," he had said would harness India's bullock-cart civilization. In short, Dalhousie had succeeded in implementing sweeping reforms in India in an attempt to create a Europe-like society in a single decade in the mid 19th century.

Dalhousie's plan for modernizing and unifying the country was indeed a selfish one. The railways could speed the process of exporting raw materials to Manchester textile mills. Swift transportation of the military to potentially troubled spots was another reason. After all, a country with a population of 200 million was being controlled by a mere 40,000 strong British troops with 232,000 Sepoys under their command. With all the annexations the country was getting too large to be safely administered without the tools of modern communication and transportation. Any miscue on the administration's part could result in quick riot and revolt that could not be contained by the minority British rulers.

This was the same reason he pushed for the expensive proposal to implement telegraphic links. Dalhousie was not prescient of the upcoming mutiny of 1857 but nevertheless, his plan of connecting the country through telegraphic wires might have saved the British Empire in India, as the news was swiftly transmitted to other areas before trouble began. In some areas, preemptive actions were taken by the British that prevented the mutineers from inflicting more damage.

The railways had been a huge success with the general population. Travel by train increased by leaps and bounds. The improved communication and transportation also connected Indians in many ways. Soon a nationalistic movement would be born but the triad of Dalhousie's ventures was not the sole cause for adding fuel to the fire that was burning among the Sepoys. It was more because of the social reforms that had been enacted at breakneck speed which threatened the very core of the existence of orthodox Hindu and Muslim societies.

Hindu and Muslim Discontentment

Dalhousie annexed Oudh with ease in February of 1856 under some pretext and complaint about the corrupt and capricious king of Oudh being not fit to rule. King Wajid Ali handed over his kingdom without any armed resistance. He petitioned Dalhousie in Calcutta, who by now was totally disinterested. Wajid Ali then travelled to London to appeal to the British authorities, but only succeeded in addressing stone faced men who were not interested in hearing his cause. He returned to India and started a conspiracy with the Brahmins and Kshatriya soldiers of Oudh, who had formed the backbone of the Sepoy Army of Bengal.

The straw that broke the camel's back was when the British introduced modern weaponry of breech-loading Enfield rifles to the army. New cartridges were greased with animal fat and lard and the soldier had to bite off the tip before loading it on to the rifle. Rumours of cattle and pig fat being used in the cartridges spread slowly and the British had paid little attention to the complaints. This was sacrilegious for Hindus who considered cows as sacred, and for Muslims handling of pigs had been considered irreligious. The "barbarians" with their archaic practices did not deserve to be heard, and sensitive matters of religious taboos were completely ignored. Soldiers who refused to load the rifles with cartridges tainted with animal fat were summarily dismissed and shamefully made to walk home without pay or pension.

Dalhousie had returned to England in 1856, a lonely and sick man, and Lord Charles James Canning was the new governor – general. Canning had enacted several unpopular measures when he took office. Most distressing was a new law called the General Services Act that forced Sepoys to be deployed away from homeland, especially to Burma. This Act alone had produced dissatisfaction among the soldiers. Brahmins and other high caste Hindus considered it pollution if made to cross the "dark waters." Dalhousie had already enacted the Caste Disabilities Act of 1850 that permitted converts to Christianity to inherit property. This had appeared as a concerted Christian conspiracy to shake the foundations of the Hindu orthodoxy. In 1856 another law allowing Hindu widows to remarry was passed by Canning that added more discord among Hindus. Sati had already been banned since 1829, and this additional meddling into Hindu customs was not welcomed in high caste Hindu society.

Rumours started by the conspirators about dead pigs in the water supply and ground cow bones in sugar added more fuel to the anger of Sepoys. A quiet recruitment, especially by people loyal to Wajid Ali and Peshwa Nana Sahib of the Marathas, went on for the first five months of 1857. Members of Bahadur Shah's (the last Mughal Emperor in Delhi) court and Dost Muhammad's agents from Kabul were also silently recruited. For five months the Sepoys organized quietly, with the aid of disgruntled monarchies which had been either dethroned or marginalized by the British.

The Sepoy Uprising

On Saturday May 9, 1857 eighty-five Sepoys were shackled and marched to prison in Meerut because they refused to load their Enfield rifles with cartridges tainted with lard. The other Sepoys silently watched the spectacle but this event served as the battle cry for the revolt. Next morning, which was on Sunday, armed Sepoys marched against their British superiors. Most of them were dragged out of churches and killed.

The prisoners were released and the frenzied mob marched thirty miles south to Delhi, shouting "Chalo Dilli" ("Let's go to Delhi"). The Mughal king Bahadur Shah II was a reluctant accomplice as he had grown old in his throne. However the revolutionists elevated him to "Emperor of India" status, and with little resistance from the British in Delhi, declared it "liberated" on May 11.

Soon the entire Ganges belt, the heartland of Hindustan, was lost to the British. Oudh (Lucknow) was well defended by chief commissioner Sir Henry Lawrence until he could get reinforcements in November. Kanpur (Kanpur) however was a disaster. Four hundred men, women and children could only hold out for eighteen days but then surrendered to Peshwa Nana Sahib. A deal was struck for safe passage to Allahabad along the river, but when the British families climbed into waiting boats, they were all massacred. This event triggered so much anger among the British that it served as a lightning rod for future atrocities by the British against the Indians, following their regaining control of Indian heartland.

Illustration of the Revolt from London Printing Company Limited

The victors failed to unite among their various factions of Muslims, Marathas and other Hindu soldiers. Moreover, the revolt failed to catch fire in the south. Madras and Bombay were quiet and showed no interest in joining forces with their northern brothers. In addition to Muslim rulers of Oudh and Delhi, local rulers like Devi Singh in Mathura and Kadam Singh of Meerut became heroes of the revolt and rallied the peasants to join in their cause. But only Delhi, Lucknow and Kanpur remained the centres of revolt, which soon lost steam from lack of sustained strategy against the British and lack of cooperation between the mutineers.

The land owners in the countryside were not too enthusiastic about the revolt as they feared losing their lands to new owners and increased burden of taxation. Bickering fights and jealousies among local rajas and nawabs, and the failure of the revolutionists to pacify traditional landowners spelt doom for the sustenance of the revolt.

The Aftermath

-British never feared a total loss, especially when the initial fury of the revolt was not maintained. Once widespread revolt was held in check, they just waited for the internal feud among the participants to fester. While they never doubted their ability to gain back control of the Ganges heartland, a fury and vengeance was well under way against the Indians. Men who were known for their patience and balanced approach towards the natives had suddenly turned into raging murderers. Indiscriminate killing of all classes of Indians began as soon as the opportunity arose. Long serving domestic servants of British families were executed under suspicion of seditious activities. Suspects were tied to the cannons and blown away. Live flaying of unsuspecting villagers and peasants was advocated. One hundred years of building bridges of confidence and trust between the British and the Indians were being abandoned only because of unfounded suspicion and innuendo. The print media, while very vocal about the atrocities of the Sepoys in Kanpur and Lucknow, were now silent about the barbaric execution of innocent people without any proof of wrongdoing or any trial.

Near Kanpur, entire villages were burnt and the people killed. Delhi was recaptured by the British, with the help of Sikh regiment by September 20, 1857 and Bahadur Shah II was exiled to Burma. His sons were murdered in cold blood, and the Emperor himself died in 1858 in exile, thus bringing an end to three hundred years of glorious Mughal history in India.

Pockets of resistance from smaller groups went on until summer of 1858. Rani Lakshmibai of Jhansi put up a gallant fight along with Tantia Topi, the artillery expert of Peshwa Nana Sahib. The Rani had lost her kingdom due to the "lapse and paramountcy" of Dalhousie, as she had no male heirs and her adopted son was not recognized as a legal heir. The Rani died fighting on her horse and Tantia Topi was captured and hung along with many other rebels.

The revolution was not as small as the British would have liked to characterize as a mutiny. However, it was much smaller than an independence struggle, as the Indians would like to call it. But it did bring about monumental changes in India.

It proved to be the nail on the coffin of the Mughal Empire, independent Oudh and the rule of the Maratha Peshwas. There was discontent in Britain about so many British citizens losing their lives and above all the whole episode of Sepoy uprising costing so much revenue to control it.

It had cost England a full year's worth of Indian revenue-36 million pounds. A debate ensued whether Dalhousie's zeal for accelerated pace of reforms or the antiquated administration of the company were to be blamed for the unfortunate turn of events. The company was the scapegoat and the administration of India came into the hands of British Crown, under Queen Victoria.

In August 1858, the British Parliament passed the Government of India Act, transferring all rights that the company had over India to the British Crown, thus effectively ending the rule of the Company Raj, which had lasted one hundred years since the Battle of Plassey, when Robert Clive defeated Siraj-ud-daula, the nawab of Bengal on June 23, 1757. Last governor-general of the company, Lord Canning, stayed on as the first viceroy of India ruled by the British Crown.

1857-What Really Happened-A Reconstruction

It is important that we in today's Pakistan once and for all clearly examine the events of 1857; arrive at a consensus and proceed further with more pressing tasks of today's life! Having close links with Punjab where my great grand father's father came in 1849 and, having both close relations both Punjabis and Hindustanis, and a deep interest in history, I feel that things in 1857 were far more complex than what many people try to assert today.

Many years ago I heard a saying in Lahore, from a thorough bred Punjabi Tarkhan (carpenter); "Lahore de Darawze Khulle; te Dilli De Darwaze Khoonee" or "Lahore despite being a fortified city, had always its gates open for the conqueror, while Delhi's possession was always contested by the invaders". Outwardly this saying, ironically coined by Punjabis, who suffer from a habit of self criticism, at least as far as the lower classes are concerned, as I personally witnessed, gives the impression that the Punjabis were docile and that the people of Delhi were brave!

Before discussing this particular Punjabi saying, I will briefly explain the frame of discussion.

A man's mind is continuously on the move, like a caravan, and our conclusions and opinion about many subjects, which we at one time accepted or took as the Gospel truth change, with the passage of time. It is generally a slow process and as time passes we discover that many of the beliefs, to which we struck like religious faith or private property, were as a matter of fact absolutely ridiculous!

To come back to the point, I thought about two decades back that Delhi was really a tough city, and all resistance was encountered by a northern invader in between the Satluj river and Delhi! India the foreigner must note before the British united it in the real sense by roads, railways, telegraph, radio and postage was never one single country in the real sense. We will confine our discussion to the Muslim time since we are discussing Hindustani Muslim claims!

Delhi was the main seat of the Mughal government and was an important city even before any Muslims came to India. It was natural that any invader who came to India was resisted by this Muslim government in power at Delhi as per its policy in vogue. The slave kings like Balban followed a strategy of resisting the invaders along the Indus or within the modern provinces of Punjab and Frontier.

Later on from 1526 when Babar the first Mughal king defeated the Muslim Lodhi Pathan kings at Panipat about 40 miles north of Delhi, a new trend emerged *i.e.* the future invasions of India were contested in between the river Satluj and Delhi.

Thus once Humayun came back to India he defeated the Suri Army near Sirhind. Nadir Shah was opposed by the main Mughal army at Panipat and similarly the Marathas were forced to fight by Abdali at Panipat.

It may be noted that there was no major siege at Delhi before 1857; *i.e.* the city gates were open for the invader. The reason why the major battles took place in between Satluj and Delhi was primarily logistic.

The government at Delhi or that controlling Delhi (as the Marathas in 1761) found it difficult to logistically sustain its main army (which by the sixteenth century was very bulky because of camp followers and luxuries) north of Satluj. It was a policy decision and that was it. In any case what did the Punjabis or the Pathans have in common with the Mughal king? This man was not the ruler of Muslims but that of India.

In terms of patronage he was more interested in wooing the Hindu Rajputs who were politically important than the Punjabi or Pathan Muslims or the Hindu Marathas who gave Aurangzeb hell from 1660 onwards! This Mughal preferred the Central Asian or Persian over the local Indian whether Punjabi, Pathan or Hindustani (a small percentage of Hindustani Muslims is of northern descent, despite whatever they claim, while about three fourth are locals just like the Punjabis etc. who converted to Islam).

The question of resistance or no resistance had little to do with docility or martial fervour!

Now lets examine 1857. Were the Hindustanis more brave or more martial or more special that they defied the British? At least this is what the Hindustani Muslims claim This claim is as ridiculous as that of Punjabi Muslims of today that they were and are the most martial race of the Indo Pak subcontinent! I believed this for many years but as my interest in the rebellion increased and I carried out more research I discovered a million loopholes in this belief which at least from 1977 to 1983 was held like a conviction by me!

The philosophical basis of this transformation was my successive drift towards the concept that all human beings regardless of race or religion are essentially the same, and that all that they do, and all their attributes, good or bad, like bravery, compassion cruelty etc. are basically situational and have nothing to do with race or religion! My belief underwent a radical transformation once I discovered many facts which changed the whole complexion of the facts of 1857!

I discovered in 1978 while reading the collection of Despatches and state papers of Fortes cue and the Aligarh district Gazetteer that the Sherwani Yusuf Zai and Shinwari Hindustani Muslim Pathans of Sikandra Rao had stayed loyal while all area between Delhi and Allahabad was out of British control!

Later as I read more I discovered that only one out of seven or eight rebel sepoys was a Hindustani Muslim while the rest were Hindustani Hindu Rajputs! By the time I finalised this work in September 1998 which I had first written as a short Term Essay as a cadet in PMA Kakul in July 1982 reached the following conclusions:-

a. The rebellion was not as simple as it appears at first sight. The first important factor about it was peculiar situation of the Bengal Army— that it was a largely homogenous force of Hindustanis who had been recruited for more than one to three generations in it and were from the same general region *i.e.* between Hissar and Patna, and had certain common perceptions and affinities which enabled them to react in unison, even without a deliberate plan. That culturally, linguistically and historically they had nothing in common with the Punjabi or Pathan Muslims although many of them were from families with Pathan Baloch (as in case of the Baloch of Rohtak and Gurgaon districts), Iranian and Central Asian ancestry.

b. The greased cartridges, the immediate and most important factor which acted as a lethal primer in igniting the fuse of revolt played an important part in propelling the Bengal Army into rebellion. Since they hurt his religious feelings, it became a far more grave matter than allowances or petty administrative matters. The Punjabi troops being an irregular second line as semi military force were never made to face this test since the first priority as far as modernisation was concerned was accorded to the Bengal Army, the most important army of the East India Company. Thus as a matter of fact, the East India Company took the risk of trusting the native soldiers without any discrimination with the Lee Enfield Rifle which at that time was the most sophisticated infantry weapon in the history of warfare since Napoleonic wars. Since the Punjabi and Pathan troops were not made to use the Enfield, they had no grievance against the company.

c. Rebellion started from the army and it was only then that the feudal and at many places the people who joined it. A novel situation emerged. Only those areas where the sepoy regiments rebelled or which they moved to after the rebellion were most seriously affected by rebellion. A vacuum like situation existed in most other areas. Here two things happened; either the local populace mostly low caste Muslims like the Joolahas or butchers raised the standard of rebellion and fought till death or a local feudal or a dispossessed Raja or Talukdar or Nawab assumed control. All other areas remained largely neutral.. In many districts which were not held by the rebel sepoys in the heart of modern UP, which led the rebellion as a province, resolute British civil servants aided by remanent of sepoy units, local levies, police and local notables like Sayyid

Ahmad Khan (the future leader of Hindustani Muslims in particular and Indian Muslims in general and the father of the Two Nation Theory) successfully held control and these included many districts like Bijnor, Etawah, parts of Aligarh, Rohilkhand, etc. Thus the rebellion had a great deal to do with the sepoys and a far less with the local population.

d. Most of the Rajas and nobles who asserted authority in absence of the British later on claimed that they were acting on the Britishers behalf! Thus many escaped Scotfree and many escaped the noose like the Nawab of Banda who had played an important part in the rebellion escaped with only confiscation of property. The vast majority of Oudh Talukdars took advantage of the clemency offer of Queen Victoria and emerged as strong as they were before 1857, with an additional guarantee that the feudal will not be touched! The only losers were the vast bulk of the rebel sepoys or the people of Delhi and some feudal and rajas of Delhi territory or the Mughal princes who payed with their life, at a time when tempers were exceedingly high because of excesses against British non combatants and the heavy British casualties in the siege of Delhi. Or there were certain men like Khan Bahadur Khan, Nawab of Farrukhabad, Tantia Topi or Rao Sahib who were executed because they were genuinely opposed to the British and were not opportunists like bulk of the feudals including landlords of Oudh and the north western provinces.

It is ironic that none of the major Talukdars who went with Hazrat Mahal into self imposed exile to Nepal, and who later refused British offers to return to Oudh, and resume their estates were Muslims. The reader may note that 99% of the landlords who did not leave India later took advantage of the British offer of clemency for all, who had nothing to do with murder of European civilians and non combatants took the plea that they had never rebelled, but had merely taken control of the civil administration, since there was anarchy, and that they were acting in this capacity on behalf of the East India Company. Thus most of them got all of their land back, and these included most of the large landholders of Oudh, both Muslim and Hindu, including men like the later famous Raja of Mahmudabad!

As a matter of fact the feudals greatly benefited from 1857, in terms of reversal of Dalhousie's policy of destroying feudalism. Later studies by many scholars including P. Hardy and Metcalfe prove that the feudals both Hindustani Muslim as well as Hindu greatly benefited from post 1858 British policies in UP and the myth that the Hindustani Muslims were the main losers of 1857, as far as the landlords is concerned, is absolutely baseless.

The British policy was situational and rewarded and punished landlords, in each region and district, in accordance with the subjective conditions and there were many districts where Muslim landlords emerged scotfree, while many Hindu landlords accused of complicity in the rebellion suffered and vice versa. Those who want to explore this may read P. Hardy or Metcalfe's book. The only loser and the one whose motives were superior and genuine, and one who had no connection with large part of the Muslims who founded the MAO College Aligarh or were active in the Muslim League, was the sepoy who was mostly from the lower classes or some feudals who were punished with confiscation or executed in the initial days immediately after siege of Delhi was over.

As a city it was Delhi and its people that suffered the most; but again not because they were more heroic but because the 3rd Light Cavalry's seizure of Meerut and the subsequent concentration of sepoy regiments at Delhi left them no choice; and the British treated whole of the city as a rebel city!

In justice to Punjabis and specially the Punjabi Muslims, it must be admitted that just 8 years after liberation by the British; and at a time when the Sikhs were in close competition with them for British recognition; psychologically the Punjabi Muslims were in no position to rebel! The British had no doubt liberated them and the Punjabi Muslim-Punjabi Sikh divide in Punjab was far more severe than the Muslim-Hindu divide in UP or Central India.

The Hindustani Muslims even today contemptuously refer to Punjabi Muslims as mercenaries. They forget that they were also performing the same role from 1757 till 1857; fighting against many Muslim powers including Hyder Ali and Tipu Sultan, against Oudh, against Rohilkhand, Afghanistan and Sindh!

And how can they condemn the Punjabi Muslims for not rebelling in 8 years service in the East India Company's army, once the Hindustani Muslims rebelled against the company after 100 years service from 1757 to 1857!

And even after this the Hindustanis were as keen to join the army as the Punjabis and as a matter of fact were in lead as mercenaries in the British Indian Army as compared to all other races in India. If after 1883 their recruitment was reduced; it was because of policy reasons and not because they were less willing to join the British Indian Army!

The hard fact of life of human mind and all intellectual activity is that there are no chosen people! At various stages various nations or groups based on ethnicity ideology or class have believed most fervently that they were the chosen people! The Punjabi Muslims and the Hindustani Muslims are victims of this intellectual hangover of being more martial or more intellectual ! The important fact for the writer or historian is to at least endeavour to be more rational and understanding.

As a great French writer once said "neither to laugh nor to cry, but to understand". I have made an attempt to be rational with the records and happening of a highly complex event. It took twenty years to analyse and yet I must have made many mistakes. It is for the readers to judge this. Although in the final analysis all judgments are subjective judgments. There is no final judgment as far as history writing is concerned!

Moments of History Redefined: Sepoy Mutiny in Perspective

India, the ancient Bharata, Hindukush or Hindustan, as we may call it; the integrated, enlightened and the formidable India, as we visualize during the illustrious Maurya and the Gupta period, passed through a protracted period (lasting many centuries over) of disintegration and anarchy till it was completely withered and worn out.

When we make an attempt to track down the road map of the

lost glories of our ancient India, we find the search terribly frustrating with the landmarks or the milestones ridiculously few and far between. After the period of the great Guptas, there is a long period of obscurity till a minor figure like a feeble light shows the way. It was Harsha. And after Harsha the glorious and the iconic India falls into the hands of a band of alien Islamic marauders. The hair-raising tales of loot, plunder, horror, arson and slaughter went on intermittently and there was no hand strong enough to resist.

In this eerie atmosphere one milestone stands out in haze-that is Prithviraj Chauhan-the last great Hindu king of Rajput stock-whose life and tenure was heavily fraught with trouble and frustration. But, against the backdrop of confusion and uncertainty, the most crowning glory of Prithviraj Chauhan's life was his victory in the first battle of Tarain (1191 A.D.) in which he beat the invader Mahmmud of Ghur very badly and the latter fled away from the battlefield grievously wounded.

But exactly a year after, Mahmmud of Ghur challenged once again Prithviraj Chauhan in the second battle of Tarain (1192 A.D.) being directly and openly supported by king Jayachandra, the king of Kanauj. In this battle Prithviraj Chauhan was defeated, imprisoned and executed.

Thus 1192 A.D. (the second battle of Tarain) is a turning point in Indian history that witnessed the routing of the imperial power of the Chauhans that spelled disaster to the whole Hindustan. Hence 1192 A.D. saw the setting of the Sun for the Hindu empire that was India. And since that ominous moment, India had been continually in and out of foreign hands till, of course, we gained our freedom in 1947.

Nearly a millennium, since Prithviraj Chauhan was vanquished in the second battle of Tarain in 1192, India writhed and bled interminably under foreign rule with their whims and caprices mercilessly imposed upon it. If we look at this terrible trend of events of Indian history we get no visible parallel to it in the entire stretch of human history, East or West, North or South. Probably such inhuman barbaric ordeal that our ancestors were exposed to made the Indians so patient.

Orissa Review August-2007

Orissa Review August-2007 tolerant, so forbearing, rather stoical and fatalists. May be our original elements of heroism and independence underwent a spell of temporary suspension or withdrawal as the Freudians or the Neo-Freudians would look at it.

Lest we should digress we must try to catchat the next visible roadmark after 1192 A.D. This would unmistakably lead us to 1526 A.D, the historic first battle of Panipat. Though for the natives nothing was to gain or to lose, the seat of power shifted from the wrecked and battered Lodhi dynasty to the Mughals. A direct descendant of the Mongol conquerors Timir and Jinghiz Khan, Babur, a crafty, cunning and ambitious Turk, was successful in establishing and consolidating the Mughal empire with his victory in the first battle of Panipat (1526 A.D.). and the battle of Kanwah (1527 A.D.) in which he gained a decisive victory over the great Rajput, Rana Sanga of Mewar. The Mughals had a long and eventful journey with tales of mostly successes and few failures here and there (hence negligible) till 1707 A.D.

The Mughal conquerors, a minority in a country the size of India, couldn't possibly hope to rule without the assistance of the Hindu majority. Hence all the historians, both Indian and Western, are unequivocal and unanimous on the point that the Mughals were not Colonists. Their role was as rulers, administrators and merchants. As a historian observes:

> *"The Mughal civil administration rested upon the Hindu clerks. Its advanced industrial undertakings depended upon Hindu labour. Trade was carried on through Hindu middle men acting on behalf of Muslim entrepreneurs. In effect, Mughal rule existed in terms of an undefined contract between the rulers and the ruled. (Michael Edwardes, 1)."*

Among the Mughals Akbar was undoubtedly the best as a specimen of good human being and an able administrator. But no historian differs on the point that Aurangzeb was the ablest. During his time an all out attempt was made to restore the Islamic character of the state which had gone slow for the liberal and conciliatory attitude of the great emperor Akbar.

Though initially Aurangzeb acted with great restraint and caution, in the latter years he became incredibly harsh and stern to the Hindu majority. At the epicenters of Muslim power proselytization became rampant and widespread. There was absolutely no consideration for the sentiments and finer feelings of the Hindus.

They were declared as 'infidels' (Kafirs) who went to the temples. A series of punitive discriminatory taxes were levied mercilessly on the Hindus. Prohibition was imposed on the great religious fairs and mass celebrations. In the process, whatever amity and goodwill Emperor Akbar had painfully built up were completely embittered and lost during the latter years of Aurangzeb (1669 A.D. onwards).

This crazy fanatic struck at the very nerve-centre of Hindu social and communal life. In a bid to execute all his orders to harass and humiliate the Hindus, Aurangzeb replaced his entire Hindu staff in administration by the Muslims. There was thus only one authority at all levels, heavily centralized and wilful. The entire fabric of administration that had been carefully developed through a long process of trial and errors by Akbar came to naught by the short-sighted, willy fanatic Aurangzeb.

Interestingly, the European traders by now had already settled in India along the entire coastline, studied its court and climate, people and religion, and were just waiting for an opportune moment. With their rational bent of mind, far-sight, cunning and diplomacy they had secured some privileges and immunity from Emperor Shah Jehan and were looking forward to a windfall in case there is no competent successor to Aurangzeb.

The European traders could clearly see through the murky situation. They were convinced that the piled up discontentment among the Hindus could be somehow contained by the military expertise and administrative competence of Aurangzeb.

In 1707 A.D. Aurangzeb died. The anarchy that followed gave both the English and the French a chance to grab power. Just us they began to feel their potential, the giant centralized Mughal empire broke apart in an ever-increasing chaos and anarchy. While this confusion prevailed, both the English and the French were stalking along to seize the Delhi throne. In this ultimate race for the throne of Delhi, interestingly, the French had entered willingly and consciously. While the English had entered rather reluctantly. But the moment it became obvious that the indigenous power was not capable of restoring the political normalcy, the English acted swiftly and took centre-stage leaving the French behind. British dominion spread slowly till 1756 A.D. Political chaos, confrontation, resistance and confusion nagged the British.

But with their victory in the battle of Plassey (1757 A.D.) things moved much faster. In 1764 A.D., the British army won the battle of Buxar and annexed Oudh to their dominion. Thus the battle of Buxar laid the foundation of British dominion in India. From that moment the British never looked behind. They consolidated their position and rose from strength to strength and smashed any resistance from the native princes or chiefs with iron hands.

As a historian insightfully comments: "Three hundred and fifty years, the English spent in India, make a story which unfolds itself like an Elizabethan play in five acts" (Philip Mason, 173) The first act is an act of exposition like any Shakespearean play in which the English introduce themselves as suave and modest traders. In act two they take out their mask and costume as they become rulers.

In the third act "the hero-who is not one man but a thousand-appears to be at the height of his glory". (Philip Mason, 173). The hero seems apparently stable and comfortable. He himself is also under the illusion that things around him are all fine. But ironically there lies the tragic flaw in his character, hamartia, as Aristotle would call it. That leads to a precipitation.

The first half of 19th Century is considered to be the high noon of the British rule in India. Having consolidated their position firmly after the battle of Plassey and the battle of Buxar the British began to break, shape and mould the age-old ancient Hindu Social and religious order/ institutions. It was on the top of their latest reform agenda. Under the regime of Lord Dalhousie all sections of Indian society felt the heavy hand of the British administration. Dalhousie, who is loudly acknowledged as the greatest reformer and the most progressive British Governor-General in India, was at heart a hard-core colonialist.

Where there was no direct heir, thus tagging Satara, Jhansi, Nagpur and a number of minor states to the British dominion. The kingdom of Oudh was thus annexed to it too. Further, the greed of Dalhousie simply refused to abate. Every second day a fresh idea, a new official release would pronounce the annexation of hundreds of estates, territories and occupations.

Thus, by some ridiculous plea or the other, more than 20,000 titles were confiscated in Deccan alone. The situation came to such a pass when the Indian princes and zamindars saw the British ghost in every bush; the atmosphere was really haunted and nightmarish. Interference was at every level; uncertainly and unpredictability was in the air. The encroachment, interference and highhandedness was not restricted to land and territory alone.

Even the poor mercenary Sepoys in British pay-roll felt jittery apprehending some cunning move from the foxy British top-brasses to encroach upon their religion. In Vellore (South India) there was already an attempt to introduce new style of head-gear, trimming of beards, and prohibition on putting tilak on the fore-heads.

The move was promptly retaliated by the Sepoys in their uprise in 1806 which was brutally put down. By the end of 1856, the whole of India, especially the north, was uneasy. Cutting across caste and class every sensitive Indian felt repressed and suffocated. On the otherhand, the British masters were completely lost in quenching their thirst and greed like a hungry lion upon its prey. As a Researcher records, a particular British high ranking officer had as many as seven native mistresses, hunted eighty-four Asiatic lions and was recognized by the crown of England as arare case of excellence and gallantry. He was not an isolated case of such conduct.

The entire British middle and high ranking officials-District magistrate and above-were recklessly indulged in such sensual gratifications with wine, women, club, gulf, hunting and such other pastimes while their Indian deputies looked upon or stood guardat such shameful and degrading acts of license and immorality. May be that spirit of subservience continues to nag the post independent bureaucratic hierarchy at the middle and the lower rungs. The deputies are still competing to play second fiddle to their bosses.

We are presently at the ending of the third act of the British occupancy in India when things seem to head to a climax. With their officers, completely drunk with colonization (maximizing British revenue collection, land encroachment) dreamt of ruling India as long as the Sun and the stars continue in sky-line. Ironically at this point of time there came a jolt, no less in intensity than an earth-shaking tremor from deep down the belly of the Earth-the Mutiny of 1857. As we all know the real trouble began with the introduction of the new Enfield rifle which needed to be heavily greased and had to be beaten to open the end and release the powder.

The muzzle of the gun was smeared with the grease that was so thick after loading. As a commenter observes very rightly:

On the lips of a Hindu Cow's fat would be an abomination for which there is no parallel in European ways of thinking; it was not merely disgusting, as excrement would be; it damned him as well; it was as bad as killing a cow or a Brahmin. To a Muslim pig's fat was almost as horrible. (Philip Mason, 158)

In the first week of January 1857 a rumour spread among the sepoys that the cartridge used in Enfield rifle was softened by the fat of cow and pig. On 24th January the danger was communicated to the Government.

The 25th was a Sunday. Though orders went out on 27th January to all the ordnance depots not to issue Enfield rifles to the natives it was too late. The rumour had spread like wild fire. It is worth nothing here that immediately prior to that came the annexation of Oudh, the main recruiting base of the army. Further, there was the mysterious relay of Chapatis (Roti) in the entire north India, the epicentre of the ritual being Oudh. One fine morning every hamlet started sending a couple of Chapatis to its neighbour. Though no conclusive evidence was found behind such a ritual, in retrospect that appears to be a meaningful piece to connect the elaborate conspiracy.

When one puts such stray pieces together one gets a coherent picture of the whole Mutiny. The emerging perspective would convince any sceptic that "the greased cartridge was only anexc use for revolt, not the cause of it" (Herbert Strang, 2). In all likelihood, unknown to the complacent, snobbish English officers who, inmost cases, had an exaggerated idea of the loyalty of their men, a great scheme was on foot for the recovery of India from the English.

Though a full century and a half has already lapsed, it remains a mystery in whose brain this plot was hatched. May be the schemers were many and their planes elaborate and cautious though not fool-proof. They, in their well-thought-out planning, had kept the Sepoys tuned to act as the prime movers in the rebellion.

And the time fixed for the zero-hour was very insightfully and strategically done. 1857, as the rumour went round, coincided with the completion of 100 years after the battle of Plassey. The rumour, further, was enriched with a credential that the astrologers predicted that the English rule would last exactly a hundred years. That appealed to the credulous, superstitious sepoys who were already under terrible pressure-moral, psychological and emotional.

Though the great uprise apparently met with failure it had its salutary effect on the despondent, fatalistic Indians to continue their struggle for another century till they were free in 1947.

Contributed by Kevin Hobson

The mid nineteenth century was a period of change and adjustment for both the popular press and the political system in Britain. In 1857, when the Indian Mutiny broke out, both the press and the politicians were caught off guard. India had been thought to be pacific; a safe and secure part of the empire.

The Sepoy were seen as obedient and docile. When the topic of India was raised in the House of Commons, it was normal for the benches to empty due to the disinterest in things Indian on the part of the members. Factional manoeuvring and infighting were far more suited to the tastes of the Parliamentarians, and

India was not an issue that seemed likely to cause or contribute to the rise and fall of ministries in Britain.

The party system was still not firmly established and with politicians busily following individuals perceived to be rising toward power, the events in India seemed of little importance. The popular press seemed to agree with this attitude of disinterest. In the year prior to the outbreak of the rebellion, very few stories ever appeared which were concerned with India. What few there were concentrated on the East India Company and its allegedly corrupt practices.

There was virtually no interest in the state of the people of India nor any real inquiry into how the rule of the Company was affecting their lives. The press was in business to sell papers and India did not interest the public enough to warrant even cursory coverage. Their concern was internal politics, not the "goings on" in some remote place like India. It was in dealing with issues that affected Britain at home that the press gained its power in influencing public opinion. So powerful was the press thought to be in this era, that it was commonly believed that "... this country is ruled by The Times."

By the middle of the century, weekly newspapers had entered this arena of political power brokering. With the rescinding of the Stamp Tax there was an opening for these smaller papers to compete with The Times by offering a product that cost less and was designed to appeal to a "lower class", such as the tradesmen, than was The Times. The Times maintained its supremacy and its influence, but it now had competition and this competition wrote for a different sector of the reading public. As a result, what was published often had a very different tone than what was written in The Times.

The concern of the present paper will be to examine what was reported during the period of July 4th to August 1st with regard to the Indian Mutiny, and how this reflected the actions and statements of the leading political figures and the sentiments of the public at large. The newspapers that will be used for this investigation will be Punch, The Spectator, The Saturday Review and to a lesser extent, The Times.

Before proceeding with an examination of the above publications, it is imperative that the positions of Disreali and Palmerston, the two key political players, be clearly stated. Moreover, it is important that the position of the East India Company also be understood. Clearly, it was the interaction of these two men and this company that precipitated much of the action and rhetoric that resulted from the outbreak of the Mutiny.

Disraeli was a consummate factionalist in the House of Commons and was notorious for seizing any opportunity to rouse the sentiments of special interest groups in his attempts to increase the power of his own position. During this period he may be viewed as the leader of the opposition, though the term is questionable since the party system had not come to full fruition. His actual knowledge of India was extremely limited but he did know that he did not like the East India Company or their policies.

This dislike seems to have originated in the fact that the directors of the Company used the positions that they controlled in India to maintain and increase their power and influence within England itself. However, Disraeli also had complaints about the way that the government had conducted itself in India. In particular he denounced Dalhousie's doctrine of lapse. Moreover, he opposed any attempt to westernize the Indian people and was vehemently anti missionary.

This viewpoint was in complete agreement with the Company but Disraeli's reasons for taking this position were quite different from those of the Company. All of this should not be taken to mean that Disraeli sympathized with, or in any way admired the Indian people. He did not.

He saw the people of India as inferior and believed that they were entirely ruled by their imagination. For this reason he felt that the most effective way to control this population was by placing it directly under the control of the British Crown. This, he believed, would have more of an effect on the "Indian imagination" than the chartered company could ever have. Therefore, under the Crown, Disraeli believed that the Indians would be easier to control. Concurrent with this notion, Disraeli believed that the Mutiny was a revolt against the policies employed by the company in the name of Britain, not a protest against the violation of religious taboos.

In the House of Commons, Disraeli clearly questioned whether or not Britain was involved in a national revolt in India. Certainly he believed that, "The rise and fall of empires are not the affairs of greased cartridges" As the rebellion progressed, Disraelis refused to believe the horror stories about English women being dishonoured and children being hacked to bits in front of their mothers. He was, in fact, even reluctant to believe the reports of the Kanpur massacre. In line with this belief, he also opposed indiscriminate reprisals against the Indians when the tide of war had turned in Britain's favour.

Palmerston was a veteran Parliamentarian and, in many ways, the antithesis of Disraeli. Having led the Government through a series of crises, Palmerston was seen by the people of Britain as invincible in the 1850s. There was a strong belief that only Palmerston could defend British prestige and honour. It was this reputation that had, in large part, facilitated Palmerston's 1857 election victory. Initially, he did not take the outbreak seriously since he could not conceive of British troops being defeated by what he thought of as native rabble.

This became particularly apparent when he objected to Canning unilaterally assuming authority and diverting troops that were bound for China. His confidence that this was not a serious problem, that the situation had been exaggerated, that it would very quickly be brought under control, and that Britain had enough strength to do virtually anything it needed to do, is further exemplified by his refusal of offers of assistance from other countries such as Belgium. However, once the situation made itself clear and it was obvious that this was a real threat to the British position in India, Palmerston was quick to commit so many troops to the conflict that there was a fear for some time that there were not enough troops left at home to defend England itself from attack from the Continent, should the need arise.

Unlike Disraeli, Palmerston favoured westernization of the Indian people and was supportive, though in a limited way, of the work of missionaries in India. Also in opposition to Disraeli's way of thinking, Palmerston was, at least publicly, in favour of mass retribution since he did believe that the Indians had committed atrocities against English women and children. The one point that the two men agreed on by the end of the war, was that India should be ruled directly by the Crown and not through a chartered company.

The East India Company's position was quite different from that of the two politicians. The board of directors clung tenaciously to the power that they held through their ability to dole out patronage appointments to the younger sons of relatives, friends and the lesser gentry. This power helped them to maintain their connections in places of power both politically and in the world of business.

Moreover, it was their opinion that the most suitable way to rule India was through the use of the commercial networks that they were involved in and through the use of the body of "experts" that they had in India. This was firmly in line with the theories and writings of John Stuart Mill which oppose any more government control of commercial operations than is absolutely necessary. For the directors of the Company, India was a commercial enterprise and should, for the sake of efficient management, remain so.

The Mutiny began on Saturday, May 9th, 1857. Communications to Britain took approximately six weeks and this time and therefore initial reports of the disturbance did not reach London until the third week of June. Initially, very little attention was paid to the incoming reports as it was assumed that the mutiny was of a very limited nature and the situation would soon be under control.

Even by the beginning of July, there seemed to be very little concern. On July 4th The Times carried a story which railed against the French press for suggesting that the Sepoy were in revolt against Britain rather than against presumed attacks on their religious sensitivities. Showing true British bluster The Times attacked the French by stating that they had been thrown out of many countries while the British had added territory after territory to their empire. To further refute the French accusations The Times stated that since the people had not joined in the revolt, they must approve of British rule and that this was strictly an isolated military mutiny.

These notions about the nature of the insurrection exactly reflected the attitude of Palmerston in the early days of the mutiny. With the same tone of optimism The Saturday Review stated that;

> *...they [the British authorities] have met the emergency with equal strength and wisdom, doing the thing best to be done with promptitude and vigour, and bringing a;; the resources of their vigorous minds to bear upon the crisis, with as little flurry and perturbation as if they had been arranging the details of a festival.*

Further, when considering the military leaders involved, it was stated that;

> *... history will record that by John Colvin and by Henry and John Lawrence, the resolute vigour of the Anglo Saxon race was nobly represented, and that bravely and wisely they anticipated the danger, and grappled with it while still in the womb.*

Finally, it was speculated that even as the paper was being written; "...the Sepoy mutiny had been suppressed", but there was still need for vigilance and more troops in case it should flair up again. Obviously, both The Times and The Saturday Review were reflecting the general view that under Palmerston, the British and their military were invincible.

It was totally inconceivable to these publications that any local "native" force could possibly pose a serious threat to British power. Moreover, it was utterly unimaginable that any group of people who had the opportunity to be governed by the British would not want this good government to continue. Such was the arrogance of the day, that this was the attitude that many had adopted.

The Spectator, while still writing with an air of total assurance that the British will be victorious, questions the inaction of the government in not sending out more troops than have been proposed and even goes so far as to question whether the government will send the troops it has promised.

Mr. Vernon Smith says "The remedy which is always suggested for every evil is to increase the European force." But the language and conduct of the government at present almost imply that Mr. Vernon Smith himself means to do nothing more than sen out the proposed 14,000 men-if even that be done; for the promise is accompanied by something like a presumption that the mutiny has already been put down.

Moreover, The Spectator called for reform in the governing of India. Civil officials and British officers were portrayed as leading a negligent life. There was a demand for more understanding of, and less interference in, the lives of the Indian people, and a call for increased and more effective recognition of Indians in the service of Britain. All of this bears a striking resemblance to the stand taken by Disraeli.

It is interesting to note that in spite of the fact that information was scarce and of dubious quality, all three of the above newspapers felt confident in predicting victory and offering opinion. The paucity of real information is clearly indicated by "Punch's Essence of Parliament" for the week of June 29th to July 3rd.

This column points out that; "The news from India brought up speakers in both houses, but nothing, of course, could be said by the Government, except that it had every confidence in the Indian authorities. The mail next week will show how far that confidence is merited."

This would tend to indicate that either the government knew more than they were willing to state publicly or that they really did not have enough information to answer the questions raised in the House. Judging by the speed of the communications and the guarded tone that tended to be used in many of the communications, it would seem likely that the latter is the case. In this case, however, the earlier reports through the press would seem to have been highly speculative rather than being based on known facts.

In any case, Punch had no other comment on the difficulties in India as of July 11 and it should be noted that this was the first occasion that the uprising had been mentioned at all in this publication.

Contrary to the reticents of Punch to indulge in any further comment on India, The Spectator did not hesitate to take this opportunity to engage in an attack on both the East India Company and the British officer corps in India.

The Company was the first to centred out for attack; Not only may it be said that defective organization is the key to the whole position in India, but the grossly deteriorated and neglected state of the regimental organization is but an example of defective system in other branches of the public service. This type of statement is a continuation of support for the replacement of the East India Company in favour of direct rule by the Crown. What is new, however, is the following statement about the British officers corps.

The more the facts of the late outbreak are considered, the more they show that-to put the case in the strongest terms-the insurrection could not have taken effect if the British officers had not connived at it by default.

At Meerut, the Sepoys numbered about 2000; and it is difficult to understand how they could have accomplished their crime-murdering their officers, burning down cantonments, marching off to Delhi and taking possession of it-when in that same station there were 2500 European soldiers. The only excuse would be, that the Europeans were so stationed as not to be effectually brought to bear upon the Native troops.

This is a wonderfully partisan report based on very little fact, and failing utterly to take into consideration circumstances that were extant on May 10th at Meerut. To begin with, the fact that it was Sunday is entirely ignored. This does not seem to be of any particular significance until one considers that it would be highly unlikely that the British officers would carry anything but side arms to church.

Thus, at the time of the outbreak they would not have had any rifles at hand. This would obviously leave the British at a great disadvantage in engaging the mutineers who were armed with rifles. The next problem is that there were not anywhere near 2500 European soldiers stationed at Meerut except perhaps on paper. However, the assumption that there was this number on the ground gave a tremendous boost to the notion that the defeat was caused by gross mismanagement on the part of the officers.

This allowed the continuation of another cherished myth of the British, and particularly Disraeli that; "The Sepoy is docile under careful and judicious management; he is irrepressible, and easily demoralized, if he be capriciously ruled, harshly treated, or neglected." The Sepoy was very much like a cocker spaniel in the minds of many of the British.

He would only bite if he was mistreated and since he had now bitten, he must have been mistreated. This attitude in itself may have been a contributing factor to the outbreak. It is rather ironic that, while the Spectator's attack on the conduct of the officer corps may considered appropriate, the reason for their attack was based on the same misconceptions of the Sepoy as contributed to the discontent.

Moreover, the very fact that the newspapers showed such signs of disbelief over the outbreak further highlights the notion that the British paid very little attention to what was happening in India.

The 1857 Mutiny was not an isolated event. It was one of many resistance actions that had occurred since the British rose to power. The main difference was one of scale, not intent. It is also interesting to note that on this date (July 11th) The Saturday Review did not run any stories about India at all. This is significant in that it reflects the attitude of Palmerston that this was not going to be a major problem and that victory was at hand. By July 18th this attitude had changed.

The Saturday Review was still predicting victory but was now warning that the battle would be long and hard; "If Government do not win in the first hour, we may be sure that they will not win in the second." Recent news from India had put Palmerston in the awkward position of being seen as failing to do enough to counter the revolt.

In contrast to the glowing praise that The Saturday Review had heaped on the authorities in India on July 4th, the paper now stated that; "...it can hardly be said that any blow has been struck." The fault, however, was not Palmerston's as the article goes on to say that the Meerut defeat was caused by the inaction of the authorities that were in place in India in that they failed to strike back boldly.

It was this inaction on their part that had resulted in the spread of the revolt to the point that; "... the whole of Northwestern is in a blaze."

Moreover, the death of the chief of the army was seen to be an additional factor that would slow down operations. All was certainly not lost though, since it was clear, according to this article, that the people had not risen to join the Sepoys and; "Of the eventual re-establishment of our authority there can be no doubt."

It should be noted that by this time Palmerston had taken action in sending out large numbers of additional troops and dispatched Sir Collin Campbell to take command of the British forces in India. The drain on the military was so great, in fact, that there was concern expressed by the Queen and the Prince Consort that Britain's defences were too weak and that the nation was vulnerable to attack. The following letter was sent to Palmerston from the Queen:

> *The Queen has just received Lord Palmerston's letter of yesterday and must say that if she had been in the House she would have joined in saying that the Government were not doing enough to 'reorganise a defensive force for home service.' The Queen will write a memorandum on the subject when she gets to Osborne, but in the meantime she must observe that she thinks the moment a critical one, and that it is not a question of a little more or less being done, but of doing all we can to avoid serious disasters! Let European complications arise (and God knows how soon they may, for the state of Europe is very bad) and we may find ourselves in an awful position of helplessness! The Queen must repeat that the Government must do all they can to keep up the army at home while they spare no means to send out a really efficient force to India.*

On the same date, July 18th, The Spectator continued its attack of the previous week, on the failure of the European officers to "study Native character". In a separate column of the same date, the attitude noted above with regard to the character of Hindus was again stated and this time the allusion to animal like qualities was even clearer than before; "...the Hindu is a tractable animal when he is managed with intelligence, intractable when his European managers are negligent or indiscrete."

In this edition, the paper takes the description a little further though, in describing the mutineers as "half children in understanding.... actuated by the same spirit that animates schoolboys in the "barring out."" It may at least be said that the Indians have reached human status, though only that of inferior children. This is much the same attitude as Disraeli had toward Asians.

Further, in a letter to the editor published on the same date, there is evidence for just how far this notion of the Hindu character had spread. Written by an individual who claims to have been a veteran of thirty years in India (no mean feat when one considers the mortality rate) this letter reiterates the notion that Hindus are children and that it has been through gross mismanagement that the insurrection occurred.

This letter also calls for more equitable treatment of native officers in the form of increased pay and prestige. The theme of mismanagement as the cause of the mutiny does indeed seem to be widely accepted. However, the paper did see cause for optimism because of the dispatching of Campbell and the increase in the strength of British forces though there was still concern that enough had still not been done because no one capable of settling the Hindus down through diplomacy had been dispatched.

Both The Spectator and Punch ran columns which outlined the significant events of the House of Parliament for the week prior to publication. It is most interesting to examine and compare these columns for the week ending July 18th. Punch intended to attract what might be referred to as the sophisticated, educated middle and upper middle classes and dealt primarily in satirical humour. The Spectator sought to attract a much wider base of readership and presented itself as a hard news publication.

As a result, Punch had a tendency to publish stories about political activities that had a direct effect on the people in Britain itself. Therefore, during the month of July, when the Mutiny did not seem like something that was going to have a profound domestic impact, very little is said about it in Punch.

However, regardless of this, it is still intriguing to look at the reports that are given about the proceedings in the House. If one reads The Spectator it would be easy to conclude that all anyone was talking and writing about was the Indian Mutiny. On the other hand, by reading Punch, one could be forgiven for wondering if there was anything of significance happening in India.

The only report that gives any indication that there is a conflict is a brief note for Monday July 6th reporting on an enquiry about how the troops were being shipped to India; by steam or by sail? According to this summary of Parliament there were no other questions or debates concerning India during the week.

Throughout the month of July this would remain the case. Punch, when it did make mention of India, did so only as it concerned local notables such as Sir Collin Campbell. It was not until well into August that this magazine devoted any serious amount of space to the crisis.

However, on the last Saturday of July, The Spectator devoted nearly three full pages to what was now being called "the war". This date is particularly significant in that it is the first time that there was any doubt voiced as to whether the mutiny could be put down. Moreover, it is the first sign that there is any doubt about the feasibility to maintain an Indian Empire.

While we have been hanging upon the next Indian mail to tell us whether or not the mutiny had been extended or suppressed, a much larger question has arisen,-whether our Indian empire is to be retained or abandoned?

Be the mutiny suppressed or not, we may still ask ourselves whether it initiates the decline of our power in the East? For our hold upon India can only be recovered by labours much greater than the mere military work of conquering the particular mutineers. There are questions also of dominion, and, deeper than this, questions of policy. We must reconsider the spirit of our government if we are to keep our Indian empire; and before we can determine that we should abandon that empire, it will behove us to consider whether imperial states can abandon their dependencies and yet retain their greatness.

This is not the same great bravado that one found in papers a week or two previous. Within this statement are signs of real self doubt. Further, the article goes on to discuss earlier attempts at mutinies and insurrections in India.

This is the first admission that the current crisis was not an isolated incident. It is also of interest to note that the Sepoys were no longer being referred to in condescending pet like terms. In this article they are called "Native mercenaries". Put in the context of the news that was reaching Britain about all the atrocities that were being committed on English women and children, this reaction on the part of The Spectator is quite understandable. The following quote from A History of Our Own Times written in 1881 captures the emotions that were generated.

Never in our time, never probably in any time, came such news upon England as the first full story of the outbreak in India. It came with terrible, not unnatural, exaggeration. England was horrified by the stories of wholesale massacres of English women and children; of the most abominable tortures, the most degrading outrages inflicted upon English matrons and maidens.

By August 1st, with rumours running rampant about Russian subversion and with the public in an uproar over the reported atrocities, Disraeli saw his moment to attack the Palmerston ministry's policies. The Spectator and The Saturday Review both reported on Disraeli's speech in the House in a highly predictable manner. The former defended Disraeli and the latter attacked him.

The Saturday Review characterized Disraeli's motion as "... Extremely ill timed and extremely unpatriotic...", but then felt that it should be pardoned because this might be the only opportunity for Disraeli to display his knowledge of India. Further, it was believed that the timing of this outpouring of information was predicated by the fear that this knowledge would soon pass back into the trivial category that it was in before the outbreak of the mutiny. There was, however, a great deal of doubt expressed as to whether most of the information given by Disraeli was actually of any use in considering why the mutiny had occurred.

In our present dearth of information, it is just possible to conceive that some few of the acts of Government stigmatized in the speech may have weakened the allegiance of the native soldier; but the larger part of Mr. Disraeli's censure is directed against measures which wise or unwise, cannot have an atom of influence on the condition of the Indian army.

In his speech Disraeli had contended that the incident involving the greased cartridges had simply been the spark to the powder and that the true causes of the rebellion, which he now referred to as a national revolt, were a combination of interference by the British in local land rights and property succession, the abolition of certain religious customs, and the displacement of ancient royal houses.

In response The Saturday Review totally ridiculed the idea that there could be any affection between the Sepoys and any of the deposed royal families and used the fact that the Sepoys had sought out the employ of a foreign power to dismiss the idea that there was any discontent with the abolition of religious customs and land rights. In a later article of the same date, The Saturday Review takes its anti Indian royal families stand a step further in proclaiming that the only mistake that had been made was in failing to dethrone all such families and to totally take away any vestiges of power. In this was they would not have been available to be used as rallying points for the rebellious Sepoys.

Disraeli's solution to the problem of the mutiny being a national revolt was to abolish the East India Company and place the Crown in direct control over India. This, he believed, would create a situation which would make control of the population easier since it would appeal to the "imagination" of the Indian mind. In one of the very few instances of its type The Saturday Review came in this case, to the defense of the Company.

Pointing out that all of the changes that Disraeli saw as causative to the rebellion had been initiated and carried out by government and not company officials the newspaper questions the logic of then taking control away from the company. The problem with this attribution of blame is that, while the government officials were responsible for these actions in a legal sense, it was more often the case than not that these actions were taken on the advice and prompting of company officials who were proported to be experts and were relied upon as advisors.

The Spectator took quite a different view of the same events and statements in the House. While stating the belief that; "The real object of the Opposition leader was to make a display, showing that the statesmanship and mastery of the subject lay on his side", it was also conceded that; "...he was by no means unsuccessful." Further, it was granted that on the basis of the latest mails, the characterization of the crisis as a national revolt was not a historical blunder or a misuse of language but an astute reading of the situation.

With regard to Disraeli's call for the dissolution of the power of the East India Company and the responses to that call from within the House, The Spectator reported with classic caustic partisan wit in stating that; "Mr. Mangles had something to say for the East India Company, Mr. Disraelis something smart in reply, and Lord Palmerston something because it was expected of him." Further columns of the same date supported Disraeli's call for direct rule by the Crown and attacked members of the Palmerston ministry, such as Vernon Smith, for being "clerklike" in their approach to the challenge of ruling India after the revolt was put down. Last, but certainly not least, in yet another column of the same date, The Spectator carried on its attack against the British officer corps for their lack of foresight and leadership in India and the recent events that still embroiled it.

Punch's response to the Disraeli speech was, while later in arriving, perhaps the most succinct of all. Both The Spectator and The Saturday Review had devoted considerable column space to the airing of their views. In contrast Punch ran a one page cartoon depicting Disraeli dressed as a Sepoy, stirring a pot labelled "For the House of Commons, July 27, 1857 to which he has apparently added what is called "King of Oude's Sauce". All of this was placed over the title; "The Asiatic Mystery. As Prepared by Sepoy D'Israeli". This one cartoon seems to convey, with greater clarity than all the inches of writing used in the other two papers, all of the mixed sentiments that the Disraeli speech aroused. Within it there was the notion of; Disraeli the factionalist stirring things up for the sake of disruption, Disraelis the expert on the Indian mind, and Disraelis the sympathiser with the King of Oude.

Of course there was also an exaggeration of Disraeli's Jewish features which was meant to convey the idea that he was more than just a little foreign himself and this was part of the reason that he was so anxious to take the side of the Sepoys. Obviously the political slant is more in line with that of The Saturday Review than that of The Spectator but it is presented in such a way that even a Disraeli supporter might have trouble suppressing a smile when presented with it. Punch definitely fulfilled its goal of appealing to the wit of the educated middle and upper middle classes with this particular cartoon.

The political tendencies of both The Saturday Review and The Spectator have been examined thoroughly enough throughout the present paper that there should be no additional need to reiterate them at this point. However, as to the question of how their stories reflected the stands of the politicians that they supported, some additional comment may be appropriate. While The Saturday Review was unabashedly pro Disraeli, anti Palmerston and anti East India Company, The Saturday Review was not so blatant in all of its stances. Early on in its coverage of the mutiny, The Saturday Review showed absolutely no sympathy for the cause of the East India Company. However, as Disraeli increasingly made the company the target of his attack in the House of Commons, The Saturday Review altered its view and printed a series of pro company statements, especially after Disraeli made his speech in the House on July 27th. This highlights the fact that this was a strongly anti Disraeli paper and that it would, at all costs to continuity of editorial policy and statements, oppose anything that Disraeli said.

This may also be a reflection of the attitudes that the newspaper's publishers perceived the public to have. As has been stated above, newspapers were primarily interested in selling copy and the publishers would have been very concerned about what the public wanted to read and make a conscious effort to satisfy that desire. Disraeli, in 1857, was not extremely popular to begin with and the speech he made in the House only served to lower his popularity since it appeared that he was siding with the enemy. When this is combined with the stories of atrocities that were circulating at the time it is not surprising that The Saturday Review would go out of its way to continue to appear to oppose Disraeli. It was perhaps for this same reason that Punch, which had very little to say about the mutiny throughout the month of July, was quick to employ its satirical wit when Disraeli made his speech.

The lack of attention to the mutiny on the part of Punch is, perhaps, less surprising than the increasingly great amount of attention paid to the crisis by The Saturday Review and The Spectator. There were, in fact, very few verifiable stories available at this time. Even The Times, which had a free lance stringer in India at the time, gave more column inches to local events in Britain, during the period under question, than to the mutiny. What is most interesting in all of these papers is that when they did write about the conflict in India, it was from the perspective of how Britain could best protect her interests or who would be best to rule India for Britain in the aftermath of the crisis. Not once was there ever any consideration given to the Indian people. This was a press that reflected the extreme self interest of the British in the mid 19th century. There was little concern for the rights of non British peoples or whether Britain had the right to rule over them.

While this comes as no great surprise to any historian of the period it is interesting when one considers the notion that Britain has been held up as an example of responsible government and as embodying and protecting the rights of free men. However none of these notions are ever evident in the press when it is discussing any other people outside of Britain itself. Moreover, the press was quite willing to sacrifice whatever notions of truth and factual reporting it may have had in the cause of copy sales and partisan politics. Perhaps, when one looks at the press today and their handling of the reporting of current conflicts, it may be truly said that the more things appear to change, the more they stay the same.

4

Battles of 1857

Battle of Agra

The Battle of Agra was a comparatively minor but nevertheless decisive action during the Indian Rebellion of 1857 (also known as the *First War of Indian Independence* or the *Indian Mutiny*). Indian rebels attacked a column of British troops which had relieved a garrison at Agra, but although they surprised the column, they were defeated and dispersed. This allowed the British to establish communications between across all of Northern India, and to concentrate troops for the vital Relief of Lucknow.

Background

Before the rebellion broke out, Agra was an important centre of British administration and commerce. Stationed in the military cantonments nearby were the 3rd Bengal Fusiliers (a "European" regiment of infantry of the British East India Company's army), a battery of artillery also manned by white troops, and two Bengal Native Infantry regiments, the 44th and 67th BNI.

The loyalty of the sepoys (Indian soldiers) of the Bengal Army had been wavering for several years, as they feared that the actions and reforms of the East India Company were threatening Indian society and their own caste and status. After increasing unrest during the early months of 1857, the sepoys at Meerut broke into rebellion on May 10. They subsequently moved to Delhi, where they called on more sepoys to join them, and for the Emperor Bahadur Shah II to lead a nationwide rebellion. News of the revolt spread fast. In Agra, the news prompted the local British commanders to disarm the two Bengal regiments on May 31, thus forestalling any uprising (although the regiments had apparently made no hostile moves in the fortnight since news of the events at Delhi had reached them.) Nevertheless, the news of the events at Delhi and increasing unrest in the countryside prompted 6,000 British civilians and their families and servants to converge on Agra and take shelter in the historic Red Fort. Although the fort was well provisioned, the sanitation and medical facilities were poor. After an uprising in the city in June, the British were blockaded in the Fort.

They endured a desultory siege for three months. Morale was poor, and the understrength Bengal Fusiliers were mainly raw and untrained troops. Delhi however, was too strong an attraction for the sepoys and other rebels. Many thousands of these moved to Delhi, where they were unable to dislodge a British force on the ridge to the northwest, but none of the rebel leaders there attempted to organise a force to clear the comparatively easy target of Agra.

Relief

On September 21, the Siege of Delhi ended with the storming of the city by the British. Within days, the victorious besiegers had organised columns which were to secure the countryside around the city. The strongest column consisted of 750 British soldiers, and 1,9C0 Sikh and Punjabi soldiers, under Brigadier Edward Greathed (formerly the commanding officer of the 8th (King's) Regiment. He moved out of the city on September 24. Several officers were surprised that the column was able to move so promptly, given the exhausted and debauched state of many units after the siege and storming of the city.

Greathed's column moved along the Grand Trunk Road, taking indiscriminate punitive measures against several Indian villages. Although Greathed intended to move directly to Kanpur, which had been recaptured by the British in July, he received several urgent requests for aid from Agra. Some of the rebels who had retreated from Delhi were said to have rallied at Muttra near to Agra, and the garrison were alarmed at what seemed to be an imminent threat.

Greathed accordingly marched his troops and his large train of elephants, camels, bullock carts forty-four miles to Agra in twenty-eight hours. On arrival, his force received a cool reception from the garrison. His battle-weary British troops in worn khaki dress were mistaken at first for Afghan tribesmen by some of the civilians; by contrast the soldiers of the garrison were still splendid in scarlet uniforms with pipeclayed white belts.

The Battle

From being in a state of panic, the senior officers of the garrison now assured Greathed that the enemy had retreated across the Khara Naddi, a stream nine miles distant. Fatigued and without any apparent danger, the column retired to rest without posting sufficient pickets. Greathed himself went to take breakfast in the fort. Taking advantage of this lapse in security, the rebels launched a surprise attack.

Round shot from 12 sepoy cannons raked the British bivouac area. Cavalry descended upon the British, musket balls filled the air and there was hand-to-hand combat between the British and their attackers. The veteran British, Sikhs and Punjabis nevertheless rallied, fell into their ranks, and returned the fire. The British cavalry outflanked the attackers on both flanks.

The rebels fled, but regrouped and tried to stand four miles down the Gwalior Road. Grape shot from British cannon and a cavalry charge broke their line. The British cavalry then pursued those fleeing for miles.

Results

This small but fierce action broke organised opposition to the British between Delhi and Kanpur. Most of the victory was due to the hardbitten British and Indian troops, who had been marching and fighting continuously for four months. They were very short of officers, and Greathed himself was regarded disparagingly by many of his junior officers. (He nevertheless led a brigade at the Relief of Lucknow and the Second Battle of Kanpur.)

Second Battle of Kanpur

The Second Battle of Kanpur was a battle of Indian rebellion of 1857. It was decisive as it thwarted the rebels' last chance to regain the initiative and recapture the cities of Kanpur and Lucknow.

Background

Kanpur had been recaptured from the rebels under Nana Sahib on July 17, 1857, by the Company forces under General Henry Havelock. Within a few days of coming to Kanpur, General Havelock received the news that the commander of the Lucknow garrison had died, and that the Company forces were facing a defeat at Lucknow.

Havelock initially decided to march ahead, and fight with the rebel forces at Unnao (or Unao) and Bashiratganj (or Bashiratgunj). However, soon he was informed that the Gwalior army had also rebelled against the Company rule. General Havelock realized that his forces were not strong enough to fight their way to Lucknow, and decided to go back to Kanpur on August 13, to await reinforcements.

The Company forces began bridging operations over the Ganges river, but the rebel soldiers attacked the bridge from the northern bank. The Company sent the Brasyer's Sikhs regiment to cover the construction. The Sikh regiment forced the rebel soldiers to retreat, and the bridge was completed without any further interference. The Company forces then set out for Lucknow. They were able to enter the city, but became besieged themselves. Another larger force under General Colin Campbell, the new Commander-in-Chief, India, was despatched to help them.

On his way to Lucknow, Campbell left a detachment of about 1,500 under Brigadier Windham to hold Kanpur, the vital bridge of boats across the River Ganges and the entrenchment constructed to protect it.

Meanwhile, the Nana Sahib's lieutenant, Tantia Topi, had gathered a large army to recapture Kanpur. The core of this army was the Gwalior Contingent. This was a body of troops in the service of the ruler of Gwalior, but which was recruited and organised on the same lines as the Bengal Presidency Army of the British East India Company. The Gwalior Contingent had mutinied against their British officers in June and July. They had since remained undecided as to their next course of action until Tantia Topi took charge of them, and led them to Kalpi on November 9, where they crossed the River Jumna and moved east on Kanpur.

Tantia Topi Recaptures Kanpur

By November 19, Tantia Topi's advance guard of 6,000 dominated all the routes west and northwest of Kanpur. Although Windham was aware that Campbell had gained success at Lucknow, he nevertheless decided to attack Tantia Topi before he could threaten the entrenchment, without waiting for Campbell to return from Lucknow.

On November 26, Windham's force drove back Tantia Topi's advance guard. However, the rebels' main body was close at hand. Windham tried to make an orderly withdrawal but some of his troops (a mixed bag of detachments of several regiments) misbehaved, retreating without orders and looting drink and supplies when they reached the entrenchment.

Meanwhile, Campbell was withdrawing from Lucknow with 3,000 troops and a convoy containing 2,000 sick, wounded and non-combatants. Hearing that Kanpur was in danger, he left his infantry to protect the convoy and moved ahead with his cavalry and horse artillery. To his relief, when he arrived on the north bank of the Ganges late on November 27, the bridge was still intact. Windham held the entrenchment, but the rebels had occupied the city of Kanpur and the ground between the city and the Ganges.

Evacuation of Civilians

Campbell crossed the bridge the next day. He deployed his artillery on the north bank of the river to fire on the rebels threatening the bridge, and then slowly filed the carts and other vehicles of the convoy across the bridge. The process took three days to complete. Although several officers urged Campbell to attack as soon as the north bank was evacuated, Campbell delayed for another five days while all the non-combatants were ferried down-river to safety. Campbell was later to be known for his caution, becoming irreverently known as "Sir Crawling Camel".

Tantia Topi Defeated

The rebels had continued to make some attacks on the British positions. An attack on December 5 was beaten off. Campbell was now ready to make his own attack, having received 5,600 reinforcements with 35 guns. On December 6, Windham opened a violent bombardment from the entrenchment to deceive the rebels that Campbell was about to attack their left. The real attack was made on their right, curling around the city of Kanpur to threaten the rebels' links to Kalpi. Campbell's heavier guns were the decisive factor, particularly the 24-pounders manned by the sailors of the Naval Brigade.

As the Gwalior Contingent broke and fled, the Nana Sahib's own retainers and adherents were defeated north of the city. The pursuit was pressed as hard as possible, capturing almost every gun and cart from the rebels. At Bithur, the Nana Sahib's treasury was captured the next day, concealed in a well.

Results

The rebels had attacked at the most favourable possible moment, under one of their most dynamic and charismatic leaders, and yet they had been defeated. From this point on, increasing numbers of British reinforcements were to arrive in India and the rebellion was doomed to defeat, although Tantia Topi and other determined leaders were to continue to resist for more than a year.

The Importance of Kanpur

Located on the Grand Trunk Road and Grand Trunk Canal and laying beside the river Ganges, Kanpur was to become a vitally important garrison town, straddling key communication lines. It lay on the approaches to the Punjab, Sind and the newly acquired Oudh provinces. Unfortunately, these new conquests had denuded the encampment of many of its European soldiers. It was thought that they were needed to help pacify the newly acquired areas.

General Wheeler was the commandant of the camp and his fine military record gave the Europeans in the area a reason to feel confident that the mutiny might pass them by. Other than the East India Officers, the European contingent was a strange collection of military families, business owners, barbers, operators of toll roads, telegraphs and railway engineers.

There was one complicating factor in the area that would come back to haunt Wheeler and the garrison. Nana Sahib was the adopted heir of the last great Mahratta king Baji Rao. Unfortunately for Nana Sahib, the East India Company decided that Baji Rao's pension and honours would die with him and would not be passed on to any successors. Nana Sahib lobbied hard sending an envoy, Azimullah Khan, to London to petition the Queen directly but to no avail. This dispossessed Hindu aristocrat would play a dangerous double game before deciding who to support in the mutiny.

The Meerut Mutiny Spreads

There had been problems and difficulties at Barrackpore and Berhampore back in February and March of 1857. But it was to be the events of May 10th in Meerut that converted the small but mostly contained disturbances into a full blown mutiny. On May 9th, eighty-five Cavalry sowars of the 3rd Bengal Cavalry refused to use the newly issued cartridges despite claims that no defiling fat had been used in their manufacture. The eighty-five were found guilty and sentenced to life imprisonment. They were shackled and led to jail.

This was too much for many of their comrades. In the heat of the following day, Sunday 10th May, a group of Sowars descended on the town and released their comrades. When some British officers tried to intervene, they were cut down or shot. Bungalows were set alight and any Europeans were considered fair game. About fifty European men, women and children lay dead by the end of the day.

With no obvious command centre or structure for the mutineers in Meerut, most of the rebellious sowars and sepoys headed for Delhi which was only 40 miles distance away. There they headed for the old Mughal Emperor and asked him to lead their rebellion and to restore the Mughal Empire so that Hindus and Muslims could live together in peace and combine forces to evict the Christian Company from India forever. The old emperor was unusually decisive in granting his patronage to the mutiny. This turned a localised army mutiny into a more significant political challenge to the rule of the East India Company. The slow response by the commander of the East India Company General Anson did not help. He underestimated the size and escalation of the challenge to the company's authority. He would not be the only one to make that mistake in 1857.

The mutiny spread from Meerut and Delhi to Agra, Muttra, Lucknow and Bhurtpore throughout the month of May. However, Kanpur appeared to remain loyal. British officers dutifully slept amongst their sepoys and sowars in order to show their confidence in their men. In fact, General Wheeler was so confident, that when a relieving force of two companies of the 84th arrived on June 2nd, he sent one of these companies plus one of the already arrived 32nd on to the besieged Lucknow. Not realising how useful they would have become to the defence of Kanpur in the days ahead.

Inadequate Preparations

The obvious defensive location in Kanpur was the magazine located in the North of the city. This had thick walls, plenty of ammunition, stores and it contained the local treasury. It was ready to defend. Unfortunately, Wheeler was expecting reinforcements to come from the South and he did not want them to have to fight their way through the city to relieve them at the magazine. He also felt that even if the Indian troops did mutiny, they would probably loot a little and then head North to Delhi as most other mutineers had done. Therefore he did not expect to need to withstand a long siege.

Conveniently, there was already a military building site to the South of the city. Nine barracks were being constructed at the Dragoon barracks. It was already full of building materials and coolies. He hoped that to redirect their construction towards an entrenchment might not unneccesarily alarm the Indian troops in the station. This would at least create a defensible area for the Europeans whilst any looting might take place before the mutineers would flee towards Delhi.

As this was the height of the hot season, digging trenches proved particularly difficult. It was almost impossible to get the trenches below waist height. There were also a large number of buildings overlooking the entrenchment that would provide cover for any would be attackers and allow them to shoot down on any defenders. The biggest problem was the lack of decent sanitatary facilities. There was only one well and that would be exposed to enemy fire.

The entrenchment would be fine to defend with a significant force of soldiers or for a very short period of time. As it was, there would be a thousand plus civilians with a pitifully small garrison of European soldiers who would end up having to defend for far longer than they had possibly anticipated.

First Signs of Discord

In a large cantonment with a thousand plus nervous and worried Europeans it was always going to be difficult to keep preparations for a defence against their own soldiers extremely difficult. As stories of various atrocities of women and children filtered back to Kanpur, the city became understandably on edge.

Although no direct threat had yet occurred in Kanpur, European families began to drift into the entrenchment and tried to find a space in one of the sturdier buildings available. The very sight of the Europeans withrawing into relative safety was not unnoticed by the Indian sepoys and sowars.

To try and disperse the number of Indian soldiers away from Kanpur, General Wheeler decided to send troops on various 'missions' to relieve garrisons in the region. One such mission was to send the surly 2nd Oudh Irregulars to Fatehgarh under the commad of Fletcher Hayes and Lieutenant Barbour. On the road to Fatehgarh they bumped into two more Englishmen named Fayrer and Carey. On the night of May 31st, Hayes and Carey left the other two Englishmen with the unit whilst they rode into a nearby town to confer with the local magistrate. The next morning they tried to rejoin the unit only to be met by an older native officer galloping towards them. He begged the two to flee. He explained that the unit had mutinied and that Fayrer had been decapitated and Barbour cut down as he tried to make his escape.

As this was being explained, Sowars raced towards them. Carey and Hayes wheeled around and attempted to gallop to safety. Hayes did not have the equestrian skills of Carey and was soon cut down by the advancing sowars. Carey on the other hand galloped over hedges and walls to try and shake off as many as he could. His horse came to a halt with exhaustion four miles later. Thinking that he was done for, Carey was amazed to see the abandoned horse of Hayes which he mounted and escaped to safety.

The cantonment was oblivious of this ominous turn of events

and life seemed to continue if apprehensively. Meanwhile, Nana Sahib had declared his loyalty to the British and sent what volunteers he could spare to be at the disposal of Wheeler and for the defence of Kanpur. He sent his units to camp just outside the magazine.

The forces at Wheeler's disposal were pitifully small. He had 49 soldiers of the 84th, 79 of the 32nd (mostly sick), 59 artillery men and 43 Eurasian drummers and fifers. Barely 250 in total. He had to defend a thousand odd civilians.

Tensions would be raised on the night of June 2nd when a drunk Lieutenant Cox fired on his own guard. He missed, was disarmed and thrown into jail for the night. The following day the sowars were less than impressed when a hastily convened court failed to convict him of firing on his own troops. This seemed to confirm that there was one rule for the English and another for the Indians.

Mutiny

Rumours of mutiny and impending treachery were becoming so widespread that it was difficult to tell the truth from the rumours. There were still Native regiments based in the city. The 1st, 53rd and 56th Native Infantry and the 2nd Bengal Cavalry. It was to be the 2nd Bengal Cavalry that were the prime instigators of the mutiny. It seemed to them as if the English were already prepared for them to mutiny. They cited the insulting fortification of the entrenchment, artillery guns being primed and aimed at them, the fact that they had to collect their pay out of uniform and one by one so as to not all turn up in the entrenchment armed and en masse, the acquittal of Lt Cox and rumours that they were to be summonsed to a parade where they were to be blown to pieces all convinced the sowars that something was seriously amiss.

At 1:30am on June 5th, three pistol shots signalled the start of the mutiny. At least one Rissaldar-Major Bhowani Singh refused to join his comrades and was cut down there and then.

As predicted by Wheeler the sowars began to burn buildings, loot and cause mayhem. The 53rd and 56th were groggily awoken by the panic and started to form up. The 56th began to panicand started to run off. European artillery opened up on the fleeing sepoys assuming they were mutineers too. If they hadn't been before, they were now. Worse than that, the 53rd, Wheelers old regiment, were caught up in the cross fire. The confusion and panic had led the British defenders to fire upon what was probably the most loyal unit in the area.

Soon virtually the entire native contingent had risen up or run off. Again, as foreseen, after a night of looting and destruction, the sowars and sepoys seemed to be making off towards Delhi to seek further orders and instructions from the Mughal Emperor there. Although deeply disappointed by the mutiny, the British officers were relieved that they would not have to survive the ordeal of a siege.

Nana Sahib's Intervention

Betrayal

During the chaos, Nana Sahib and his contingent entered the magazine/treasury. The 53rd guarding the magazine were unsure of what was going on elsewhere in Kanpur and had nominally remained loyal. At this time it was thought that Nana was volunteering to guard the magazine on behalf of the British. As it was, once they were on the inside he announced his loyalty to the mutiny and his desire to become a Hindu vassal of the Muslim Mughal Empire.

After looting the treasury, Nana Sahib advanced up the Grand Trunk Road with his elephants and loot. He caught up with the bulk of the mutineers at Kalyanpur. He realised that if he wanted to resurrect the old Mahratta Confederacy then Kanpur would need to be captured. He therefore pleaded with the mutineers to about-turn and come back with him to besiege and capture the city on behalf of the Mughal Emperor. Reluctant at first, the sepoys and sowars were convinced by the treasure he was carrying and a promise to double their pay and reward them with gold if they were to destroy the British encampment.

Ominously for the British, the mutineers trundled back into town. This time, they made sure that they had expunged all the Europeans from outside of the entrenchment and systematically plundered and destroyed all European owned property. Native Christians were also singled out for gruesome fates. Whilst all this was happening Nana Sahib took the time to write a letter to General Wheeler informing him to expect an attack the next morning at 10am!

Assaulting the Entrenchment

Life in the Entrenchment

The attack started half an hour late at 10:30 on June 6th. It would actually take the form of a prolonged artillery bombardment but this offered little comfort to the defenders who realised quickly that the mutineers had more and better guns available to them and that the entrenchment offered woefully inadequate cover from overlapping fire from all sides. It did not help the morale of the British to realise that the mutineers were putting their training to good account. The British artillery men fired back, but with smaller guns it was always going to be difficult. Additionally, the British had to keep their guns ready and primed with canister in case of an infantry assault. Fortunately for the British, the mutineers were reluctant to test the defences in an all out assault. In fact, they had been led to believe (falsely) that the entrenchment had gunpowder filled trenches preceding them to explode if the mutineers got too close to the defences. The British defenders could give a sigh of relief, but they had been given a taste of what a miserable siege they were in for.

The following days, and indeed weeks, would only confirm what a difficult position this was to defend. The fact that it was the hottest time of the year only added to the miseries of the defenders. The one well was exposed to the enemy artillerymen and snipers who took delight in aiming at the desperately thirsty defenders. Water extraction would have to take place at night to stand any chance of success.

A second dried-up well would have to serve as the make-shift burial chamber. The solid ground was too difficult to dig individual graves. Dead bodies would have to be piled up outside the buildings awaiting nightfall when they would be dragged and dumped with as much ceremony as could be summonsed given the circumstances. Even with this one particular precaution, diseases such as Smallpox and Cholera broke out and would ravage the steadily weakening defenders.

Savada Koti

Over the first week of the siege the mutineers completed the encirclement. They created loopholes and firing positions from surrounding buildings. They probed the defences for weaknesses. Captain John Moore retaliated and kept the defenders on their toes by launching dangerous but successful night time sorties to disrupt the attackers or spike their guns. One consequence of these sorties was that it convinced Nana Sahib that he should retreat his HQ to Savada House some two miles away in relative safety lest he become a target himself.

Provoked by these sorties, Nana Sahib attempted to lead a direct assault on the entrenchment. However a combination of lack of enthusiasm by the mutineers and some well timed artillery shot by the defenders dispersed the attack before it even began. So the pattern of artillery bombardment and sniper fire was resumed with some new heavier mortars adding to the misery of the defenders. It was calculated by Jonah Shepherd that one round was landing every eight seconds on average.

On the 11th June, the mutineer artillery decided to change tactic by concentrating their fire on particular buildings and firing incendiary round shot. They had some success with some of the smaller barrack buildings. To increase their chances of success, they also sent greased natives to try to set fire to the buildings.

The first assault of substance took place on the evening of June 12th. Musket fire was ferocious and the British had to use canister extensively to even out the imbalance in personnel. The final charge never did come through. The mutineers were still genuinely convinced that the British had laid some sort of trap; gunpowder filled trench or something along those lines and did not want to be the first ones to discover it.

The loss of the hospital to fire on the 13th June was a major blow to the defenders. It hurt their morale, but it also destroyed most of their medical supplies and removed one of the major structures from the defenders. As people scurried out of the hospital barrack for safety, the mutineers gathered for an attack. However, Lieutenant George Ashe used his few artillery pieces to devastating effect with well aimed canister round after canister round. The mutineers were convinced that there were more defenders than there actually were. The bombardment and sniper fire continued until the 23rd June. This was a date designated to host a major assault to coincide with the anniversary of Plassey. It had been foretold that the British would leave India on the 100th anniversary of this battle. Nana Sahib wished to take advantage of such a favourable omen.

The 2nd Cavalry led the charge but they did so at the gallop. This left the horses winded in the final stretch over open ground. British discipline allowed the mutineers to approach to within 50 yards when all hell let loose. The British fire was so well directed and the canister so devastating that the cavalry wheeled and fled before hitting home.

The danger was not yet over as men of the 1st Native Infantry advanced behind cotton bales and mobile parapets. Again, fortune smiled on the British when their opening volley brought down the 1st's commanding officer Radhay Singh. Canister blew away any cover that the infantrymen had hoped to gain from the cotton bales. Indeed many of them combusted and became an additional hazzard to the attackers. On the other side of the entrenchment by the barracks, mutineer numbers allowed them to overwhelm and engage the defenders in hand to hand combat. Lieutenant Thomson led 17 men to fight back and regain the position in desperate fashion.

The defenders cannons were wheeled around to help clear this flank of mutineers. By midday, it was clear that this assault too had failed to gain entry into the entrenchment. Although it had come close and the defenders could ill afford to lose any of more men.

Surrender

Although the attackers were becoming frustrated at their lack of success, it did seem as if time was on their side, at least in the short to medium term. It was known that Havelock was advancing up from Allahabad, but he had become severely bogged down and would not arrive imminently.

The defenders on the other hand were becoming increasingly desperate, their already small quantity of soldiers was being steadily whittled down by the combined attritional effects of successive bombardments, snipers, assaults, disease and poor to non-existent medical supplies. Food and water were dangerously low and the hot season was still beating down the sun unmercifully on the defenders. By the 21st of June, they had probably lost a third of their number. Personal tragedy had afflicted General Wheeler when his son Lieutenant Gordon Wheeler had been decapitated in the last assault on the barracks. His own personal morale was at its lowest ebb.

With the prospect of relief seemingly as far away as ever, General Wheeler assented to Jonah Shepherd slipping out of the entrenchment in disguise to ascertain the condition of the mutineer army. Jonah was picked up pretty quickly by the mutineers although they failed to appreciate that he had been part of the defending force and merely imprisoned him as a wastrel. Whilst this was all taking place, Nana Sahib and his advisers had come up with a plan of their own to end the deadlock. They used a female European prisoner, Rose Greenway, to approach the entrenchment with the idea of initiating negotiations. She conveyed to the defenders a note that said that Nana Sahib was willing to offer safe passage to Allahabad for all those who lay down their arms.

This offer was rejected by General Wheeler ostensibly because it hadn't been signed and that therefore no personal guarantee had been offered. However, the very fact that it had been made meant that the defenders began to debate the merits of holding out or capitulating and returning under the truce being offered. The following day, June 25th, a second note was brought, this time by a different female prisoner, a Mrs. Jacobi. This letter was signed by Nana Sahib himself. Debate swirled amongst the survivors and it was clear that there were two camps forming: Those determined to hold out versus those wishing to lay their trust in Nana Sahib's assurance.

Wheeler, already in a poor state of mind, was actually in favour of holding out, but when some of his officers began to talk of the sense in escorting the surviving women and children to safety, the old general relented and offered to lay down his arms in return for safe passage.

The next 24 hours saw an immediate improvement in the condition of the defenders. No longer having to brave the bombardment just to get a bucket of water meant that the defenders could drink their fill and wash and bathe for the first time in three weeks. Additionally, as the remaining rations would no longer be required for a long siege, allowances were doubled and the defenders could eat satisfying quantities for the first time in a long time. Probably most blissfully of all, the defenders could sleep without the din of cannons or the apprehension of an attack.

Betrayal at Sati Chowra

With a day for preparation and laying to rest any remaining fallen comrades, the morning of the 27th June was designated as the day to board the boats to take them down the Ganges to Allahabad. A large column was formed with General Wheeler leading from the front. They tried to show as much dignity as they could muster but the privations and conditions were unable to be concealed from the Indian onlookers. The respect shown to the front of the column gradually broke down as looters and pilferers tried their luck in grabbing the personal effects of those further down the column. More locals swarmed into the entrenchment hoping to find things of value left behind by the defenders.

Within an hour, the lead elements reached the embarkation point of Sati Chowra. One unanticipated problem was that the river was unusually dry and the boats were left fairly high and dry. It would take some serious dragging and effort to find the deeper parts of the Ganges. Nonetheless the hapless Europeans tried as best they could to find a place on one of the boats provided. General Wheeler and his party, being the first to arrive, were the first aboard and the first to manage to set their boat adrift. It was at this point that some of the mutineers began to look nervously at the general's boat floating downstream. It was clear that not all the boats were yet loaded and there were still a lot of Europeans waiting to board the at all.

There was a bit of confusion as the Indian boatmen jumped overboard and made for the banks. They knocked over the cooking fires on the boats before jumping in, thus setting some of the boats ablaze. Then, all hell broke loose. Tatya Tope ordered the 2nd Bengal Cavalry unit and some artillery pieces to open fire on the hapless Europeans.

The massacre was merciless. Bullets flew from all directions as the Europeans desperately attempted to scramble into the burning boats. There was no return fire as the British had been disarmed as part of the surrender terms. The relative shallowness of the river caused further difficulties in getting the boats moving as they scraped along the bottom of the riverbed. Bodies were falling everywhere as grapeshot and musket fire raked the boats from both banks. Mutineer cavalry sowars moved into the water to try and finish off any remaining Europeans with swords and pistols.

Women and children were inevitably caught up in the deadly fire. Two boats seemed to drift off-General Wheeler's boat-which had started the mutineers in their murderous fire in the first place and a second boat which was quickly holed beneath the waterline with round shot fired from the bank. There was a panicked exodus from this second boat to try and attempt to make it General Wheeler's boat which was slowly drifting to safer waters. Meanwhile back at the boarding point, the carnage continued. It then stopped almost as suddenly as it started when the mutineers suddenly ceased fire. Any remaining women and children were taken prisoner and escorted to Savada House. Any remaining men were cut down where they stood. Approximately 120 women and children were thus taken away.

Thomson's Party

The danger was not yet over for Wheeler's little ark with approximately sixty fugitives aboard. Mutineers pursued it down the riverbanks and the boat frequently grounded on unseen sandbanks. Trying to dislodge the boat under fire was particularly onerous to the remaining soldiers and officers on the boats. Not all were able to rejoin the boat whenever it floated free-General Wheeler's own family members were probably killed in the water trying to free the boat.

The boat would be freed only to hit other sandbars further down the river. On one such sandbar with withering fire being provided by mutineers pursuing them along the banks, Lieutenant Thomson led a last gasp desperate charge out of the river into the mutineers. Unbelievably, the suicidal charge worked and in fact allowed them to capture some vital ammunition. The next morning yet another grounding resulted in another charge by Thomson and 11 volunteers. Yet again, the fighting was fierce. Thomson's party was forced to find a long way around the mutineers to get back to the boat, but when they got to where they expected to find it, they could not locate it. Whilst Thomson had been fighting, an attack had been launched from the opposite bank and the remaining defenders were on their last legs.

After many of the remaining men had been shot or wounded, the remainder had decided to fly the white flag. They were unceremoniously escorted off the boat and taken back to Savada house. It was here that Nana Sahib ordered the execution of all the remaining men (including General Wheeler) whilst the women and children were taken to Savada House to be reunited with their remaining colleagues.

Thomson's ordeal was not yet over. The survivors decided to run barefoot for three miles to try and evade any pursuing mutineers. Mutineers pursued but were wary of getting too close as Thomson's party laid several ambushes and mini-counter attacks. The party found some refuge in a small shrine. They blocked the doorway with the bodies of mutineers who had hastily charged the position. Appreciating the difficulties of a frontal assault, a group of mutineers went around the back and started digging from behind.

Another group attempted to smoke the British out-but the wind took the smoke in the opposite direction. Gunpowder was added to the fire to thicken the fire later in the day. This prompted the British to try a last gasp charge through the thick black acrid smoke. Six of the British were cut down, but the rest managed to bayonet their way to the riverbank where they flung themselves into the river and tried to swim to safety. A group of villagers beckoned the five soldiers to their side of the bank only to start clubbing them as they reached that bank. One was killed leaving just the four-including Thomson-to swim to the centre of the river. They drifted downstream as best they could-although they now had to worry about crocodiles too. They came exhaustedly ashore a few hours later. Their fortunes finally turned for the better when they were discovered by Rajput matchlockmen who worked for the Raja Dirigibijah Singh who had remained loyal to the British.

They were taken, or rather carried, to the Raja's palace. With the exception of Jonah Shepherd, these were the only male survivors of the ordeal.

The Bibighar

The dazed, shocked and confused women and children were moved from Savada House to the Bibighar. It was called this as in happier times a British officer had housed his Indian Bibi (mistress) in this villa-type house. It was terribly cramped for the women and children. The original 120 women and children would later be joined by other women and children from Wheeler's boat, some from a second flotilla from Fatehgarh (with three men) which had been captured and some other women and children who were already being held captive. In total there were about 200 souls crammed into the house. Nana Sahib placed the care for these survivors under one of his mistresses serving girls who would become known as the Begum. Her real name was Hussaini Khanum. She seemed particularly unmoved by the plight of her captives and did little to help them. Food was provided but little thought was given to the dignity or care of the prisoners.

Nana Sahib had decided to use these prisoners as bargaining chips to try and keep back the relieving force of Havelock and Neill. They demanded that the British retreat to Allahabad. Havelock's force though advanced relentlessly towards Kanpur. An army was sent by Nana Sahib to intercept the relatively small but determined flying column. They met at Fatehpur on July 12th where Havelock's forces quickly out-manoeuvred the larger mutineer force and captured the town.

Storming Positions

Furious with this setback, Nana Sahib sent his brother Bala Rao with another force to intercept and turn back the British. On July 15th, British scouts came across a heavily fortified position just outside the village of Aong. A frontal assault dislodged the mutineers and sent them fleeing across the river to yet another defensive position. An attempt by the mutineers to blow the bridge was only partially successful so the bridge remained usable for the infantry at least. Being in a hurry, Havelock urged his soldiers on and at 4am on July 16th they moved to clear the way to Kanpur itself. Scouts were fortunate to capture some mutineers who informed Havelock that there was an army Highlanders of 5,000 rebels with 8 artillery pieces awaiting them further up the road. Havelock decided that a frontal assault would be suicidal and so moved his infantry up on the flank whilst keeping his irregular cavalry in front of the mutineers as if they were still screening an infantry force. The plan was only partially successful as the mutineers spotted the flanking manoeuvre and opened fire. Desperate charges from the Highlanders carried the day but with high casualties on both sides. The road to Kanpur had been cleared, but the cost of these victories had not yet been fully tallied.

As it became clear that the British were going to enter Kanpur, Nana Sahib, Tatya Tope and Azimullah Khan debated about what to do with their captives. As mutineers scurried out of the city, it was not clear how 200 women and children could be escorted anywhere and their use as bargaining chips had patently failed. Azimullah Khan was also worried that Nana Sahib might flee and abandon the mutiny altogether. The order was given to eliminate their prisoners.

At first the guarding Sepoys refused to obey the order. They had executed the remaining men without much thought, but murdering women and children was another matter. It was only when Tatya Tope threatened to have the sepoys themselves executed for dereliction of duty that they agree to try and remove the women and children from the courtyard for their execution. The women had already realised what was going on with the execution of the remaining menfolk. They barricaded themselves in as best they could by tying the door handles with clothing. This did seem to work. The furore and screams were such that Nana Sahib left the building rather than be a witness to the enfolding massacre.

Meanwhile, the sepoys moved to the opposite wall to the far verandah. Some twenty soldiers opened fire into the cramped compound. A second squad that was to fire the second volley was so disturbed by what they saw that they discharged their shots into the air and staggered away. The sepoys now adamantly refused to finish the job off. The Begum was so irate at what she called the cowardice of the sepoys that she had to get recruit her lover Sarvur Khan to finish the job off. He went into town and hired butchers with cleavers to finish off the nasty business. The remaining women and children were in such a sorry state that they found it impossible in their squalid, sickly state to fight off the cleavers of the strong, well built men finishing them off as a team. The murderers finally retired when it seemed as if the job had been completed, although remarkably some of the women and children had actually survived and lay for the night of the 15th amongst the scene of carnage. The following day, orders were given by Nana Sahib to clean up the scene of the massacre. They were surprised to come across the half dozen or so women and children who were still alive. The women actually threw themselves down the well rather than be murdered on the spot. The children, who were only five and six years of age, tried to evade the scavengers and mutineers until exhausted. They were then chased around the corner into waiting executioners who decapitated them. Eventually, all the bodies were looted of whatever pitiful possesions that they still had on their bodies and were then dragged to the nearby well and thrown down it. The horror was indescribable. There was so much blood that they could not clean the walls and floors despite their attempts at scrubbing.

Relief

On the 16th of July, a group of British officers and soldiers were directed by fearful local Indians to the Bibighar. They were horrified by the smell and sight that greeted them. They had assumed that they were arriving to rescue the women and children. Any feelings of elation at the victories and relief quickly turned to feelings of despair and then through to vengeance. It was beyond comprehension for Victorian soldiers to believe that innocent women and children could be butchered in such a manner. Most pitiful were the tiny hand and footprints of the children who had been slaughtered. Their tiny shoes brought tears to the eyes of the battle-hardened Highlanders and veterans of the 64th.

Torching Villages

Word soon got back to Havelock, Neill and all the remaining soldiers. Havelock actually had to worry about the large numbers of mutineers still in the area and he was also supposed to go on to Lucknow to relieve the force besieged there too. However, discipline had all but collapsed amongst the British who were in utter despair at the massacre. The Bibighar became a place of pilgramage for the British soldiers who then turned their indignation on any local Indians who happened to be in the way. They wondered how any of the locals could have let this massacre occur and do nothing to intervene and stop it. Neutrals became hostiles in the minds of the British soldiers. Looting, burning of houses and murder became acceptable as old testament-style vengeance was meted out indiscriminately. Looted alcohol fueled the despair and destruction.

Hanging Suspects

The worst vengeance was applied to any mutineer captured. No mercy was shown to them at all. A set of nooses was set up next to the well at the Bibighar, so that they could die within sight of the massacre. Colonel Neill decided that the crime was so serious, that all captured mutineers would be expected to clean up the scene of the massacre literally with their tongues. They were beaten and clubbed into licking the floor of the Bibighar compound. They would then be forced to eat Beef if Hindu or Pork if Muslim and then hanged at the gallows adjacent. Sweepers were employed to execute high-caste Brahmins. Some Muslims were sown into pig skins before being hung. The idea was to ritually humiliate and defile the victims to preclude any reward they might have expected to find in the afterlife.

Within days more bad news greeted Havelock with news that the commander of the Lucknow garrison had died and that garrison was now seriously facing defeat. Havelock had to remotivate his tired and disconsolate soldiers and ferry them across the Ganges and go on the march again. Havelock's forces were motivated by thoughts of righteous indignation to destroy a mutineer force lying in wait at Unao and one at Bashiratgunj.

News reached the British that the Gwalior army had joined the mutineers despite the attempt of the Raja of Gwalior to keep them loyal to the British. This meant that Havelock's exhausted and diseased force was perhaps not strong enough to fight its way through to Lucknow. Reluctantly he withdrew back to Kanpur on August 13th to await reinforcements.

When word reached Calcutta of the atrocities at Kanpur, the political imperative to exact revenge became overwhelming.

Europeans flooded to join the newly raised regiments and some of these were hastily despatched to attempt to avert any more massacres or disasters. Sir James Outram led such a force to the aid of Havelock. His small relieving force arrived in Kanpur on September 5th. They then set out to force their way through the huge force besieging Lucknow. They were able to fight their way through to Lucknow, only to become besieged themselves! The manpower was helpful to the defenders, but escape was impossible.

In fact, a second larger force under General Colin Campbell had to be despatched. He had dropped off General Windham in Kanpur en route to Lucknow. Windham, however, was over confident of his position and disobeyed Campbell's instructions by leaving his defensive positions and trying to engage a huge force of Gwalior soldiers and other mutineers being led by Tatya Tope. General Windham ordered a small advance on November 25th but did not press home his advantage, mainly due to his lack of numbers.

Tatya Tope correctly interpreted that the British must be fairly weak and launched a sophisticated attack the following day. Tatya Tope had some 25,000 men plus eighty guns at his disposal. The British were outgunned, outmanned and outmanoeuvered. They began to flee back to the relative safety of a new fort that had been hastily thrown up over the last couple of weeks-directed by the remarkable Lieutenant-now Captain-Thomson no less.

It seemed as if Kanpur was about to be re-besieged! Street-fighting reignited but this time help was at hand. General Campbell had not dilly-dallied in Lucknow. When he had got there, he emptied the compound and got the garrison to come back to what was considered to be the relative safety of Kanpur. They were surprised to come back to find it being besieged, but Campbell calmly took command of the situation. He engaged the mutineer artillery in a deadly duel across the river as Tatya Tope's men attempted to destroy the bridge of boats in vain.

A 30 hour duel reduced the mutineer artillery and convinced the mutineers to retreat to give fight another day. Before going though they did set light to much of the city as a departing gift. Only now, on December 6th 1857, did the city of Kanpur finally become pacified. Despite this, the women and children rescued from Lucknow were hastily sent down the river to the far more secure Allahabad. Kanpur would finally return to its original job of being a significant military cantonment in a strategically important communications choke point. More expeditions would have to be sent out to try and bring Tatya Tope and other mutineers to heel, but Kanpur itself would never be threatened again.

Historical Sikh Events: 1857

Anglo Sikh Wars brought an end to the Khalsa rule in Punjab. These two series of wars, First Anglo Sikh War and Second Anglo Sikh War left Sikhs leaderless. The Dogra generals who lead Sikh armies were in alliance with British and reaped a profit of their own by getting small kingdoms (like Kashmir). In the years that followed the Anglo-Sikh wars of 1849, sikh armies were disbanded by the British imperialists. Then happened the mutiny of 1857, which was nothing more then an attempt by Marathas to bring back the old order of Mughals. Mutiny in British armed forces was encouraged and several hundreds of British women, children were murdered by these mutineers, all over North India.

Eighty Years Bahadur Shah Zafar, from the lineage of Mughals was asked to take up the leadership of mutineers, which he reluctantly agreed. He had actually no other choice. During the Mutiny of 1857, the Muslims sought restoration of the rule of Muslim princes and rulers, and the Hindus hoped to put the Maratha rulers back into power. The princes of the two communities had a unity of purpose in putting up a common front against a common enemy, the British. Because of the earlier British repression of the Sikhs, they were too disorganised to think of putting up a united leadership to reclaim their lost kingdom. Sikh community was leaderless.

Moreover, the situation in the Punjab was quite different from the one that prevailed in the rest of India. An important and the main factor was that the Sikhs had nursed a serious grudge against the Purbias who, despite the Sikhs having never given them any cause for offence, had by their betrayal and other overt and covert acts, helped the British during the Anglo-Sikh wars and later in the annexation of Punjab. The British used the Sikh grievance and the consequent "natural hatred" towards the Purbias. Kavi Khazan Singh in his work, 'Jangnama Dilli', written in 1858, mentions that the Sikh participation against the Purbia soldiers was in reaction to their boast that they had vanquished the Sikhs in 1845-46 and in 1848-49. Another contemporary observer noted: "The animosity between the Sikhs and the Purhias is notorious.

The former gave out that they would not allow the latter to pass through their country. It was, therefore, determined to take advantage of this ill feeling and to stimulate it by the offer of rewards for every Hindostanee sepoy who should be captured. The bitter memories of Purhia cooperation with the British were so fresh in Sikh minds that any coalition between the two became impossible. The people who now claimed to be fighters for freedom were the same who, eight years earlier, had actively helped the British to usurp Sikh sovereignty. On top of that they were trying to bring back the same Mughal empire which over the years had wreak havocs on Sikh Gurus and famous Gursikhs.

The pleas of Purbias were so hollow and incongruous with their earlier conduct, that they fell on deaf ears of the agprieved Punjabi Sikhs, Hindus and Muslims whose independence they had helped the British to roh. Besides, it is a well-accepted view that the risings in 1857 were just revolts by the princes to regain their feudal or territorial rights. It was far from being any ideological struggle for any common Indian interest. In this context, the Sikhs in the background of their rule in Punjab and egalitarian tradition could hardly be expected to side with Muslim and Hindu princes to regain their kingdoms, nor could religious taboos which affected Hindu and Muslim sentiments, against many of which the Sikh Gurus had led a crusade, in any measure inflame Sikh sentiments.

It was on account of all this that the Punjab was not affected by the rebellion which convulsed the rest of northern India. Punjabi Mussalmans turned a deaf ear to their Hindustani co-religionists exhortation of Jihad against the pig-eating despoilers of Islam. Punjabi Hindus and, with greater reason, the Sikhs refused to listen to the belated appeal to save Hindu Dharma from beefeating foreigners who used cow fat to grease their cartridges. However, there were stray cases of Sikhs joining the mutineers. It was reported that a large number of Sikhs gathered at Ropar and declared the Khalsa Raj for which the leader of the band was immediately put to death. A Sikh Chief, Raja Nahar Singh, was executed for supporting the cause of the rebels. After annexation Bhai Maharaj Singh had moved from village to village in Majha region and incited the people to rebel.

The Cis-Satluj chiefs of Patiala, Malerkotla, Kalsia, Nabha, Faridkot and Jind, along with their mercenary forces, rendered full help to the British in suppressing the rebellion. These chiefs owed their existence to the British and were always outside the main Punjab, being hostile to Ranjit Singh. They still remembered with gratitude the support extended to them by the British against Maharaja Ranjit Singh. But for the British protection, Ranjit Singh would have overpowered them long ago.

This mutiny led British to recruit for their armed forces heavily among the communities which had been neutral to this rebellion. Especially, Gurkhas, Rajputs of Rajasthan, Punjabi Muslims and Sikhs. Sikhs started enlisting with British forces and were thus back to the profession of their liking, the military services.

Ninety Years later when India became independent Indian leaders decided to call the Mutiny of 1857 as "The first war of Independence", which in reality was the last war of Mughals.

Allahabad

Although everything was quiet at Allahabad at this time, the situation was very confused and the news of the mutiny in the north caused considerable anxiety and doubt. However, no precautionary measures were considered necessary until the 5th of June, when all civilians and women and children were ordered into the fort. This was just in time, for, at 10 p.m. on the 6th of June, the 6th Native Infantry, which was stationed in the cantonments two miles from the fort, unexpectedly mutinied. The men attacked their officers in the mess and then plundered the treasury. Incendiary, rapine and murder followed. The mutineers were joined by all the town rabble, and their savagery was terrible and continued for days.

Although the Commissioner and other senior officers were unprepared, Lieutenant Brasyer was ready and, as soon as the firing started in the cantonment, he quietly assembled his men and gave them instructions and encouragement. There were three guards of the 6th Native Infantry, numbering about two hundred men, in the fort in charge of the different gates. Lieutenant Brasyer, entirely on his own initiative, decided to disarm these men. He immediately went to the main gate with a party of Sikhs and instructed the officer in command of the guard to order his men to give up their arms.

The guard, who, it was afterwards learnt, had been given ammunition to hold the gate for the rebels, defiantly refused. Lieutenant Brasyer saw that determined action was necessary, so he caused his Sikhs to support him and advanced towards the guard. It was thought that the Sikhs might join the mutineers, but Brasyer had an irresistible influence over his men and the Sikhs did not waver.

Lieutenant Brasyer immediately ordered the guard to pile arms and stand clear. The guard hesitated and one man lunged forward at Brasyer with his bayonet, but the officer's orderly knocked aside the musket and saved his life. The Sikhs now adopted a determined attitude and the mutinous guard, seeing that the Sikhs were firm; gave way. Brasyer then personally disarmed all the men of the 6th Native Infantry in the fort and his Sikhs supported him throughout. The guards were made prisoners and turned out of the fort the next day.

As soon as the guards had been disarmed, Lieutenant Brasyer organized the defence of the fort, which he held against the rebels with his four hundred Sikhs, a party of invalid British artillerymen and a small number of volunteer civilians until reinforcements arrived.

The following is an extract from the London Times of that time Lieutenant Brasyer commanded the Seikhs at Allahabad. It was to him that the Europeans were indebted for preventing the rebels from taking the fort.

This was the first important British success in the Mutiny and it was a stroke which has never been properly appreciated. Allahabad was the key to the northwest and, once secured, it formed an advanced base of operations. But for Brasyer's initiative and intrepidity, the war against the mutineers would have taken a very different course.

The importance of Lieutenant Brasyer's success is borne out

by this extract from a report by Lord Canning, the Governor-General, to the Government

I shall not be surprised if that strong fortress Allahabad, with all its valuable stores and war munitions, has fallen into the hands of the insurgents. That would indeed be a climax to our misfortunes, more serious than the seizure of Delhi.

After the 6th of June the fort was subjected to a desultory siege, for the place was surrounded by a large force of rebels, who remained in possession of the bazaar and city. The rebels were well armed and had two guns. Brasyer wrote as follows about his Sikhs at this time.

All this time my faithful Seikhs, on whom so much depended, were craving to be led against the enemy outside, or anywhere, rather than be kept idle within the Fortress, so I found it necessary to temporise with them a little. 'Now, as we are all on special duty, doing hard work, and in hot weather,' said I, 'let us discard the cap and heavy clothing. Adopt your national dress, and show how Seikhs can fight, and save this Fort and all within it.

The Ferozepore Sikhs therefore from this time on discarded their caps and heavy coats and wore red turbans and Sikh blouses throughout the Mutiny. This pleased the men immensely, especially as Brasyer himself adopted the dress.

A few days later Colonel James Neill arrived with a British battalion, the 1st Madras Fusiliers, and took over command at Allahabad. By this time the whole countryside had broken out into revolt, so from the 12th of June Colonel Neill carried out a series of vigorous sorties against the rebels. The Ferozepore Regiment, now known as Brasyer's Sikhs; played a prominent part in these operations and won further distinctions. These sorties met with considerable success and the district was soon in a state of submission. On the 17th of June the rebels were defeated and driven out of the city and the British administration was reestablished.

Before the end of the month Lieutenant Montague arrived from Mirzapore with the remainder of the Regiment and joined Brasyer, who had been promoted to captain for his gallantry at the beginning of the month.

The situation at Kanpur was now serious and it was essential to send a force to relieve the British garrison as soon as possible. Transport was immediately collected and an advance column, consisting of Madras Fusiliers and Ferozepore Sikhs, set out for Kanpur; on the 30th of June.

On the same day General Havelock arrived in Allahabad with the 64th and 84th Foot and the 78th Highlanders, and he set off for Kanpur a few days later, taking with him his British troops and a detachment of the Ferozepore Sikhs. By this time Kanpur had been captured by the rebels, so General Havelock decided to drive them out and then march to the relief of Lucknow, where the British were besieged in the Residency.

A portion of the Ferozepore Sikhs were left behind in Allahabad, under Lieutenant Montague, to hold the fort and patrol the surrounding district. Here the Sikhs did excellent work and fought several successful engagements with parties of mutineers in the area. On one occasion a guard of two non-commissioned officers and eight sepoys, surrounded by about a thousand rebels at Sahunga, gallantly rescued a wounded British officer and fought their way back through the rebels to the main guard.

Kanpur

General Havelock joined forces with the advanced column on the 12th of July and moved on towards Kanpur in very trying conditions in the hot weather. On the following day, just as the combined force was preparing to camp near the village of Fathepur, a large party of mutineers advanced from the village to attack the British force.

Although his men were exhausted after a long march under a scorching sun, Havelock decided to attack. He immediately deployed his troops and utterly routed the enemy in a short, sharp fight. After a much-needed rest on the next day, the force continued the march early on the 15th of July. However, it was found that the enemy had re-formed and was holding the village of Aong in strength. General Havelock immediately attacked the enemy positions and threw back the mutineers at the point of the bayonet.

It was now learnt that the enemy was preparing to blow the important bridge over the Pandu river, six miles farther on, so

Havelock had to push on without resting in order to save the bridge and secure a passage over the river. Brasyer's Sikhs moved forward in skirmishing order and occupied the cliffs overlooking the bridge. This enabled the guns to come forward and cover the Madras Fusiliers, who stormed the bridge and put the enemy to flight.

The same evening General Havelock learnt that a number of women and children had been made prisoner at Kanpur and had to be rescued at all costs. He therefore decided to continue the advance without delay, even though his men had no rest and the column was still twenty-two miles from Kanpur On the 16th of July the force advanced to within a few miles of the town before meeting any resistance.

Here some ten thousand rebels opposed the British advance on the town. General Havelock personally led his now-small force of nine hundred men round the enemy's left flank and took the enemy by surprise from the rear. The 78th Highlanders were in the lead and rolled up the enemy's left flank with a brilliant charge. The 64th and 84th Foot and Brasyer's Sikhs then passed through and carried the enemy's position. They captured the guns on the right and the enemy retreated. Leaving the guns behind, protected by Brasyer's Sikhs, the British infantry regiments followed up their success and inflicted further losses on the enemy, who eventually lost heart and fled in disorder.

General Havelock and his men camped for the night in the open and entered Kanpur early on the 17th of July, but they were too late to stop the brutal murder of the women and children by the mutineers.

Forest, in His History of the Indian Mutiny, Wrote as Follows about Havelock's Advance from Allahabad

In nine days Havelock and his veterans had marched 126 miles under an Indian sun in the hottest season of the year, each man carrying a heavy weight of ammunition, and had won four pitched battles and sundry combats against highly disciplined troops far exceeding them in number. During four days' fighting they had killed or wounded many hundreds of their enemies, and had captured twenty-three pieces of artillery. Their advance had been one of suffering, of privation, and of fatigue.... Battle after battle was won by desperate fighting; the cholera and the sunstroke slew many survivors of the combat, but on they went with unflinching resolution until Kanpur was reached.

After a few days' rest Havelock, leaving General Neill with a small force to hold Kanpur, crossed the River Ganges by boat and set out to march to the relief of Lucknow, forty-five miles away. His force, which was only fifteen hundred strong and included Brasyer's Sikhs, moved out on the 29th of July and almost immediately encountered a large force of the enemy opposing their advance. Havelock drove the enemy out of the villages of Unao and Basiratganj and utterly defeated them in two brilliant battles. However, Havelock's force was seriously depleted by sickness and battle casualties and he had to withdraw to Mangalwar; a few miles north of the river, and await reinforcements. It was quite obvious that the remnants of his force had little chance of forcing the way to Lucknow and carrying out the relief of the besieged garrison in the Residency. Forrest wrote in his History

Two victories had been won. But if the road to Lucknow was to be so roughly contested there was little chance of reaching the Residency. What soldiers could do Havelock's men had achieved. But they could not fight the pestilence of the tropics. For some days cholera and dysentery had done deadly work among them. A sixth of his force had perished-half on the battlefield, half by disease.

A few days later Havelock received a small number of reinforcements and a few guns, so he moved forward again on the 5th of August. He encountered the enemy in Basiratganj and utterly routed the rebels for a second time, but again was forced to withdraw to Mangalwar. He was still not strong enough to fight his way to Lucknow, which was reported to be held by thirty thousand mutineers.

On the 11th of August Kanpur was threatened by four thousand mutineers, who had arrived in Bithur from Saugor, and General Neill called for aid, while, at the same time, the enemy was also reported to be collecting again in Basiratganj. Havelock was determined to strike another blow before recrossing the river to Kanpur, and he set out with his force the same evening. He once again defeated the enemy in a fierce battle a few miles north of Basiratganj during the next morning, and then withdrew for a third time and crossed the river to Kanpur.

On the 16th of August Havelock led his much-depleted force against the mutineers in Bithur. After a long march of eight hours the weary force gained contact with the enemy, who were holding one of the strongest positions that Havelock had ever seen, around the village. Havelock decided not to wait, and his men assaulted the position with great gallantry. After some hard hand-tohand fighting the position was carried and the enemy utterly routed. Brasyer's Sikhs were on the left flank and threw back a large force of the enemy, entrenched in the bank of a nullah, at the point of the bayonet and captured his guns.

After the battle Havelock returned to Kanpur and issued his famous order of the day in which he said:

> *Soldiers, your labours, your privations, your sufferings and your valour will not be forgotten by a grateful country.*

This quotation is inscribed on his statue in Trafalgar Square, and on the reverse The Regiment of Brasyer's Sikhs is included amongst the units listed as the Defenders of Lucknow. The 14th Sikhs are the only unit of the Indian Army mentioned on a monument in England.

Owing to casualties and the serious sickness from cholera and other diseases amongst his British troops, Havelock had to remain in Kanpur for nearly a month awaiting reinforcements. There was very little fighting and the Ferozepore Regiment was detailed to escort a convoy of sick and wounded to Allahabad. The Sikhs escorted the wounded safely back, in spite of encountering a number of rebels during the journey, and then returned to Kanpur.

In the middle of September Sir James Outram arrived in Kanpur with a large force of reinforcements and bridging operations over the Ganges were begun. The mutineers attacked the bridge from the northern bank and Brasyer's Sikhs were sent over to cover the construction. The Sikhs drove the enemy back and the bridge was completed without further interference.

On the 21st of September two brigades, about three thousand strong all told, set out for Lucknow under General Havelock, accompanied by Sir James Outram. The enemy opposed the advance at Mangalwar and at Alambagh, in the southern outskirts of Lucknow, and were utterly defeated by the British in two gallant battles. Havelock and Outram halted at Alambagh on the 24th of September while they decided the best means of extricating the British forces in the Residency.

Relief and Defence of Lucknow

The sick and wounded, heavy baggage and large supply train were left at Alambagh, protected by a guard of three hundred men drawn from all units, in the force.

On the 25th of September the advance from Alambagh began. General Neill's Brigade was in the lead and the 78th Highlanders and Ferozepore Regiment were detailed as rearguard and ordered to hold the bridge at Charbagh until everything had passed. The Madras Fusiliers, with the 84th Foot, forced the bridge and Havelock then led his force round east of the city. This move evidently surprised the rebels, for he met no serious opposition until he arrived a short distance from the Residency. Meanwhile, the Highlanders and Sikhs were heavily engaged at Charbagh, where they were attacked by a large force of rebels. After three hours' fighting they defeated the enemy and were able to push on. However, they had lost touch with the main British column and took the wrong road. This mistake proved most fortunate, for they suddenly encountered the rear of some guns which were holding up Havelock's advance and rushed them without ceremony.

The 78th Highlanders and Ferozepore Regiment were now in front. The Residency was only some five hundred yards away, but since it was now dusk and the column was strung out over a considerable distance General Outram suggested halting. General Havelock, however, was determined to reach the Residency without delay and ordered the 78th High-landers and Brasyer's Sikhs to advance. This column, led by Sir James Outram and General Havelock, dashed forward through the narrow streets of flat-roofed, loopholed houses held by the mutineers. The Highlanders and Sikhs fought their way forward with desperate gallantry under continuous fire from the enemy and eventually reached the Bailey Guard Gate of the Residency to the deafening cheers of the gallant garrison. In describing the assault Brasyer wrote

Onward went the devoted band into a fire that seemed, as General Havelock said, as if nothing could live under it. The Highlanders, being Europeans, were placed in front, but the Seikhs followed them closely, pressed eagerly forward, and loudly cheered. Eventually it became a pell mell race for who should be first. Here Neill fell. Continuing this rushing, the troops were all intermixed, jumping over cuttings, and other obstacles in the street, until they finally reached the gateway of the Residency. But this was not only shut, but barricaded. A scramble ensued, the enemy firing from the roofs and windows of houses at us in every direction. At this moment I caught sight of a gap at the side of the gate, forced my way through this, and in reality was the first European of the relieving force who entered the beleaguered Lucknow Residency.

During the day's desperate fighting many acts of gallantry were performed and the Regiment suffered a very large proportion of casualties. One noteworthy feat of gallantry was that of Sepoy Nihal Singh, of the Ferozepore Sikhs, who carried General Neill, when he was mortally wounded in the final charge, to the rear under heavy fire.

The rearguard, with a number of sick and wounded, had not been able to reach the Residency and had remained in the Moti Mahal. So, on the next day, a detachment of the 5th Fusiliers and Brasyer's Sikhs was sent to reinforce them and help them to withdraw to the Residency. Although the Sikhs and Fusiliers fought their way through and drove the enemy back from the buildings and gardens adjacent to the Mod Mahal, the enemy fire from the Kaiserbagh was found to be too heavy to admit of the rearguard convoy being moved back. Further reinforcements from the 78th Highlanders were then sent forward and the rearguard was safely withdrawn to the Residency after dark.

After arriving in the Residency area Sir James Outram took over, from General Havelock, the command of the British forces. Although the rebels had been outwitted, they had not been decisively defeated and still occupied the city in great strength. It was found to be quite impracticable to carry out the original intention of withdrawing the besieged people in the Residency and all the relieving force could do was to aid its defences. Although this was not really a relief of the Residency, it was a very gallant rescue from a situation of the gravest peril. There were now 2,000 additional troops, so there was no longer an imminent danger of the garrison being overwhelmed. However, the Residency was besieged as closely as ever, and Sir James Outram had to stand on the defensive and await relief in his turn.

With the increased number of troops in the Residency positions had to be enlarged and so for the next few days several sorties were made to improve the position. The Regiment of Ferozepore was in General Havelock's sector and took part in the sorties along the eastern face of the Residency to clear the enemy from the gardens and houses up to the Chata Manzil. These sorties were entirely successful and improved the defences of the Residency. Lieutenant Cross, of the Ferozepore Sikhs, was wounded in one of these sorties, but otherwise the Regiment suffered very few casualties.

On account of the Sikhs' good service, General Havelock promoted each man to a grade higher in rank, and all subadars were granted the 1st Class Indian Order of Merit.

For the next two months Brasyer's Sikhs were put in charge of the Bailey guard, one of the most important positions in the Residency, and they also held the defences on the right of General Havelock's sector bordering the Pyne Bagh. Outram's force was given no rest by the enemy and it had always to be on the alert. Duties were constant and arduous, while rations were scanty throughout the siege. On one occasion, when the enemy blew a breach in the defences, a detachment of the Ferozepore Sikhs checked a large force of the enemy who stormed the breach, and gave the garrison time to form and repulse the enemy. Jemadar Gowahir Shah was in command of the guard and was awarded the Indian Order of Merit for his gallant conduct.

At last, on the 17th of November, a relieving force under General Sir Colin Campbell, Commander-in-Chief in India, arrived at Lucknow. The situation at Kanpur, however, had again become: critical and General Campbell had to return there as quickly as possible. He therefore decided to evacuate the Residency and return to deal with the rebels at Lucknow at a later date. On the night of the 22nd November all the British forces were withdrawn successfully from the Residency together with all the women, children and wounded. The enemy were taken completely by surprise by this operation, which had been carefully planned and boldly executed.

General Outram was left with a force of some four thousand men to hold Alambagh and contain the enemy at Lucknow. The Ferozepore Regiment was included in General Outram's force and held defensive works at Alambagh for three months. Duties were very arduous on account of the large perimeter to be held while the enemy kept in constant touch and there were almost daily skirmishes and minor encounters. The enemy delivered a number of attacks, but these were all beaten off with losses to the rebels.

On the 22nd of December General Outram took the offensive and threw back a large enemy force which had attempted to sever his communications to Kanpur. Reporting on this action, Outram wrote:

> *The gallant way in which, with a, cheer, the 78th and the Regiment of Ferozepore, led by their commanders, dashed at a strong position held by the enemy (30,000 men and 6 heavy guns), excited much admiration.*

On another occasion a most determined attack was made by the enemy on the defences held by the Ferozepore Regiment. Before dashing off to counter-attack the enemy Captain Brasyer sent the following message, scribbled on an envelope, to General Outram: General, the enemy is in force on our right picket; I am off. This action was completely successful and five thousand of the enemy were driven off. Later General Outram told Brasyer that his scribbled report satisfied him more than all the documents tied with red tape he had ever received. Forrest, in his book, wrote:

> *Full justice was not done by Sir Colin Campbell or the Chief-of-Staff to Outram's defence of Alambagh, which must be viewed as a fine example of courage and good conduct and will always stand out as a glorious episode in the annals of the Indian Mutiny.*

Capture of Lucknow

At the beginning of March, 1858, Sir Colin Campbell, with a large, well equipped force, joined General Outram at Alambagh and started methodical operations against the rebels at Lucknow,, The enemy were holding three lines of defences north of the city covering the Kaiserbagh, their citadel. These had been strengthened since the relief of the Residency, and houses were now fortified and roads barricaded.

Sir Colin's plan was to send General Outram with his division north of the River Gumti to turn the rebels' position, while his main force attacked the Kaiserbagh from Dilkusha Park.

For a few days the Ferozepore Regiment, now only three hundred and twenty strong, protected the Commander-in-Chief's camp, but it was soon in action against the enemy and took part in the operations to force back the rebels from their first line of defences along the canal. By the 13th of March the British had reached the Little Emambarra, which was held in strength and had to be captured. On the 14th of March one hundred men of the Ferozepore Regiment, under Captain da Costa, with two companies of the 10th Foot, assaulted breaches in the walls of the Little Emambarra, while Captain Brasyer and a hundred more Sikhs assaulted some houses to a flank. Since he had no other British combatant officer available, Captain Brasyer placed the Colours with an escort in charge of the medical officer, Surgeon J. Browne, and ordered him to keep close to him. These orders were faithfully carried out.

Brasyer's party captured and set fire to the houses on the flank and then, climbing 'up on to some flat roofs, set out towards the Little Emambarra itself. It arrived just as the assault was launched. This diversion enabled the storming troops to advance with unexpected ease. They soon captured the Emambarra, and the Colours of the Ferozepore Regiment were planted over the gateway. The day's objective had been captured, but the Sikhs were eager to follow up their success and Captain Brasyer described the next phase of the battle as follows:

> *The men were excited and eager to go on. Without orders, my Seikhs like monkeys climbed a wall and opened a large gate which gave outlet from the smaller Emambarra, while I, with other officers, joined them. A rush such as nothing could stop followed. The General (Franks) smiled as he cheered my men, but issued no order. This acquiescence was enough, I knew what*

he wanted. My Seikhs like greyhounds let loose, passed into the street, deafening cheers encouraged us, while the General and his staff followed in support. We rushed onwards, cleared 40 guns in battery en route, driving all before us. Pickaxe and shovel were next at work, and soon a breach was opened in an outer wall.

The Sikhs and the 90th Light Infantry, led by Captains Brasyer and Havelock (Son of General Havelock.), rushed forward and fought their way into an enclosure adjoining the Kaiserbagh under terrible fire. Havelock ran back for reinforcements, and a party of the 10th Foot advanced and captured a small bazaar in rear of the Tara Kothi and mess-house, which were held by some six thousand rebels. This bold move completely surprised the enemy, who made as though they would rush Brasyer's party and force their way out into the city. However, Havelock, seeing the danger, dashed forward with a party of Sikhs and captured two bastions in the last line of defences, turned the guns on to the rebels and drove them towards the Chatar Manzil. Reinforcements followed up quickly and before long the whole of Kaiserbagh was in British hands. Meanwhile, Brasyer had dashed into the centre of the palace, climbed on the top and pushed the Queen's Colour through a gunshot hole in the highest dome, as a signal that the citadel had been captured. The Ferozepore Regiment suffered heavy casualties in this battle and Captain da Costa was among those killed.

General Franks, in his report of that day, wrote:

No words of mine could give due credit to Major Brasyer's courageous conduct. Ever to the front, he was to be seen courageously leading his men wherever the enemy were to be found.

On the 16th of March Brasyer's Sikhs formed part of General Outram's force which captured the Residency and the iron bridge. Major Brasyer was seriously wounded in these operations, but refused to relinquish command of his Sikhs and had to be carried on a litter at the head of the Battalion for several days.

The rebels had been completely defeated in these battles and Lucknow was once again safely in British hands.

After the capture of Lucknow the Ferozepore Regiment joined the Oudh Field Force and took part in a number of minor encounters in rounding up parties of rebels and pacifying the countryside. During this period Lieutenant Montague, with the Allahabad detachment, arrived back in the Battalion.

Operations came to an end in June, 1859, and the Regiment marched to Ferozepore, its home station. Brasyer wrote:

> *The remnant of the gallant four hundred marched into Ferozepore on the 7th September, with drums and fifes playing, and colours all tattered and torn, after an arduous campaign of two years and four months, and thirteen years of faithful service under the British Government.*

For its service in the Indian Mutiny the Regiment was allowed to bear on its Colours the inscription Lucknow, Defence and Capture, while as a special mark of distinction for its outstanding conduct the Governor-General issued orders that the men of the Regiment of Ferozepore were permitted to wear red safas (turbans), like those in which they had fought, instead of native infantry caps-a privilege of which the Regiment still avails itself on ceremonial parades.

The staff of one of the Colours was broken by a bullet at the relief of Lucknow and was mended with a plain brass ring. This staff still carries the Regimental Colour today, although the actual Colour has been renewed on two occasions since that time.

Only five British officers served with the Ferozepore Regiment during the Mutiny: of these one was killed and three wounded. Brasyer commanded the Regiment throughout the Mutiny, starting as a lieutenant and ending up as a lieutenant-colonel.

Siege of Kanpur

The Siege of Kanpur was a key episode in the Indian rebellion of 1857. The besieged British in Kanpur (now Kanpur) were unprepared for an extended siege and surrendered to rebel Indian forces under Nana Sahib, in return for a safe passage to Allahabad. However, under ambiguous circumstances, their evacuation from Kanpur turned into a battle, and most of them were killed or captured. Those captured were later executed, as an East India Company rescue force from Allahabad approached Kanpur; in what came to be known as the Bibighar Massacre, 120 British women and children captured by the Sepoy forces were hacked to death and dismembered with meat cleavers, with the remains being thrown down a nearby well in an attempt to hide the evidence. Following the recapture of Kanpur and the discovery of the massacre, the outraged British forces engaged in widespread retaliatory counter-atrocities against the captured rebel Indian soldiers and civilians. The murders greatly embittered the British rank-and-file against the Sepoy rebels and inspired the war cry *"Remember Kanpur!"*.

Background

Kanpur (now Kanpur) was an important garrison town for the East India Company forces. Located on the Grand Trunk Road, it lay on the approaches to Sindh (Sind), Punjab and Awadh (Oudh).

By June 1857, the Indian rebellion had spread to several areas near Kanpur, namely Meerut, Agra, Mathura, and Lucknow. However, the Indian sepoys at Kanpur initially remained loyal. The British General at Kanpur, Hugh Wheeler, knew the local language, had adopted local customs, and was married to an Indian woman. He was confident that the sepoys at Kanpur would remain loyal to him, and sent two of British companies (one each of the 84th and 32nd Regiments) to besieged Lucknow.

The British contingent in Kanpur consisted of around nine hundred people, including around three hundred military men, around three hundred women and children, and about one hundred and fifty merchants, business owners, drummers, engineers and others. The rest were the native servants, who left soon away after the commencement of the siege.

In the case of a rebellion by the sepoys in Kanpur, the most suitable defensive location for the British was the magazine located in the north of the city. It had thick walls, ample ammunition and stores, and also hosted the local treasury. However, General Wheeler decided to take refuge in the south of the city, in an entrenchment composed of two barracks surrounded by a mud wall. There was a military building site to the south of Kanpur, where nine barracks were being constructed at the dragoon barracks. The British soldiers found it difficult to dig deep trenches, as it was hot summer season. The area also lacked good sanitary facilities, and there was only one well and that would be exposed to enemy fire in case of an attack. Also, there were several buildings overlooking the entrenchment that would provide cover for the attackers, allowing them to easily shoot down on the defenders.

General Wheeler's choice of this location to make a stand remains controversial, given the availability of relatively safer and more defensible places in Kanpur. It is believed that General Wheeler was expecting reinforcements to come from the southern part of the city. He also assumed that in case of a rebellion, the Indian troops would probably collect the arms, the ammunition and the money, and would head to Delhi and therefore, he did not expect a long siege. There is also another theory that Wheeler had simply chosen this location because it was closer to his personal residence at the time.

Rebellion at Fatehgarh

The first sign of the rebellion at Kanpur came in the form of a rebellion at Fatehgarh (or Futteghur), a military station on the banks of Ganges. To disperse the Indian troops away from Kanpur and lessen the chances of a rebellion, General Wheeler decided to send them on various "missions". On one such mission, he sent the 2nd Oudh Irregulars to Fatehgarh. On the way to Fatehgarh, General Wheeler's forces under the command of Fletcher Hayes and Lieutenant Barbour met two more Englishmen, Fayrer and Carey.

On the night of May 31, 1857, Hayes and Carey departed to a nearby town to confer with the local magistrate. After their departure, the Indian troops rebelled and decapitated Fayrer. Barbour was also killed, as he tried to escape. When Hayes and Carey came back next morning, an older Indian officer galloped towards them and asked them to run away. However, as the Indian officer explained the situation to them, the rebel Indian sowars (cavalry troopers) raced towards them. Hayes was killed as he tried to ride away, while Carey escaped to safety.

Outbreak of Rebellion at Kanpur

There were four Indian regiments in Kanpur: the 1st, 53rd and 56th Native Infantry, and the 2nd Bengal Cavalry. Although the sepoys in Kanpur had not rebelled, the European families began to drift into the entrenchment as the news of rebellion in the nearby areas reached them. The entrenchment was fortified, and the Indian sepoys were asked to collect their pay one by one, so as to avoid an armed mob.

The Indian soldiers considered the fortification, and the artillery guns being primed and aimed at them, as insulting as well as threatening. On the night of June 2, 1857, a British officer named Lieutenant Cox fired on his Indian guard while drunk. Cox missed his target, and was thrown into the jail for a night. The very next day, a hastily convened court acquitted him, which led to discontent among the Indian soldiers. There were also rumours that the Indian troops were to be summoned to a parade, where they were to be massacred. All these factors instigated them to rebel against the East India Company rule.

The rebellion began at 1:30 AM on June 5, 1857, with three pistol shots from the rebel soldiers of the 2nd Bengal Cavalry. Elderly Risaldar-Major Bhowani Singh, who refused to hand over the regimental colours and join the rebel sepoys, was killed. The 53rd and 56th Native Infantry, which were the most loyal units in the area, were awoken by the shootings. Some soldiers of the 56th panicked and started to run off into the city. The European artillery assumed that they were rebels too, and opened fire on them. The soldiers of the 53rd were also caught in the crossfire.

The 1st N.I. rebelled and left in early morning on June 6, 1857. On the same day, the 53d N.I. also went off, taking with them the regimental treasure and as much ammunition as they could carry. Around 150 sepoys remained loyal to General Wheeler.

After obtaining arms, ammunition and money, the rebel troops started marching towards Delhi to seek further orders from Bahadur Shah II, who had been proclaimed the *Padshah-e-Hind* ("Emperor of India"). The British officers were relieved that they would not face a long siege.

Nana Sahib's Involvement

Nana Sahib was the adopted heir to Baji Rao II, the ex-peshwa of the Maratha Confederacy. The East India Company decided that the pension and honours of the lineage would not be passed on to Nana Sahib, as he was not a natural born heir. Nana Sahib sent his envoy Dewan Azimullah Khan to London, to petition the Queen against the Company's decision, but failed to evoke any favourable response. Amid the chaos in Kanpur, Nana Sahib entered the British magazine with his contingent. The soldiers of the 53rd Native Infantry, which was guarding the magazine, were not fully aware of the situation in the rest of the city. They assumed that Nana Sahib had come to guard the magazine on behalf of the British, as he had earlier declared his loyalty to the British, and had even sent some volunteers to be at the disposal of General Wheeler. However, once Nana Sahib was inside the magazine, at the urging of the rebels, he announced that he was a participant in the rebellion against the British, and intended to be a vassal of Bahadur Shah II.

After taking possession of the Company treasury, Nana Sahib advanced up the Grand Trunk Road. His aim was to restore the Maratha confederacy under the Peshwa tradition, and he decided to capture Kanpur. On his way, Nana Sahib met with rebel soldiers at Kalyanpur. The soldiers were on their way to Delhi, to meet Bahadur Shah II. Nana Sahib wanted them to go back to Kanpur, and help him in defeating the British. The rebels were reluctant at first, but decided to join Nana Sahib, when he promised to double their pay and reward them with gold, if they were to destroy the British entrenchment.

Attack on Wheeler's Entrenchment

Photograph entitled, "The Hospital in General Wheeler's entrenchment, Kanpur." (1858) The hospital was the site of the first major loss of British lives in Kanpur (Kanpur).

On June 5, 1857, Nana Sahib sent a polite note to General Wheeler, informing him that he intended to attack the following morning, at 10 AM. On June 6, Nana Sahib's forces (including the rebel soldiers) attacked the British entrenchment at 10:30 AM. The British were not adequately prepared for the attack, but managed to defend themselves for a long time, as the attacking forces were reluctant to enter the entrenchment. Nana Sahib's forces had been led to falsely believe that the entrenchment had gunpowder-filled trenches that would explode if they got closer.

As the news of Nana Sahib's advances over the British garrison spread, several of the rebel sepoys joined him. By June 10, he was believed to be leading around twelve thousand to fifteen thousand

Indian soldiers. The British held out in their makeshift fort for three weeks with little water and food supplies. Many died as a result of sunstroke and lack of water. As the ground was too hard to dig graves, the British would pile the dead bodies of their killed outside the buildings, and drag and dump them inside a dried well during the night. The lack of sanitation facilities led to spread of diseases such as dysentery and cholera, further weakening the defenders. There was also a small outbreak of smallpox, although this was relatively confined.

During the first week of the siege, Nana Sahib's forces encircled the entrenchment, created loopholes and established firing positions from the surrounding buildings. British Army Captain John Moore of the 32nd Cornwall Light Infantry countered this, launching night-time sorties. Nana Sahib retreated his headquarter to Savada House (or Savada *Kothi*), which was situated about two miles away. In response to Moore's sorties, Nana Sahib decided to attempt a direct assault on the British entrenchment, but the rebel soldiers displayed a lack of enthusiasm.

On June 11, Nana Sahib's forces changed their tactics. They started concentrated firing on specific buildings, firing endless salvos of round shot into the entrenchment. They successfully damaged some of the smaller barrack buildings, and also tried to set fire to the buildings.

The first major assault from the Nana Sahib's side took place on the evening of June 12. However, the attacking soldiers were still convinced that the British had laid out gunpowder-filled trenches, and did not enter the area. On June 13, the British lost their hospital building to a fire, which destroyed most of their medical supplies and caused the deaths of a number of wounded and sick artillerymen who burned alive in the inferno. The loss of the hospital to fire on the 13 June was a major blow to the defenders. Nana Sahib's forces gathered for an attack, but were repulsed by the canister shots from artillery under the command of Lieutenant George Ashe. By June 21, the British had lost around a third of their numbers.

Wheeler's repeated messages to Henry Lawrence, the commanding officer in Lucknow, could not be answered as that garrison was itself under siege.

Assault on June 23

The sniper fire and the bombardment continued until June 23, 1857, the 100th anniversary of the Battle of Plassey. The Battle of Plassey, which took place on June 23, 1757, was one of the pivotal battles leading to the expansion of the British rule in India. One of the driving forces of the rebellion by sepoys, was a prophecy that predicted the downfall of East India Company rule in India exactly one hundred years after the Battle of Plassey. This prompted the rebel soldiers under Nana Sahib to launch a major attack on the British entrenchment on June 23, 1857.

The rebel soldiers of the 2nd Bengal Cavalry led the charge, but were repulsed with canister shot when they approached within 50 yards of the British entrenchment. After the cavalry assault, the soldiers of the 1st Native Infantry launched an attack on the British, advancing behind cotton bales and parapets. They lost their commanding officer, Radhay Singh, to the opening volley by the British.

They had hoped to get protection from cotton bales; however, the bales caught light from the canister fire, and became a hazard to them. On the other side of the entrenchment, some of the rebel soldiers engaged in a hand combat against 17 British men led by Lieutenant Mowbray Thomson. By the end of the day, the attackers were unable to gain an entry into the entrenchment. The attack left over 25 rebel soldiers dead, with very few casualties on the British side.

Surrender of the British Forces

The British garrison had taken heavy losses as a result of successive bombardments, sniper fire, and assaults. It was also suffering from disease and low supplies of food, water and medicine. General Wheeler's personal morale had been low, after his son Lieutenant Gordon Wheeler was decapitated by a roundshot. With approval of General Wheeler, a British civil servant called Jonah Shepherd slipped out of the entrenchment in disguise to ascertain the condition of Nana Sahib's forces. He was quickly imprisoned by the rebel soldiers.

At the same time, Nana Sahib's forces were wary of entering the entrenchment, as they believed that it had gunpowder-filled trenches. Nana Sahib and his advisers came up with a plan to end the deadlock. On June 24, they sent a female European prisoner, Mrs. Rose Greenway, to the entrenchment and conveyed their message. In return for a surrender, Nana Sahib had promised the safe passage of the British to the Satichaura Ghat, a dock on the Ganges from which they could depart for Allahabad. General Wheeler rejected the offer, because it had not been signed, and there was no guarantee that the offer was made by Nana Sahib himself.

Next day, on June 25, Nana Sahib sent a second note, signed by himself, through another elderly female prisoner, Mrs. Jacobi. The British camp divided into two groups with different opinions-one group was in favour of continuing the defence, while the second group was willing to trust Nana Sahib. During the next 24 hours, there was no bombardment from Nana Sahib's forces. Finally, General Wheeler decided to surrender, in return for a safe passage to Allahabad. After a day of preparation, and burying their dead, the British decided to leave for Allahabad on the morning of June 27, 1857.

Satichaura Ghat Massacre

1858 picture of Sati Chaura Ghat on the banks of the Ganges River, where on 27 June 1857 many British men lost their lives and the surviving women and children were taken prisoner by the rebels.

On the morning of the June 27, a large British column led by General Wheeler emerged out of the entrenchment. Nana Sahib sent a number of carts, dolis and elephants to enable the women, the children and the sick to proceed to the river banks. The British officers and military men were allowed to take their arms and ammunition with them, and were escorted by nearly the whole of the rebel army. The British reached the Satichaura (or Sati Chowra) Ghat by 8 AM. Nana Sahib had arranged around 40 boats, belonging to a boatman called Hardev Mallah, for their departure to Allahabad.

The Ganges river was unusually dry at the Satichaura Ghat, and the British found it difficult to drift the boats away. General Wheeler and his party were the first aboard and the first to manage to set their boat adrift. There was some confusion, as the Indian boatmen jumped overboard after hearing bugles from the banks, and started swimming toward the banks. As they jumped, some fires on the boats were knocked off, setting a few of the boats ablaze.

Though controversy surrounds what exactly happened next at the Satichaura Ghat, and who fired the first shot, it is known that soon afterwards, the departing British were attacked by the rebel sepoys, and were either killed or captured.

Some of the British officers later claimed that the rebels had placed the boats as high in the mud as possible, on purpose to cause delay. They also claimed that Nana Sahib's camp had previously arranged for the rebels to fire upon and kill all the English. Although the East India Company later accused Nana Sahib of betrayal and murder of innocent people, no evidence has ever been found to prove that Nana Sahib had pre-planned or ordered the massacre. Some historians believe that the Satichaura Ghat massacre was the result of confusion, and not of any plan implemented by Nana Sahib and his associates. Lieutenant Mowbray Thomson, one of the four male survivors of the massacre, believed that the rank-and-file sepoys who spoke to him did not know of the killing to come.

After the conflict began, Nana Sahib's general Tatya Tope allegedly ordered the 2nd Bengal Cavalry unit and some artillery units to open fire on the British. The rebel cavalry sowars moved into the water, to kill the remaining British soldiers with swords and pistols. The surviving men were killed, while women and children were taken into captivity, as Nana Sahib did not approve of their killing. Around 120 women and children were taken prisoner and escorted to Savada House, Nana Sahib's headquarters during the siege.

By this time, two of the boats had been able to drift away: General Wheeler's boat, and a second boat which was holed beneath the waterline with a round shot fired from the bank. The British people in the second boat panicked and attempted to make it to General Wheeler's boat, which was slowly drifting to safer waters.

General Wheeler's boat had around 60 people aboard, and was being pursued down the riverbanks by the rebel soldiers. The boat frequently grounded on the sandbanks. On one such sandbank, Lieutenant Thomson led a charge against the rebel soldiers, and was able to capture some ammunition. Next morning, the boat again stuck at a sandbank, resulting in another charge by Thomson and 11 British soldiers. After a fierce fighting on the ground, Thomson and his men decided to return to the boat, but didn't find the boat where they expected to find it.

Meanwhile, the rebels had launched an attack on the boat from the opposite bank. After some firing, the British men on the boat decided to fly the white flag. They were escorted off the boat and taken back to Savada house. The surviving British men were seated on the ground, as Nana Sahib's soldiers got ready to fire on them. The women insisted that they would die with their husbands, but were pulled away. Nana Sahib granted the British chaplain Moncrieff's request to read prayers before they died. The British were initially wounded with the guns, and then killed with the swords. The women and children were confined to Savada House, to be reunited later with their remaining colleagues, who had been captured earlier, at Bibighar.

After being unable to find the boat, Thomson's party decided to run barefoot to evade the rebel soldiers. The party took refuge in a small shrine, where Thomson led a last charge. At the end, six of the British soldiers were killed, while the rest managed to escape to the riverbank. They tried to escape by jumping into the river and swimming to safety. However, a group of rebels from the village started clubbing them as they reached the bank. One of the soldiers was killed, while the other four, including Thomson, swam back to the centre of the river. After swimming downstream for a few hours, they reached ashore, where they were discovered by some Rajput matchlockmen, who worked for Raja Dirigibijah Singh, a British loyalist.

They carried the British soldiers to Raja's palace. These four British soldiers were the only male survivors from the British side, apart from Jonah Shepherd (who had been captured by Nana Sahib before the surrender). The four men included two privates named Murphey and Sullivan, Lieutenant Delafosse, and Lieutenant (later Captain) Mowbray Thomson. The men spent several weeks recuperating, eventually making their way back to

Kanpur which was, by that time, back under British control. Murphey and Sullivan both died shortly after from cholera, Delafosse ironically went on to join the defending garrison during the Siege of Lucknow, and Thomson took part in rebuilding and defending the entrenchment a second time under General Windham, eventually writing a firsthand account of his experiences entitled *The Story of Kanpur* (London, 1859).

Another survivor of the Satichaura Ghat massacre was Amy Horne, a 17-year-old Eurasian girl. She had fallen from her boat and had been swept downstream during the riverside massacre. Soon after scrambling ashore she met up with Wheeler's youngest daughter, Margaret. The two girls hid in the undergrowth for a number of hours until they were discovered by a group of rebels. Margaret was taken away on horseback, never to be seen again, and Amy was led to a nearby village where she was taken under the protection of a Muslim rebel leader in exchange for converting to Islam. Just over six months later, she was rescued by Highlanders from Sir Colin Campbell's column on their way to relieve Lucknow. It is rumoured that the youngest daughter of General Wheeler survived the massacre and married a Muslim soldier. On her deathbed, she confided to a Christian priest that she was the daughter of General Wheeler.

Bibighar Massacre

The surviving British women and children were moved from the Savada House to Bibighar ("the House of the Ladies"), a villa-type house in Kanpur. Initially, around 120 women and children were confined to Bibighar. They were later joined by some other women and children, the survivors from General Wheeler's boat. Another group of British women and children from Fatehgarh, and some other captive European women were also confined to Bibighar. In total, there were around 200 women and children in Bibighar. Nana Sahib placed the care of these survivors under a prostitute called Hussaini Khanum (also known as Hussaini Begum). She put the captives to grinding corn for *chapatis*. Poor sanitary conditions at Bibighar led to deaths from cholera and dysentery.

Nana Sahib decided to use these prisoners for bargaining with the East India Company. The Company forces, consisting of around

1000 British, 150 Sikh soldiers and 30 irregular cavalry, had set out from Allahabad, under the command of General Henry Havelock, to retake Kanpur and Lucknow.

The first relief force assembled under Havelock included 64th Regiment of Foot and 78th Highlanders (brought back from the Anglo-Persian War), the first arrivals of the diverted China expedition, 5th Fusiliers, part of the 90th Light Infantry (seven companies), 84th from Burma, and EIC Madras European Fusiliers, brought up to Calcutta from Madras. Havelock's initial forces were later joined by the forces under the command of Major Renaud and Colonel James Neill, which had arrived from Calcutta to Allahabad on June 11. Nana Sahib demanded that the East India Company forces under General Havelock and Colonel Neill retreat to Allahabad. However, the Company forces advanced relentlessly towards Kanpur. Nana Sahib sent an army to check their advance. The two armies met at Fatehpur on July 12, where General Havelock's forces emerged victorious and captured the town.

Nana Sahib then sent another force under the command of his brother, Bala Rao. On July 15, the British forces under General Havelock defeated Bala Rao's army in the Battle of Aong, just outside the Aong village. On July 16, Havelock's forces started advancing to Kanpur. During the Battle of Aong, Havelock was able to capture some of the rebel soldiers, who informed him that there was an army of 5,000 rebel soldiers with 8 artillery pieces further up the road. Havelock decided to launch a flank attack on this army, but the rebel soldiers spotted the flanking manoeuvre and opened fire. The battle resulted in heavy casualties on both sides, but cleared the road to Kanpur for the British.

By this time, it became clear that the Company forces were approaching Kanpur, and Nana Sahib's barganing attempts had failed. Nana Sahib was informed that the British troops led by Havelock and Neill were indulging in violence against the Indian villagers. Some historians, such as Pramod Nayar, believe that the forthcoming Bibighar massacre was a reaction to the news of violence being perpetrated by the advancing British troops.

Nana Sahib, and his associates, including Tatya Tope and Azimullah Khan, debated about what to do with the captives at Bibighar. Some of Nana Sahib's advisors had already decided to kill the captives at Bibighar, as revenge for the murders of Indians by the advancing British forces. The women of Nana Sahib's household opposed the decision and went on a hunger strike, but their efforts went in vain.

Finally, on July 15, an order was given to kill the women and children imprisoned at Bibighar, despite strong objection from Nana Sahib. The details of the incident, such as who ordered the massacre, are not clear. According to some sources, Azimullah Khan ordered the killings of women and children at Bibighar.

The rebel sepoys executed the four surviving male hostages from Fatehghar, one of them a 14 year old boy. But they simply refused to obey the order to kill women and the other children. Some of the sepoys agreed to remove the women and children from the courtyard, when Tatya Tope threatened to execute them for dereliction of duty. Nana Sahib left the building because he didn't want to be a witness to the unfolding massacre.

The British women and children were ordered to come out of the assembly rooms, but they refused to do so and clung to each other. They barricaded themselves, tying the door handles with clothing. At first, around twenty rebel soldiers opened fire on the outside of the Bibi-Ghar, firing through holes in the boarded windows. The soldiers of the squad that was supposed to fire the next round were disturbed by the scene, and discharged their shots into the air. Soon after, upon hearing the screams and groans inside, the rebel soldiers declared that they were not going to kill any women and children.

An angry Begum Hussaini Khanum termed the sepoys' act as cowardice, and asked her lover Sarvur Khan to finish the job of killing the captives. Sarvur Khan hired some butchers, who murdered the surviving women and children with cleavers. The butchers left, when it seemed that all the captives had been killed. However, a few women and children had managed to survive by hiding under the other dead bodies. It was agreed that the bodies of the victims would be thrown down a dry well by some sweepers.

The next morning, when the rebels arrived to dispose off the bodies, they found that three women and three children aged between four and seven years old were still alive. The surviving women were cast into the well by the sweepers who had also been told to strip the bodies of the murder victims. The sweepers then threw the three little boys into the well one at a time, the youngest first. Some victims, among them small children, were therefore buried alive in a heap of dead corpses.

Recapture and Violence by the British Soldiers

The Company forces reached Kanpur on July 16, and captured the city. A group of British officers and soldiers set out to the Bibighar, to rescue the captives, assuming that they were still alive. However, when they reached the site, they found only dead bodies of the British women and children.

Brigadier General Neill, who took the command at Kanpur, decided to sentence the arrested rebels immediately, unless they could prove a defence. They were forced to clean the blood from the floor of the Bibighar compound. Then, they were forced to eat beef (if Hindu) or pork (if Muslim) — something they considered unholy. Some of the Muslim sepoys were sown into pig skins before being hung, and sweepers were employed to execute the high-caste Brahmin rebels. The idea was to humiliate the religious victims and prevent any reward they might have expected in the afterlife. After that, the rebels would be hanged and then buried in a ditch at the roadside. A set of nooses was set up next to the well at the Bibighar, so that they could die within sight of the massacre. Some rebels were tied across the mouths of cannon that were then fired; an execution method initially used by the rebels, and the earlier Indian powers, such as the Marathas and the Mughals.

The British soldiers, angry after learning of the massacre, indulged in indiscriminate violence, including looting and burning of houses. They were angry even at the neutral locals for not doing anything to stop the Bibighar massacre. *Remember Kanpur!* became a war cry for the British soldiers for the rest of the conflict. In one of the villages, the Highlanders caught around 140 men, women and children. Ten men were hanged without any evidence or trial. Another sixty men were forced to build the gallows of wooden logs, while others were flogged and beaten. In another village, when around 2,000 villagers came out in protest with lathis, the British troops surrounded them and set the village on fire. The villagers trying to escape were shot to death.

Aftermath

On July 19, General Havelock resumed operations at Bithoor. Nana Sahib's palace at Bithur was occupied without resistance. The British troops seized guns, elephants and camels, and set Nana Sahib's palace to fire.

In November 1857, Tantia Topi gathered a large army, mainly consisting of the rebel soldiers from the Gwalior contingent, to recapture Kanpur. By November 19, Tantia Topi's advance guard of 6,000 dominated all the routes west and northwest of Kanpur. However, Tantia Topi's forces were defeated by the Company forces under Colin Campbell in the Second Battle of Kanpur, marking the end of the rebellion in the Kanpur area. Tantia Topi then joined Rani Lakshmibai.

Nana Sahib disappeared and by 1859, he had fled to Nepal. His ultimate fate was never determined. Up until 1888, there were rumours and reports that he had been captured and a number of individuals turned themselves in to the British claiming to be the aged Nana. As the majority of these reports turned out to be untrue further attempts at apprehending him were abandoned.

British civil servant Jonah Shepherd, who had been rescued by Havelock's army, spent the next few years after the rebellion attempting to put together a list of those killed in the entrenchment. He had lost his entire family during the siege. He eventually retired to a small estate north of Kanpur in the late 1860s.

Memorials

A memorial erected (circa 1860) by the British after the Mutiny was crushed at the Bibi Ghar Well. After India's independence the statue was moved to the Memorial Church, Kanpur. Albumen silver print by Samuel Bourne, 1860.

After the revolt was suppressed, the British dismantled Bibighar. They raised a memorial railing and a cross at the site of the well in which the bodies of the British women and children had been dumped. The inhabitants of Kanpur were forced to pay £30,000 for the creation of the memorial; this was partially their punishment for not coming to the aid of the women and children in Bibighar.

The remains of a circular ridge of the well can still be seen at the Nana Rao Park, which was built after India achieved independence. The British also erected the All Souls Memorial Church, in the memory of their deceased. An enclosed pavement outside the church marks the graves of over 70 British men captured and executed on July 1 1857, four days after the Satichaura ghat massacre. The marble gothic screen with "mournful seraph" was transferred to the churchyard of the All Souls Church after the Indian independence in 1947, and a bust of Tantia Topi was installed in its place.

In Popular Culture

- Julian Rathbone describes the brutality of both British and Indian forces during the siege of Kanpur in his novel *The Mutiny*. In the novel, the Indian nurse Lavanya rescues an English child, Stephen, during the Satichaura Ghat massacre.
- In *Massacre at Kanpur*, V. A. Stuart describes the siege and the British defence through the eyes of the characters Sheridan, and his wife Emmy.
- George MacDonald Fraser's *Flashman in the Great Game* also contains lengthy scenes set in the entrenchment during the siege.

The Battle of Kanpur-December 1857

Tantia Topi's attack on Kanpur in December 1857 was the only worthwhile sepoy countermove against the British at the strategic level. Unlike the Delhi sepoys, the fact that Tantia's force reached the British line of communication and seriously threatened it proves Tantia's ability as a first rate strategist and tactician.

We have seen that Tantia left Gwalior on 15 October 1857. They marched via Jalaun to Kalpi and crossed the Jumna River opposite Kalpi on 15 November 1857. Many of the sepoy Regiments at Banda joined him. Here it is important to note that bulk of Tantia's troops belonged to the Gwalior contingent which was not as well trained as Regular Bengal Army Infantry Regiments.

The Gwalior contingent comprised seven infantry and two cavalry regiments and its total strength before the rebellion was

8,318 men. All British writings repeatedly refer to Tantia Topi leading the Gwalior contingent to Kanpur, but we must remember that the term "Gwalior Contingent" is misleading, keeping in view the fact that in December 1857 this contingent was not the same as a military entity what it was in May 1857. Following factors greatly reduced its strength:-

1. The 7th Infantry Regiment of the Gwalior Contingent marched to Delhi with the 72 NI and Ist LC after having rebelled at Nimach on 3 June 1857.
2. Major part of 6th Infantry Regiment of the Gwalior Contingent rebelled in May 1857 and marched to Kanpur. Later on parts of this regiment retreated to Gwalior after having been defeated by Havelock in July 1857.
3. Part of the Ist Infantry Regiment of the contingent at Etawah rebelled in May 1857. Parts of it marched to Kanpur and to Delhi. However a large part of this regiment never rebelled and survived the rebellion being renumbered as 41 Bengal Native Infantry.

Roughly by December 1857 the Gwalior Contingent which may have accompanied Tantia to Kalpi and Gwalior could not have exceeded 3,000 infantry and 300 cavalry. The sepoys who may have joined him at Kalpi similarly could not have been more than 2,000. Delhi the focal point of rebel expectations by this time had fallen and the major part of the sepoy strength was committed at Lucknow. Tantia's move against Kanpur at a time when the initiative had firmly been regained by the British was a titanic effort in terms of morale since the sepoy cause in Decmber 1857 was almost hopeless. All territory south of Ganges and north of Jumna had been recaptured by the British and their final victory was now just a matter of few months. Strategically the Grand Trunk Road was firmly in British control and steady reinforcements were arriving from Britain and China via the port of Calcutta. Viewed in face of these odds when the so-called martial races of India were swelling the ranks of the irregular regiments of the newly raised British Regiments and the fiery Afghans had been cooled down with a cool retainer of 12 lakh per annum; we can only salute this indomitable Mahratta who was still thinking like the ultimate Greek Hero!

Meanwhile, the following had been the situation at Kanpur during November-December 1857:

1. Sir Colin Campbell had proceeded with the major part of his force to Lucknow for the final relief of Lucknow in November 1857. He had left General Windham at Kanpur with a small force of 500 Europeans and some Sikh troops. Fitzgerald Lee and Radcliffe specified that there were 500 Europeans and 500 Madras infantry and nine guns. Fortescue another very conservative man admits that 350 men of 2nd Royal Battalion reinforced Windham on 25 November. Windham's assigned task was to defend the Bridge over the Ganges by deploying his force behind an entrenchment just next to the bridge.
2. By 19 November according to Michael Edwardes Tantia had severed Kanpur's communication with the area west of Kanpur. It may be noted that Windham had requested Campbell permission to retain reinforcements passing through Kanpur. Campbell had authorised Windham to retain these reinforcements on 14 November.
3. On 24 November 1857 Windham decided to move south and stall Tantia Topi before he could enter Kanpur. He therefore, moved south on the Kalpi road with 1,200 men and 12 guns if we can believe the contemporary British accounts. On the 26th a small battle book place few miles south of Kanpur. Windham was forced to retreat and the British historians were forced to inflate Tantia's strength to 25,000 men! (This exceeds the total number of sepoy regiments and Gwalior contingent troops present in Central India before the rebellion started!). We must not forget that there were about nine sepoy regiments in Central India and seven Gwalior contingent infantry Regiments. This makes 16 regiments of infantry. Out of these five regiments of sepoys (12 NI, 15 NI, 30 NI, 23 NI and 72 NI) went to Delhi. One Regiment of Gwalior contingent went to Delhi and one to Kanpur. One regiment of sepoys *i.e.* the 31 NI never rebelled. This leaves about three sepoy regiments *i.e.* 42 NI 50 NI and 52 NI. These went to Banda. Four regiments arrived from Dinapur and Orissa. There could not have exceeded 2,000 men after a long march and

considerable fighting in Dinapur (and these went to Lucknow in November 1857 and were never at Kanpur). The British ego, however, scoffs at odds lower than ten to twenty times when Indians are concerned!

4. Our hero Windham defeated those 25,000 sepoys he encountered on 26 November but was forced to retreat due to shortage of Cavalry! This Honourable Fortescue wants us to believe us as we read page 329 of his book. We believe him because the British very cleverly hanged Tantia at Sipri!
5. Windham retreats and Tantia with his 25,000 lazy sepoys follows hi! Tantia enters Kanpur and advances towards the entrenchment on a five mile wide front because Fortescue has to do something with 25,000 men! This happens on 28 November when Windham is finally forced to retreat behind his entrenchment! Providence sends four companies of the third battalion of the Rifle Brigade. By 29 November Tantia's artillery was fully operational and had opened fire on Windham's entrenchment!
6. Meanwhile Sir Colin Campbell with part of his force from Lucknow arrived at Kanpur on 28 November and by 29 November Campbell had started engaging Tantia's obsolete 9 and 12 pounders with the vastly superior and sophisticated Heavy Naval guns of Peel's heavy brigade from across the Ganges. Thus by midday 29 November 1857 Tantia's artillery was completely silenced. The British authorities especially Fortescue underplayed the havoc created by Peel's eight heavy guns and two rocket launchers.

The situation by 30 November was steadily favouring the British. The 24 pounder heavy guns of Peel had silenced and effectively neutralised Tantia's artillery. Some 3,000 soldiers had reinforced Windham bringing British strength over 5,000 troops.

Tantia's position had some serious drawbacks. He was occupying built up area along the west bank of the Ganges canal. His numerical superiority if he ever had any keeping in view the dubious British claims was turned into inferiority because of the fact that Tantia could not reinforce his vulnerable right flank by shifting troops from his centre or left. This fact has been somehow admitted by the British authors ! We are very grateful to them for having been a little intellectually honest for a change in this case. In this Campbell left no choice to subsequent British historians by admitting this fact in despatch written about the battle of Kanpur.

Campbell's plan of battle was as following:

- Adrian Hope's brigade to cross the Ganges bridge and take position to the south east of Kanpur so that communication with Calcutta could be reopened. Deploy facing the west and ensure safe passage of British non-combatants of Lucknow Residency which were being evacuated to Calcutta after the withdrawal of Lucknow Residency garrison.
- Six companies of 34th Foot to escort convoy of non-combatants to Allahabad.
- Main attack on 06 December 1857 after the non-combatants were safely away from Kanpur organised as following:
    1. Feint from entrenchment and artillery fire in order to convince the rebels into believing that the main British attack would come from the north or the British Right.
    2. Brigadier Greathed to attack the rebel Centre based in General Ganj area
    3. Main attack on the sepoy right by Brigadier Inglis's and Brigadier Adrian Hope's Brigades.
    4. Cavalry Brigade to threaten the rebel communication with Kalpi.
        - Order of Battle:-

1. Cavalry Brigade (600 Sabres)
    - HM 9th Lancers
    - Ist Punjab Cavalry (Parts) (Authors unit)
    - 2nd " " "
    - 5th " " "
    - Hodson's Horse
2. Greathed's Brigade
    - HM 8 Foot

- HM 64 Foot
- 2nd Punjab Infantry

3. 4th Infantry Brigade
   - HM 42 Foot
   - HM 53 Foot
   - HM 93 Highlanders
   - 4th Punjab Rifles
4. 5th Infantry Brigade
   - HM 23 Foot
   - HM 32 Foot
   - HM 82 Foot
5. 6th Infantry Brigade

- Parts of Rifle Brigade
- Detachment of HM 38 Foot
- In all the British had about 5,000 infantry, six hundred cavalry and thirty five guns, if we are to believe Fortescue. But nowhere does Fortescue mention superiority in terms of being armed with the Enfield Rifles which automatically reduced the rebel potential to one fourth and multiplied the British hitting power by four times. It may be noted that the main British attack was going south of the built up area where the advantage of close quarter battle and thereby reduced engagement ranges which benefited the sepoy was nullified. In addition the tremendous British artillery superiority must not be under estimated.

The rebel left rested on the Ganges and their centre was based on the built up area of Kanpur which was located on both east and west bank of the Ganges canal. The Sepoy right extended for about one and half to two miles south of the Kanpur city on the west bank of the Ganges canal.

The British attack commenced after a heavy artillery preparation at nine O'clock on the morning of 06 December 1857. All praise to Tantia Topi who with all the tremendous odds against him managed to march all the way from Gwalior to Kanpur with a obsolete pre-1815 Brown Bess whereas we so miserably failed to advance more than ten miles despite having the most sophisticated tank of 1960s. Those who have any doubt must visit a village called "Patton Nagar" near Valtoha in Indian Punjab! The British victory was a foregone conclusion and Tantia's defeat as inevitable as that of Russians in the Crimean War or the Afghans in the First Afghan War!

Despite all this superiority Brigadier Mansfield who had been specifically ordered by Campbell with blocking the retreat of Tantia's centre miserably failed in his assigned task! Thus the rebel centre was able to execute an organised withdrawal along the Bithur road. Fortescue compares this inexcusable blunder with John Stuart's at Wellington's passage of the Douro River during the Peninsular war.

The British casualties were nominal, *i.e.* just 98 killed or wounded. Pursuit continued till 08 December 1857. Tantia escaped towards Kalpi while his centre and left escaped towards Bithur. From here some of them withdrew towards Farrukhabad whereas some crossed the Ganges and withdrew into Oudh.

The Rohailkhand Campaign

Rohailkhand was the last major sepoy stronghold after capture of Lucknow in March 1858. Sir Colin Campbell made the following plan to recapture Rohailkhund:

a. The attacking force was divided into four columns which were to advance from the west the south west the south and the south west and to ensure that the sepoys were pushed towards the Himalayan rain forest of Terai.

b. The south eastern force consisted of General Walpoles column originating from Lucknow consisting of:-

    1. HM 9th Lancers
    2. 2nd Punjab Cavalry
    3. 42 Highlanders
    4. 79 Highlanders
    5. 93 Highlanders
    6. 4th Punjab Infantry
    7. Two Troops Horse Artillery

8. Two 18 Pounders
9. Two 8 Inch Howitzers
10. Some Mortars

c. Walpole was to march from Lucknow towards west and clear the northern bank of Ganges River and the districts bordering the western bank of Ganges River. Subsequently he was to join forces with the force commanded by Seaton attacking from Fatehgarh and little south of Shah Jahanpur. Walpole's force was about 6,000 men of all arms.

d. Seaton Commanding a column consisting of 82 Foot, a Sikh Battalion and some irregular troops was to march north from Fatehgarh and effect a junction with Walpole short of Shahjahanpur.

e. The Third Column commanded by General Penny was to advance from Meerut and advance Eastwards joining the two other columns east of Bareilly.

f. The fourth column commended by General Coke was to cross the Ganges from Rurki side and was to ensure that no sepoys escaped west of Bareilly.

Theoretically in April 1858 the British situation was excellent and all should have proceeded like clock work. But the British had one very gifted general by the name of Walpole. He left Lucknow with his column on 7th April 1858. All proceeded well till this outstanding general arrived at a small fort Ruiya about 51 miles south west of Lucknow on 15 April 1858. Walpole was told by his spies that the Talukdar Nirpat Singh occupying the fort had no intention of opposing the British but only wanted by putting up a token resistance order to preserve appearances and to save his honour.

Walpole refused to believe this and decided to assault the fort without bothering to carry out any type of reconnaissance of the fort. Subsequently it was discovered that the rear wall of the fort in contrast with the front wall was so low that even a child could climb it ! Walpole's frontal assault on the front failed with a casualty figure of over 100 killed and wounded including a very promising officer by the name of Brigadier Adrian Hope. While Walpole was planning a future assault Nirpat Singh abandoned the fort during the night with his entire force ! Meanwhile Brigadier Coke crossed the Ganges a little west of Hardwar and moving south east twice defeated the sepoys halfway between Ganges and Bareilly on 17 and 21 April and finally arrived on 26 April about five miles west of Muradabad. At Moradabad Coke carried out a house to house search to find prince Feroze Shah but Feroze Shah had already escaped towards Shahjahanpur.

Meanwhile, Brigadier Penny was killed in a night ambush short of Badaun and was succeeded by Brigadier Jones. On 27 April Campbell effected a junction with Walpoles column while marching north. On 30 April they entered Shahjahanpur and left a garrison of 500 men under Colonel Hale. They joined Penny's column at Miranpur Kattra on 3rd May 1858 and marched towards Bareilly.

Cokes Column defeated a sepoy force at Nagina on 21 April 1858 and reached Mirganj on 5 May about 14 miles west of Bareilly.

Campbell had now about 8,000 men from the following units:-

a. 64 Foot

b. 78 Foot

c. 42 Highlanders

d. 79 Highlanders

e. 93 Highlanders

f. 4 Punjab Rifles

g. 2nd Punjab Infantry

h. 22nd Punjab Infantry

i. Baluch Battalion

Khan Bahadur Khan contested Campbells force about two miles south of Bareilly but was defeated on 05 May 1858. He withdrew towards Pilibhit near the Terai.

Meanwhile, the Maulvi of Faizabad *i.e.* Maulvi Ahmadullah had attacked Hale with 500 men and had forced Hale to fortify himself in jail. This situation continued till Shahjahanpur was relieved by Brig. Jones on 11 May 1858. The Maulvi was soon joined by Firoz Shah and Hazrat Mahal and the battle continued till 15 May 1858 once after being reinforced again Jones was finally able to recapture Shahjahanpur. Thus ended the last major resistance in Northern India.

Battle of Badli-ki-Serai

The Battle of Badli-ki-Serai was fought early in the Indian rebellion of 1857, or *First War of Indian Independence* as it has since been termed in Indian histories of the events. A British and Gurkha force defeated a force of sepoys who had rebelled against the British East India Company. The British victory allowed them to besiege and ultimately capture Delhi.

Outbreak of the Rebellion

Tension between the East India Company and the sepoys of its Bengal Army had been growing for several years, and increased rapidly during 1857. The rebellion finally broke out when the Company attempted to introduce a new Enfield rifle. The cartridges for this were believed by the sepoys to be greased with beef and pork fat. A Hindu soldier who bit the cartridge open to load the rifle would lose caste, and a Moslem soldier would be defiled. The sepoys believed that the Company was attempting to force them to become Christians.

The revolt occurred on May 10 at Meerut, 60 miles northwest of Delhi. After killing many of their British officers and some civilians, three regiments of Bengal infantry and cavalry marched to Delhi. When they arrived on May 11, they called on the three Bengal infantry regiments there to join them, and for the Mughal King, Bahadur Shah II to lead them. By the end of the day, Delhi was in rebel hands, and news of the rebellion was spreading rapidly over northern India.

British Moves

Most of the units of the British Army in India, and the "European" units of the Bengal Army, were in the "hill stations" in the foothills of the Himalayas. At Simla, the Commander in Chief, General Anson, began collecting a force to recapture Delhi. Although aged, Anson nevertheless acted swiftly, but was handicapped by lack of transport and supplies. He succeeded in collecting a force at Ambala on May 17, and they began advancing to Karnal, where most of the British civilians who had escaped from Delhi were taking shelter. On the way, his men indiscriminately hanged or blew from the guns, many suspected rebels or sympathisers.

Another small British force was advancing from Meerut to meet Anson. It was commanded by Major General W. Hewitt, whose health had been broken by his age and many years' service in India. He eventually had to hand over command to Brigadier Archdale Wilson.

On May 30, some Indian forces from Delhi attacked Wilson's force at the River Hindon. Wilson's infantry, the 60th Rifles, made good use of their Enfield rifles to drive the Indians from the field and capture five light guns. The rebels tried another attack the next day and were again driven back, though they lost no more of their artillery.

The Battle

General Anson had died of cholera at Karnal on May 27. He was succeeded by Major General Sir Henry Barnard, who had recently fought in the Crimean War. Barnard's force advanced to join with Wilson's at Alipur (NW Delhi) on June 1. The combined force advanced along the Grand Trunk road towards Delhi.

The rebel sepoy regiments had dug in at Badli-ki-Serai to oppose their advance. Their strength was estimated in some works as 30,000, but was put closer to 4,000 by historian A.H. Amin. It is of course possible that the sepoy regiments were accompanied onto the battlefield by irregular contingents from Delhi, and scavengers and sight-seers, making effective numbers difficult to estimate.

The rebels' right flank, with most of their artillery, occupied a serai (a walled enclosure) and a village, also surrounded by a wall. Their left flank consisted of a "sandbagged" battery. Both flanks were supposedly protected also by areas of marshy ground. On the left however, there was a gap of a mile between the end of the swamp and the Western Jumna canal, which was not defended. The right flank was similarly vulnerable.

When the British advanced against this position early on June 8, they suffered heavy casualties from the rebel artillery, which was heavier than most of the British guns and very well-handled.

Barnard sent his cavalry under Colonel James Hope Grant to outflank the rebel left and a brigade of infantry under Colonel Graves (temporarily replacing Brigadier Jones, who was ill) around the rebel right. As these forces began to threaten the enemy flanks and rear, Barnard ordered his other brigade under Colonel Showers (which included a Gurkha regiment) to charge and capture the enemy artillery with the bayonet. There was severe fighting for the village and serai, but the rebels fled to avoid being surrounded, abandoning thirteen guns.

The sepoys retreated to Delhi in disorder, and some of the citizens thought that the British would follow close on their heels and capture the city before resistance could be organised. The British were too exhausted by the heat and their exertions, and contented themselves with occupying Delhi Ridge north of the city. This led to a costly siege lasting three and a half months, but the city was eventually stormed and the rebels were defeated.

Results

The battle had exposed the rebel weaknesses. The most damaging was their lack of competent leaders. Bahadur Shah had nominated his son Mirza Mughal as commander in chief of his army, but the sepoys treated him and the King disrespectfully.

Mirza Mughal was preoccupied with the administration of Delhi, and showed himself to be most unwilling to lead a force to attack Meerut or confront Barnard. He had not been present at the battle, and later issued a rather fatuous statement that *"...as a castle in the game of chess, he was firmly seated beyond all fear of check being given."*

The sepoys' officers had attained rank by seniority only, and none of them proved to be gifted generals, as opposed to platoon commanders. At Badli-ki-Serai, they deployed no forces to protect against outflanking moves, and left themselves no reserves. The sepoys refused to use the Enfield rifle (for which they lacked ammunition in any case), and were forced to use the Brown Bess, which was much less accurate than the Enfield rifle. (Some of the British units at Badli-ki-Serai also had the Brown Bess, but the weapon's short range and inaccuracy hampered the defenders more than the attackers.)

Delhi

The British were slow to strike back at first but eventually two columns left Meerut and Simla. They proceeded slowly towards Delhi and fought, killed, and hanged numerous Indians along the way. At the same time, the British moved regiments from the Crimean War, and diverted European regiments headed for China to India. After a march lasting two months, the British fought the main army of the rebels near Delhi in Badl-ke-Serai and drove them back to Delhi. The British established a base on the Delhi ridge to the north of the city and the siege began. The siege of Delhi lasted roughly from the 1st of July to the 31st of August. However the encirclement was hardly complete—the rebels could easily receive resources and reinforcements. Later the British were joined by the Punjab Movable Column of Sikh soldiers and elements of the Gurkha Brigade.

Eagerly-awaited heavy siege guns did not guarantee an easy victory against the numerical superiority of the sepoy. Eventually the British broke through the Kashmere gate and began a week of street fighting. When the British reached the Red Fort, Bahadur Shah had already fled to Humayun's tomb. The British had retaken the city.

The British proceeded to loot and pillage the city. A large number of the citizens were slaughtered in retaliation for the Europeans killed by rebel Indians. Artillery was set up in the main mosque in the city and the neighbourhoods within the range of artillery were bombarded. These included the homes of the Muslim nobility from all over India, and contained innumerable cultural, artistic, literary and monetary riches. An example would be the loss of most of the works of Mirza Asadullah Khan Ghalib, thought of as the greatest south Asian poet of that era.

The British soon arrested Bahadur Shah, and the next day British officer William Hodson shot his sons Mirza Mughal, Mirza Khizr Sultan, and Mirza Abu Bakr under his own authority. Their heads were presented to their father the next day.

Kanpur

In June, sepoys under General Wheeler in Kanpur, (known as Kanpur by the British) rebelled — apparently with tacit approval of the Nana Sahib — and besieged the European entrenchment. The British lasted three weeks of the Siege of Kanpur with little water, suffering constant casualties. On the 25th of June the Nana Sahib requested surrender and Wheeler had little choice but to accept. The Nana Sahib promised them safe passage to a secure location but when the British boarded riverboats, their pilots fled, setting fire to the boats, and the rebellious sepoys opened fire on the British, soldiers and civilians. One boat with 4 men escaped.

The surviving women and children were led to Bibi-Ghar (the House of the Ladies) in Kanpur. On the 15th of July, worried by the approach of the British forces and believing that they would not advance if there were no hostages to save, the Nana Sahib ordered their murders. Three men entered it and killed everyone with knives and hatchets and hacked them to pieces. Their bodies were thrown down a well.

The butchering of the women and children proved to be a mistake. The British public was aghast and the pro-Indian proponents lost all their support. Kanpur became a war cry for the British soldiers for the rest of the conflict. The Nana Sahib disappeared and was probably killed trying to escape India.

When the British retook Kanpur later, the soldiers took their sepoy prisoners to the Bibi-Ghar and forced them to lick the bloodstains from the walls and floor. Then they hanged all of the sepoy prisoners.

Lucknow

Rebellion erupted in the state of Awadh (also known as Oudh, in modern-day Uttar Pradesh) very soon after the events in Meerut. The British commander of Lucknow, Henry Lawrence, had enough time to fortify his position inside the Residency compound. British forces numbered some 1700 men, including loyal sepoys. The rebels initial assaults were unsuccessful, and so they began a barrage of artillery and musket fire into the compound. Lawrence was one of the first casualties. The rebels tried to breach the walls with explosives and bypass them via underground tunnels that led to underground close combat. After 90 days of siege, numbers of British were reduced to 300 loyal sepoys, 350 British soldiers and 550 non-combatants. This action quickly became known as the

Siege of Lucknow. On the 25th of September a thousand soldiers of the Highlanders under General Sir Henry Havelock joined them, in what was known as 'The First Relief of Lucknow'. In October another Highlander unit under Sir Colin Campbell came to relieve them and on the 18th of November they evacuated the compound women and children first. They fled to now-retaken Kanpur.

Jhansi

Jhansi was a Maratha-ruled princely state in Bundelkhand. When the Raja of Jhansi died without an male heir in 1853, Jhansi was annexed to the British Raj by the Governor-General of India under the Doctrine of Lapse. His widow, Rani Lakshmibai, protested the annexation on the grounds that she had not been allowed to adopt a successor, as per Indian custom.

When the Rebellion broke out, Jhansi quickly became a centre of the rebellion. A small group of British officials took refuge in Jhansi's fort, and the Rani negotiated their evacuation. When the British left the fort, they were massacred by the rebels. Although the massacre might have occurred without the Rani's consent, the British suspected her of complicity in the slaughter, despite her protestations of innocence.

In September and October 1857, the Rani led the successful defence of Jhansi from the invading armies of the neighbouring rajas of Datia and Orchha. In March 1858, the British Army, led by Colonel Rose advanced on Jhansi, and laid siege to the city. The British captured the city, but the Rani fled in disguise.

Other Areas

On 1 June 1858, Rani Lakshmibai and a group of Maratha rebels captured the fortress city of Gwalher (Gwalior) from the Shinde (Sindhia) rulers, who were British allies. The Rani was killed three weeks later at the start of the British assault, when she was hit by a spray of bullets after fleeing Gwalior. The British captured Gwalior three days later.

The Rohillas centred in Bareilly were also very active in the war and this area was amongst the last to be captured by the rebels.

Retaliation—The Devil's Wind

From the end of 1857, the British had begun to gain ground again. Lucknow was retaken in March 1858. On 8 July 1858, a peace treaty was signed and the war ended. The last rebels were defeated in Gwalior on 20 June 1858. By 1859, rebel leaders Bakht Khan and Nana Sahib had either been slain or had fled. The British adopted the old Mughal punishment for mutiny and sentenced rebels were lashed to the mouth of cannons and blown to pieces. It was a crude and brutal war, with both sides resorting to what would now be described as war crimes. In the end, however, in terms of sheer numbers, the casualties were significantly higher on the Indian side.

Due to the bloody start of the rebellion, and the violence perpetrated upon the Europeans by the Indian forces especially after the apparent treachery of Nana Sahib and butchery in Kanpur, the British believed that they were justified in using similar tactics. As a result, the end of the war was followed by the execution of a vast majority of combatants from the Indian side as well as large numbers of civilians perceived to be sympathetic to the rebel cause. The British press and British government did not advocate clemency of any kind, though Governor General Canning tried to be sympathetic to native sensibilities, earning the scornful sobriquet "Clemency Canning". Soldiers took very few prisoners and often executed them later. Whole villages were wiped out for apparent pro-rebel sympathies. The Indians called this retaliation "the Devil's Wind."

Reorganization

The rebellion also saw the end of the British East India Company's rule in India. In August, by the Queen's Proclamation of 1858, power was transferred to the British Crown. A secretary of state was entrusted with the authority of Indian affairs and the Crown's viceroy in India was to be the chief executive. The British embarked on a program of reform, trying to integrate Indian higher castes and rulers into the government and abolishing the East India Company.

The viceroy stopped land grabs, decreed religious tolerance and admitted Indians into civil service, albeit mainly as subordinates. The British also increased the number of British soldiers in relation to native ones; henceforth 'Indian' regiments would be made-up of at least one-third British soldiers and only these would be allowed to handle artillery. In 1877 Queen Victoria took the title of Empress of India on the advice of her Prime Minister, Benjamin Disraeli. Bahadur Shah was tried for treason by a military commission assembled at Delhi, and exiled to Rangoon where he died in 1862, finally bringing the Mughal dynasty to an end.

Causes

This has been a subject of much speculation and divided historical opinion. But quite undoubtedly, the rebellion had diverse political, economic, religious and social causes. It is against this backdrop that the war of 1857 is to be seen.

The sepoys (from *sipahi,* Hindi for soldier, used for native Indian soldiers) had their own list of grievances against the Company Raj, mainly caused by the ethnic gulf between the British officers and their Indian troops. Other than Indian units of the British East India Company's army, much of the resistance came from the old aristocracy, who were seeing their power steadily eroded under the British.

Frictions

Due to the missionary activity, some Indians came to believe that the British intended to forcibly convert them to Christianity, a view which was perhaps not entirely unfounded, as the British religious fashion of the time was Evangelism, and many British East India Company officers took it upon themselves to try to convert their Sepoys. This was strongly discouraged by the Company, which was aware of the attempts' potential to become a flashpoint, but in spite of official disapproval conversion attempts continued unabated.

The jewels of the royal family of Nagpur were publicly auctioned in Calcutta, a move that was seen as a sign of abject disrespect by the remnants of the Indian aristocracy.

Indians were unhappy with the heavy-handed rule of the Company which had embarked on a project of rather rapid occupation and westernisation. This included the outlawing of many religious customs, both Muslim and Hindu, which were viewed as uncivilized by the British. This caused outrage amongst the Indian population. They abolished child marriage-without realizing that child marriage was simply a betrothal agreement between families: the children continued to live with their respective families until the age of consent and the marriage was not consummated until both spouses formally went to their matrimonial home. The British also abolished Sati and claimed to have ended female infanticide, but this claim is doubtful without accompanying demographic data. The removal of Thuggees is perhaps true, but may have been done with the intent of removing obstacles to British imperialism.

Many of the Company's modernising efforts were viewed with automatic distrust; for example, it was feared that the railway, the first of which began running out of Bombay in the 1850s, was a demon. However, the common misconception that the British undertook these changes in social system themselves is largely inaccurate, as there were many Indian reformers, notable among them Raja Ram Mohan Roy, who were really the driving force behind these reforms.

In fact, one lesson learned by the British after 1857 was to not enact reforms, but to instead further strengthen social divides in order to maintain their supremacy; and also to appease the gentry, who had been major instigators in the 1857 revolt. After 1857, Zamindari (regional feudal officials) became more oppressive, the Caste System became more pronounced, and the communal divide between Hindus and Muslims became marked and visible, all due in great part to British efforts to keep Indian society divided. This tactic is infamously known as Divide and rule.

The justice system was inherently unfair to the Indians, as can be expected from any foreign occupation. In 1853, the British PM Aberdeen opened up the Indian Civil Service to native Indians; however, this was widely viewed in India as an insufficient reform. The official Blue Books — entitled "East India (Torture) 1855–1857" — that were laid before the House of Commons during the sessions of 1856 and 1857, revealed that British officers were allowed an extended series of appeals if convicted or accused of brutality or crimes against Indians. The Company also practised financial extortion through heavy taxation. Failure to pay these taxes almost invariably resulted in appropriation of property.

The British policy of expansionism was also greatly disliked by the Indians. In eight years James Andrew Broun-Ramsay, 1st Marquess of Dalhousie, the Governor-General of India, had annexed a quarter of a million square miles (650,000 km^2) of land to the Company's territory.

Economics

The British East India Company was a massive export company that was the force behind much of the colonization of India. The power of the Company took nearly 150 years to build. As early as 1693, the annual expenditure in political "gifts" to men in power reached nearly 90,000 pounds. In bribing the Government, the Company was allowed to operate in overseas markets despite the fact that the cheap imports of South Asian silk, cotton, and other products hurt domestic business. By 1767, the Company was forced into an agreement to pay 400,000 pounds into the National Exchequer annually.

By 1848, however, the Company's financial difficulties had reached a point where expanding revenue required expanding British territories in South Asia massively. The Company began to set aside adoption rights of native princes and began the process of annexation of more than a dozen independent Rajas between 1848 and 1854. In an article published in The New York Daily Tribune on July 28, 1857, Karl Marx notes that "... in 1854 the Raj of Berar, which comprise 80,000 square miles of land, a population from four to five million, and enormous treasures, was forcibly seized".

In order to consolidate and control these new holdings, a well-established army of 200,000 South Asians officered by 40,000 British soldiers dominated India by 1857. The last vestiges of independent Indian states had disappeared and the Company exported tons of gold, silk, cotton, and a host of other precious materials back to England every year.

The land was reorganised under the comparatively harsh Zamindari system to facilitate the collection of taxes. In certain areas farmers were forced to switch from subsistence farming to commercial crops such as indigo, jute, coffee and tea. This resulted in hardship to the farmers and increases in food prices.

Local industry, specifically the famous weavers of Bengal and elsewhere, also suffered under British rule. Tariffs were kept low, according to traditional British free-market sentiments, and thus the Indian market was flooded with cheap clothing from Britain. Indigenous industry simply could not compete, and where once India had produced much of England's luxury cloth, the country was now reduced to growing cotton which was shipped to Britain to be manufactured into clothing, which was subsequently shipped back to India to be purchased by Indians.

The Indians felt that the British were levying very heavy taxation on the locals. This included an increase in the taxation on land.

Political Interference

If a landowner did not leave a male heir thorugh natural process *i.e.* own child, not the adopted one, the land became the property of the British East India Company via the doctrine of lapse carried out by Lord Dalhousie and his successor, Charles John Canning, 1st Earl Canning. Lord Dalhousie used this doctrine to possess a number of Indian kingdoms, most notably those of Pune, Nagpur and Jhansi, causing the disenfranchised rulers of these kingdoms to join sides with the rebellious Indian troops. This was applied to feudal lands as well as to the states.

Sepoys

Sepoys were native Indian soldiers serving in the army of the British East India Company under British officers trained in the East India Company College, the company's own military school in England. The presidencies of Bombay, Madras and Bengal maintained their own army each with its own commander-in-chief. They fielded more troops than the official army of the British Empire. In 1857 there were 257,000 sepoys.

The Company also recruited Indians of other castes than the Brahmin and Rạjputs; the latter is a traditional warrior caste in the Western part of North India, now Rajasthan. In 1856 sepoys were required to serve overseas during a war in Burma. Hindu tradition states that those who 'travel the black waters' will lose their caste and be outside the Hindu community. Sepoys were thus very displeased with their deployment to Burma.

The sepoys were dissatisfied with various aspects of army life. Their pay was relatively low and after the British troops conquered Awadh and the Punjab, the soldiers no longer received extra pay for service there, because they were no longer considered "foreign missions". However, they were not subject to the penalty of flogging as were the British soldiers. Sepoy soldiers found themselves constantly pitted against their countrymen in an army which the common soldiers increasingly began to feel was governed by wholly foreign influences. In a colonial setting, this is the prime breeding ground for a conflagration.

Into this conflagration, the Pattern 1853 Enfield (P/53) rifle was introduced into India. Its cartridge was covered by a greased membrane which was supposed to be cut by the teeth before the cartridges were loaded into the rifles. There was a rumour that the membrane was greased by cow or pig fat. This was offensive to Hindu and Muslim soldiers alike, who considered tasting beef or pork to be against their respective religious tenets.

The British claimed that they had replaced the cartridges with new ones not made from cow and pig fat and tried to get sepoys to make their own grease from beeswax and vegetable oils but the rumour persisted. A new drill was also introduced in which the cartridge was not bitten with the teeth but torn with the hand: the sepoys argued that they might very well forget and bite. The Commander in Chief in India, General George Anson reacted to this crisis by saying, "I'll never give in to their beastly prejudices", and despite the pleas of his junior officers he did not compromise.

Some began to spread the rumour of a prophecy that the Company's rule would end after a hundred years. Their rule in India had begun with the Battle of Plassey in 1757.

1857-The Story on Stamps

The Rising of 1857 was an important landmark in the history of India. It marked the beginning of the country's struggle for freedom after a century of uninterrupted foreign domination. The violent outbreak of the Sepoys at Meerut on the evening of 10 May was not a mutiny similar to those which had occurred earlier in the British Indian Army to ventilate certain local grievances of the soldiers. It did not remain an isolated incident. The rebellion soon spread beyond the Bengal Army and assumed the character of a general revolt, which was enthusiastically joined by the civil population of Hindustan. The country witnessed a popular upsurge of deep-seated and widespread bitterness against the alien rulers. The East India Company's Government was swept from large parts of North India and the very foundations of British rule were shaken. It appeared for some time that the Company's Raj had disappeared from the land.

What was the cause of this great convulsion? Some historians attribute it to the 'greased cartridge'. But it is unbelievable that such a vast and popular uprising could have been brought about merely by the new cartridge, howsoever offensive it might have been to the Sepoys. It was the immediate cause, the spark that set ablaze the smouldering fire of discontent. The basic causes of the revolt were complex, embracing all aspects of the impact of alien rule on Indian polity and society.

Mangal Pande (1831-1857): No. 1446 Sepoy Mangal Pande of the 5th Company, 34th Native Infantary fired the bullet that marked the beginning of the great uprising of 1857. The shot fired at Barrackpore resounded all over the country and soon the cavalry corps at Meerut responded adding a new dimension to the revolt. Twenty six year old Mangal Pande was deeply religious and had a good service record. He was disturbed by some happenings like the court-martial of Jamadar Saligram Singh for refusing to use the greased cartridge and the disbanding of the 19th Native Infantry.

There was also a general feeling among the sepoys that despite long years of loyal and devoted service to East India Company, the 'native' soldiers were unfairly dealt with and treated with arrogance and their genuine grievances were not redressed. After the impulsive act, Mangal Pande tried but could not shoot himself dead. He was court martialled on 6 April 1857. On 8 April, when he was sent to the gallows he was calm and unruffled as befitted a martyr to a noble cause. Ever since the battle of Plassey (June 1757) the Company's territorial power had been growing very fast.

By 1818, when the last Peshwa was dethroned, practically all the Indian States had either been annexed or had entered into treaty alliances with the Company on humiliating conditions. The British had become the suzerain power and the Indian princes were mere puppets in their hands.

The policy of expansion did not stop there and the few independent principalities on the frontiers were also annexed whenever an opportunity presented itself. In 1843, Sind was attacked and added to the British dominion; it was an act of wanton aggression to cover the terrible disaster which the British armies had suffered in the Afghan war. The revolt of Diwan Mulraj of Multan was used as a pretext for the annexation of the Punjab in 1849. The rights of the minor Maharaja, Dalip Singh, who was under the protection of the British, were set aside.

Lord Dalhousie annexed States whenever an occasion arose and often in disregard of solemn engagements. Under his 'Doctrine of Lapse' the princes were denied the long-cherished right of adoption; in this way Dalhousie annexed the Maratha States of Satara, Nagpur and Jhansi and several minor principalities. On the death of the ex-Peshwa, Baji Rao 11, the pension granted to him was abolished and the claims of his adopted son, Nana Dhondu Pant, were disregarded. In 1856, the kingdom of Oudh was annexed. The Nawabs had been the faithful allies of the Company for a long time; but such considerations did not weigh much with Dalhousie, who had a calculated plan to abolish all the Indian States.

The result of his policy was that no Indian prince felt secure, and there was widespread resentment. The annexations also caused discontent among the subjects of the dispossessed princes, as they were bound to them by old ties of tradition. For an Englishman like Dalhousie it was not possible to realize that the people had genuine respect for old dynasties and that they might prefer the old tyranny to the oppression of the new rulers.

The ever widening frontiers of the Company's dominion also resulted in the shutting out of Indians from all avenues of honourable employment. The administrative reforms of Cornwallis, introduced at the close of the 18th century, meant the virtual exclusion of Indians from high posts. The administration assumed an English character. There was perhaps no other case of foreign rule in which the people were "so completely excluded from all share of the government of the country as in British India". To make matters worse, the English administrators gradually became arrogant and there was a wide gulf between them and the people. They could hardly know the feelings of the vast multitude, which providence had placed under their rule.

Rani Lakshmibai (1835-1857): Born in a Maharashtrian Brahmin family, 'Manu' was married to Raja Gangadhar Rao of Jhansi and became Lakshmibai. The Raja died childless and, despite an assurance given before his death, the company did not permit the adopted child to succeed him and annexed the kingdom. Rani Lakshmibai found it hard to bear this humiliation. She stoutly opposed the British expansionist policies with regard to Indian states and was among the principal organisers of the 1857 uprising. In June 1857, she actively led the Jhansi troops against the British army. She demonstrated a rare organising capacity with military leadership, valour and indomitable courage. The Times' correspondent reported on 3 Aug 1858 that *"the battle plans were effected mainly under the direction and personal supervision of the Ranee who, clad in military attire... was constantly in the saddle, ubiquitous and untiring."* General Hugh Rose regarded her as *"... the woman who was the only man among the rebels"*. She laid down her life for the freedom of the country on 17 June 1857.

This lack of understanding of the feelings of the people is nowhere better illustrated than in the agrarian changes which were introduced in the first half of the 19th century, particularly in the North-Western Province. In the settlement of this province, many landowners were deprived of their lands as they failed to establish their proprietary rights by documentary proof. Investigations were even made into the titles of those who had held estates for many generations before the advent of the Company's rule. At the same time enquiries were held in regard to rent-free tenures. Many failed to satisfy the authorities in regard to the original validity of their titles and their tenures were resumed to augment the Government's revenue. Similarly, in the Bombay Presidency the Inam Commission carried out investigations into a large number of titles to land and many estates were abolished on the failure of the Jagirdars to produce satisfactory documentary evidence in support of their claims.

The landed aristocracy was alienated by these ill-conceived measures. Further bitterness was aroused by the working of the Sale Law and excessive taxation which ruined the landlord and peasant alike. Under the old system land was inalienable, but now it could be sold in default of payment of rent. In the auctions the estates of many land owners were acquired by money-lenders, whose power was growing under the new system but who were total strangers to the rural population. As a result of this 'agrarian revolution' village communities were broken up. The landlords were not merely deprived of their estates but of all hope of honourable.employment. The peasants did not benefit under the new dispensation and were equally aggrieved. Ideas of individual rights and personal freedom did not occur to them and they were opposed to changes in traditional socioeconomic relations. The British administrators failed to realize that there was a traditional bond between the talukdars and their retainers arid they all blamed the alien rulers for their impoverishment. When the revolt broke out, the rural population naturally swelled the ranks of the rebels.

Economic distress was also caused in another way by the policies of the Government. The political authority which the Company wielded was employed to serve its commercial interests for many years. Indian handicrafts were ruined as a result of its oppressive policy and the loss of patronage caused by the dissolution of the princely states. The adverse effects of the Industrial Revolution on the Indian economy were also being felt. These factors naturally added to the rising wave of discontent in the country.

The British were different from the Indian people in race, religion, habits, ideas and sentiments. In the 18th century they exhibited a friendly attitude towards Indian society and religions. They had no particular zeal for their own religion and the Company even acted as trustees of some Hindu temples. Missionary activity was discouraged. In the 19th century this attitude underwent a radical change and the British began to interfere with the religious and social usages of the people. Some of the social reforms were indeed introduced with lofty motives, to put an end to evil customs and to ameliorate the condition of the people; but the feelings of those whom the reforms affected were not taken into consideration. The result was that even the abolition of Sati (1829) was not welcomed by the mass of the people. When this evil custom had been banned more than 250 years earlier by Akbar there was no such feeling of resentment on the part of his Hindu subjects. But in the 19th century people looked on the foreign Government with suspicion and they feared that their ancestral faith and caste were in peril. Their fears were undoubtedly based on their own observations.

After 1813 there was a definite increase both in the numbers and proselytising activities of the Christian missionaries, whose avowed object was to convert people to their faith. Missionaries were to be seen everywhere-in bazars, schools, hospitals and even prisons. They ridiculed in public the tenets of Hinduism and Islam. The teaching of the Bible was introduced in some Government schools, and orphans and victims of calamities were often converted to Christianity. The missionaries received support and patronage from highly placed Government officals and the people naturally believed that the Government was in collusion with them to eradicate their caste and convert them to Christianity. The passing of Act XXI of 1850, which enabled converts to inherit ancestral property, confirmed this belief; the new law was naturally interpreted as a concession to Christian converts. Another unpopular act was the one of 1856, permitting Hindu widows to remarry. This was a salutary reform, but according to the sentiments of those days the people apprehended that their religion and society were in imminent danger.

Kunwar Singh (1777-1858): Kunwar Singh epitomises not only the spirit of liberty but also unparalleled courage and the will to resist injustice at all costs and under any circumstances. He played a major role in the First War of Independence of 1857. Born at Jagadishpur in Shahabad District of Bihar, Babu Kunwar Singh was nearly eighty and in failing health when he was called upon to take up arms. The great warrior that he was, he gave a good fight and harried British forces for nearly an year and remained invincible till the end. While crossing the Ganga on way to his ancestral seat at Jagadishpur, he was wounded in the arm. Undaunted, he severed the injured limb and flung it into the river-as his last offering to Ganga. Soon after, he completely routed the British forces in the battle on 23 April 1858 and passed away the next day.

The princes lived in an atmosphere of insecurity, the landed aristocracy had been alienated and the mass of the people were disaffected; but their antagonism would not have led to a serious insurrection so long as the Sepoy Army remained loyal. The Sepoys of the Bengal Army were mostly men of high caste from Oudh and the North-Western Province; they shared the general apprehensions regarding the Government's intentions. The Sepoys had won many wars for the Company. They had fought for their masters with unflinching devotion in the most difficult and perilous circumstances. In spite of this, they did not get a fair deal. Their emoluments were very low in comparison with those of the British soldiers and their chances of promotion negligible. They also had grievances regarding the payment of extra cillowances for service in newly conquered territories, like Sind, which were foreign lands to them.

The Sepoy's trust in the Government was fast waning. Their bitterness against the foreign masters was intensified by the arrogant attitude of their European officers, and the fellow feeling between Sepoys and officers which had once existed in the Company's Army was a thing of the past. The loyalty of the Sepoys was further undermined by certain military reforms which outraged their religious feelings. They had an aversion to overseas service, as travel across the seas meant loss of caste for them: Their feelings had previously been respected in this matter; but in accordance with the new enlistment regulations issued in July 1856 overseas service was made obligatory on all new recruits. The Sepoys construed this as another attack on their caste and religion; their loyalty was severely shaken.

While the country was thus seething with discontent and the Sepoys, too, were agitated, the affair of the greased cartridge came up, One day in January 1857 a rumour went round at Calcutta that the new cartridges to be used in the Enfield Rifle, recently introduced in India, were greased with cow's fat and lard and that this had been done to defile both the Hindu and Muslim Sepoys who would use the cartridges, There was reason to believe that the grease used was of an offensive nature, and the news soon spread to all the military stations. This roused a storm of indignation and kindled the embers of discontent. The introduction of the cartridges hastened the revolt which had long been brewing.

The authorities soon discovered their error and attempted to allay the feelings of the Sepoys, which had been roused by their ill- conceived measure. Orders were issued that the new cartridges should not be issued to the Indian regiments and the drill was changed so that the cartridges need not be bitten. But it was too late. Once the suspicions of the Sepoys were aroused it was not possible to soothe them. They were not satisfied even when they were told to grease their cartridges themselves.

The rising wave of discontent manifested itself in several cases of incendiarism at Barrackpore and several other military stations. On 26 February the 19th Native Infantry at Barhampur refused to accept the cartridges given to them. The authorities decided to disband the regiment as a warning to others. Then on 29 March Mangal Pande, a sepoy of the 34th Native Infantry at Barrackpore, attacked the Adjutant of his regiment. His action was a result of the fear in the Sepoy's minds regarding loss of their caste and religion. Mangal Pande was executed after a court-martial; but the trouble which had started could not be stopped by such measures. He was not a felon or a criminal in the eyes of his fellow Sepoys; he was regarded a martyr in the cause of his religion.

Bahadur Shah 'Zafar' (1775-1862): The last Mughal Emperor, Abdul Muzaffar Muhammad Siraj-ud-din Bahadur Shah, had, for all practical purposes his authority confined to the four walls of the Red Fort-thanks to the machinations of the East India Company. Following the outbreak of revolt in Meerut, troops proclaimed him the Emperor of Hindustan. This resulted in his deposition, imprisonment, trial by military court and exile. A man of aesthetic temperament, Bahadur Shah was a sensitive poet who had adopted "Zafar" as a poetic sobriquet. Before his death in Rangoon, he had lamented the fact that he will not be buried in his homeland -

On 24 April Colonel Smyth of the 3rd Native Cavalry at Meerut called to parade ninety selected sowars of his regiment to demonstrate how they could load their rifles without biting the cartridges. When the cartridges were issued, eighty-five of the sowars refused to accept them. The cartidges were of old pattern, but the Sepoys could not be persuaded to handle even the material which they had used on previous occasions. The offenders were tried by court-martial and sentenced to imprisonment. On 9 May the men were stripped of their uniforms and put in fetters in the presence of the whole brigade and sent to prison. This humiliation drove their Sepoy brethren to frenzy. The following evening, the standard of rebellion was raised. The station was taken by surprise. Led by the sowars of the 3rd Cavalry, the Sepoys broke open the prison and released their comrades, shot many of their British officers and set their bungalows on fire. Chaos followed in the city and there was indiscriminate plunder and killing.

The Sepoys had risen without any plan; but they did not stay very long at Meerut. The majority of them took the road to Delhi forty miles away. Early next morning, after crossing the Jamuna by the bridge of boats, they appeared before the palace of the titular King of Delhi, Abu Zafar Siraj-ud-din Bahadur Shah, a worn-out man of eighty. The King, though shorn of all ruling authority, was still the legal sovereign of Hindustan, and the East India Company held sway over the country on the basis of grants made by his ancestors. There was still a lingering memory of the glorious Mughal Raj, and the last representative of the dynasty was the natural choice of the Sepoys for leadership of the revolt. They urged the old monarch to accept their leadership. He hesitated but finally agreed to their request. This gave legal sanction to the 'mutiny' and the struggle assumed a political colour. Henceforth the Sepoys were fighting in the name of their sovereign.

Nana Saheb (1824-NR): Adopted by Peshwa Baji Rao 11, Nana Dhundhu Pant-Nana Saheb-was the heir presumptive but was denied the title and the pension on the Peshwa's death in 1857. Naturally hostile to the British, he assumed the leadership of the troops at Kanpur and declared war on the Company. Having suffered serious upsets in July 1857, he went to Nepal and was not further heard of.

The city of Delhi passed into the hands of the 'rebels' in a few hours. The Meerut Sepoys were soon joined by their brethren in the cantonment and the civilian population led by the princes of the royal family. The city was denuded of all Europeans; many were killed and others escaped in disguise when darkness fell at the end of the day. On 12 May the revival of the Mughal Empire was proclaimed with the booming of guns, and the news went round that the English Raj had come to an end. Tidings of the disaster had, however, been flashed to the British authorities in the Punjab before the telegraph office was captured.

The loss of Delhi was a severe blow to the prestige of the Company's Government. There was a comparative respite for a fortnight, however, and the English heaved a sigh of relief. The Punjab, where trouble was expected, remained peaceful. The regiments of Purbiah Sepoys of the Bengal Army posted in different cantonments of the province were disarmed to render them harmless. Those among them who chose to revolt at Ferozepore, Peshawar, Mardan, Sialkot and Lahore, were wiped out. Preparations were set afoot by the Punjab authorities to help in the recovery of the imperial city.

But before the English made an attempt to restore their authority in Delhi rebellions broke out over a wide area covering the North--Western Province, Oudh, Central India and Western Bihar. There were outbreaks of the Sepoys at Nasirabad and Nimach in Central India, and at Jhansi on 5 June. By the second week of June practically the whole of Oudh, was up in arms. The Sepoys had risen at Lucknow on 30 May and the British residence, led by Sir Henry Lawrence, the Chief Commissioner of Oudh, had to take refuge in the Residency. In Rohilkhand, the Sepoys rose at Bareilly on 31 May under the leadership of Subadar Bakht Khan, who later became the Commander-in-Chief of the 'rebel' forces at Delhi. Banaras witnessed a sporadic rising on 4 June and the next day a rising started at Kanpur. Allahabad followed on 6 June.

Apart from Delhi, the main centres of the rebellion were Kanpur, Lucknow and Jhansi. At Kanpur the leadership of the rebels was assumed by Nana Dhondu Pant, popularly called Nana Saheb, the adopted son of the ex-Peshwa, Baji Rao II. He established his government there. He was assisted by his friend and adviser Azimullah Khan, Tantia Tope, Jwala Prasad and Tika Singh. In Oudh, Begam Hazrat Mahal, the wife of the ex-King of Oudh, led the revolt. Her minor son, Birjis Qadr, was proclaimed Wali-i-Oudh. The most outstanding leader of the revolt in Oudh was, however, Ahmad-ullah Shah, the Moulvi of Faizabad. At Bareilly, Khan Bahadur Khan, a descendant of Hafiz Rahmat Khan, proclaimed himself Viceroy on behalf of the Mughal Emperor. In Allahabad, Moulvi Liakat Ali, a man of humble origin, took over the administration. Rani Lakshmibai, the young widow of Raja Gangadhar Rao, began to rule at Jhansi. All these chiefs, however, professed allegiance to the Mughal Emperor who was the symbolic head of the struggle.

The rebellion spread very fast and its suppression proved to be a difficult problem. With the arrival of reinforcements, the task was taken up by the British authorities with determination. Neill was dispatched from Calcutta with a strong force to relieve Kanpur and Lucknow. He arrived at Banaras on 3 June 1857, and after ruthlessly suppressing an outbreak, caused by his own aggressive policy, he left for Allahabad. He reached the latter place on 11 June and within a week the city was secure in the hands of the British force. The Moulvi had to leave the city.

In the meantime, General Sir Henry Havelock had been dispatched with fresh reinforcements to restore British authority at Kanpur and Lucknow. He came by rapid marches and encountered Nana's forces at Fatehpur on 12 July. Havelock's advance on Kanpur was fiercely contested by the Indian troops, but superior equipment and better leadership helped him to enter the city on 17 July at the head of a victorious army. Nana Saheb evacuated Bithtir on 18 July and escaped to Oudh. Havelock soon started preparations for the relief of Lucknow, and on 25 July he crossed the Ganga and entered Oudh territory.

Tantia Tope (1814-1859): Ramchandra Pandurang Tope was a close friend of Nana Saheb, the Peshwa's adopted son. When Nana was deprived of his father's pension, Tantia Tope also became a sworn enemy of the British. In May 1857 he won over the Indian troops of the Company at Kanpur and commanded the revolutionary forces. After reoccupation of Kanpur by the British troops, Tantia Tope led the revolt in Bundelkhand. Suffering reverses, he reached Gwalior but had to move again. He carried on a guerilla campaign against the British for over an year. Unfortunately, betrayed by a friend, he was captured and executed on 18 April 1859.

The recovery of Delhi was of supreme importance to the British. On 8 June a combined force from the Punjab and Meerut defeated the rebels at Badli-ki-Serai, near Delhi, and occupied the Ridge the same day. The British force had to wait there for more than three months for reinforcements and heavy artillery to enable them to make a successful assault on the city. During this period they maintained their position on the Ridge with great difficulty in the face of incessant fire from the troops within the city walls and repeated attacks on their positions. More than twenty actions were fought here during June and July.

The British force was strengthened in August with the arrival of John Nicholson. On 3 September the siege-train arrived, and on 14 September the British delivered their assault. The fiercest battle of the campaign was fought on that day and there were heavy casualties on both sides; but by nightfall the British troops had entered the city after blowing up the Kashmir Gate. The fury of battle raged for another six days; the defenders fought courageously but could not prevent the occupation of the city. The palace was taken on 20 September. The following day Bahadur Shah surrendered to Captain Hodson in the shadow of the tomb of his great ancestor, Emperor Humayun. At the same place three of the princes were captured on 22 September and mercilessly shot by Hodson outside Delhi Gate. The city was sacked and thousands of innocent people perished.

Begum Hazarat Mahal (NR-1879): Hazarat Mahal, the Begum of Avadh, was the wife of Nawab Wajid Ali Shah of Lucknow (who was exiled to Calcutta by the East India Company). She had an inborn genius for organisation' and command. During the 1857 uprising, she seized control of Lucknow with the help of Nana Saheb and other supporters. She suffered reverses with fortitude and rejected with contempt, British offers of status and allowances. She sought asylum in Nepal where she died in 1879.

Meanwhile, Henry Havelock had crossed the Ganga from Kanpur with the object of relieving the besieged troops in the Residency at Lucknow. But his task was a very difficult one. The people of Oudh opposed his advance every inch of the way to Lucknow and twice he had to retreat. It was not till 25 September that he was able to reach the Residency, but he could do no more than add to the garrison. The siege of Lucknow continued, and the rebel forces were augmented by the arrival of numerous retainers of the Oudh talukdars who had joined the struggle.

Meanwhile, Sir Colin Campbell had assumed the office of

Commander-in-Chief and with a strong contingent arrived at Kanpur on 3 November. He was joined by the troops from Delhi, and after very hard fighting succeeded in reaching the Lucknow Residency on 17 November. He felt, however, that his force was inadequate to hold the city, so he returned to Kanpur with the sick and wounded and the women and children.

On his return to Kanpur on 28 November, Sir Colin found that the town had been occupied by Tantia Tope, who had defeated General Windham on 27 November and obliged him to take shelter in the entrenchment. Tantia had assumed command of the rebel Gwalior contingent at Kalpi (45 miles from Kanpur) and taking advantage of the absence of the British Commander-in-Chief, advanced on Kanpur and joined the troops of Nana Saheb there. Tantia could not hold the city for long; the 'rebel' forces were routed on 6 December. Tantia and many of his troops were, however, able to return to Kalpi.

Veer Narayana Singh (1795-1857): Narayana Singh Binjhwar, the scion of the Zamindar family of Sonakhan in Chhattisgarh, was born in 1795. During a severe famine, in 1856, he helped the people to save them from starvation. He was falsely implicated and arrested in October, 1856. When the flames of 1857 war reached Chhatisgarh, the masses elected the imprisoned Narayana Singh as their leader and liberated him from the jail. After organising the local people, Narayana Singh had an encounter with the British army near Sonakhan.

Moved by the atrocities of the British and the resultant devastation and destruction, Narayana Singh surrendered to the British to protect the lives of his people. His public execution on 10 December 1857 provoked the public and the army contingent at Ranipur, which rose in yet another revolt. Veer Narayana Singh's martyrdom was a memorable event in the history of Chhattisgarh and lent momentum to the freedom struggle.

In March 1858 Sir Colin returned to Lucknow. The city was regained after three weeks of hard fighting. Begam Hazrat Mahal and other leaders of the revolt were able to make their escape with numerous followers. The fighting in Oudh continued till the end of the year, and many talukdars refused to surrender on the terms offered to them. The rebels were finally driven to the Nepal frontier, to die there in the inhospitable climate or to be captured as prisoners by the Gurkhas who had come to succour the British at a very critical stage of their campaign.

In Rohilkhand, Khan Bahadur Khan's rule came to an end within two months of the capture of Lucknow. Bareilly was occupied by the British force on 5 May. Bahadur Khan escaped, but was later captured on the Nepal frontier, brought to Bareilly, tried and hanged. The Moulvi of Faizabad had entered Rohilkhand after his defeat at Lucknow. He continued to fight undaunted for some time. On 5 June 1858, he attacked Powain and was shot dead by the garrison in the fortress. His head was severed and exposed at the Kotwali of Shahjahanpur, a town which he had attacked a few days earlier. His body was burnt and the ashes thrown into the Ramganga, the worst punishment his enemy could possibly inflict after his death.

In Bihar, the most formidable challenge to British authority came from Babu Kunwar Singh, an old Rajput chieftain of Jagdishpur, in Shahabad district. He assumed command of the Sepoys who had revolted at Danapur on 25 July. Two days later he occupied Arrah, the headquarter of the district. Major Vincent Eyre relieved the town on 3 August, defeated Kunwar Singh's force and destroyed Jqgdishpur. Kunwar Singh left his ancestral village, and after passing through Rewa, Banda, Kalpi and Kanpur, he reached Lucknow in December 1857. In March 1858 he occupied Azamgarh, for which he had been granted a farman by the Wali of Oudh. He had to leave the place soon; pursued by Brigadier Douglas, he hastily retreated towards his home in Bihar. On 23 April Kunwar Singh won a signal victory near Jagdishpur over the force led by Captain Le Grand, but the following day he died in his village.

Rani Avantlbai (NR-1858): Avantibai, the queen of Ramgarh in Mandla District of Madhya Pradesh, was looking after the affairs of the State when the British took over the administration in 1851. She vowed to win back her land, organised the local zamindars and rulers and raised an army of about four thousand. In 1857, the Rani led her army and in the first encounter with the British defeated Wadington, their commander. However, in subsequent engagements, despite her courage and skill, the Rani could not hold out against the large and well-equipped British army. Faced with the prospect of defeat and surrender, Rani Avantibai chose to sacrifice her life. She joined the ranks of martyrs on 20 March 1858.

The mantle of the old chief now fell on his brother Amar Singh who, in spite of heavy odds, continued the struggle and for a considerable time ran a parallel government in the district of Shahabad. In October 1859 Amar Singh joined the rebel leaders in the Nepal Terai.

After his defeat at Kanpur in December 1857, Tantia Tope carried on a desperate struggle in Central India. Meanwhile Sir Hugh Rose had taken over command of the Central India Field Force. Starting from his base at Mhow. he relieved Sagar in February and on 22 March laid siege to Jhansi, where the indomitable Rani held the reins of government. Tantia Tope came to the assistance of the Rani, but he was defeated in the battle of the Betwa. Jhansi fell on 4 April after a heroic resistance, in which even women and children took part. Lakshmibai fled to Kalpi to join Tantia Tope and Rao Saheb. The 'rebels' now suffered a series of defeats and Kalpi was evacuated on 23 May.

Surrounded by British forces on all sides, they were now in sore straits. However, they had courage enough for an act of great daring. Marching to Gwalior, they captured the city and fortress practically without striking a blow on 1 June The Maharaja remained loyal to the British and fled to Agra, but his army joined the rebels, Rao Saheb proclaimed the Peshwa's rule at Gwalior.

Sir Hugh Rose immediately marched to Gwalior and arrived there on 16 June. Three days later the British force occupied the fortress. The Rani of Jhansi fell in a battle on 17 June but Tantia Tope and Rao Saheb were able to escape. Tantia now resorted to guerilla warfare, and baffled the British commanders for many months. He was finally betrayed early in April 1859 by a friend named Man Singh. After a hurried trial, he was hanged at Sipri on 18 April. By that time the revolt had been suppressed.

Raja Nahar Singh (NR-1858): Ruler of the small state of Ballabhgarh, Nahar Singh was a farsighted person and a votary of Hindu/-Muslim unity. He played an important role in the uprising of 1857. Nahar Singh tried to bring together all the neighbouring rulers, especially Begum Samaroo of Gurgaon, Nawabs of Jhajjar, Farrukh Nagar and Rewari. He organised a secret' meeting in the fort of Mukteshwar at the time of Kartik mela which was attended, among others by Tantia Tope.

Emperor Bahadur Shah 11 had appointed Raja Nahar Slngh as the Internal Administrator of Delhi. Raja Nahar Singh had tirelessly organised the neighbouring princes and chieftains during the uprising. The British forces had a tough time in controlling the second revolt in the region-Ballabgarh, Gurgaon, Jhajjar and Rewari. He was tried and hanged on 9th Jan 1858.

The Indian struggle of 1857 was marked by merciless savagery and many innocent men, women and children were slaughtered on both sides. From the beginning, when the British heard of the excesses committed at Meerut and Delhi, they were seized with the desire for vengeance. Wherever the British forces advanced cities were sacked, villages burnt and people slaughtered irrespective of their guilt. Such inhuman behaviour was ascribed to the indignation which the news of the murder of British women and children had aroused. It may, however, be noted that the two massacres-at Kanpur-came after the inhuman acts of Neill at Banaras and Allahabad. The massacres at Sati Chaura Ghat and Bibighar were to a large extent the direct result of the provocation offered by the slaughter of innocent people by Neill.

It would be appropriate to quote in this connection the words of Michael Edwardes. He writes: "From the first murder of European civilians at Meerut and Delhi, the English threw aside the mask of civilization and engaged in a war of such ferocity that reasonable parallel can be seen in our own times with the Nazi occupation of Europe and, in the past, with the hell of the Thirty Years' War. No quarter was given to suspected mutineers. Justice became a dirty word, and reason and humanity, feminine frippery."

All Englishmen were not in favour of such cruel treatment of Indians and many raised their voices of protest. Lord Canning, the Govemor-General, genuinely attmpted to put an end to this madness and ordered the proper trial and punishment of those who were suspected of being guilty. For this his countrymen nick-named him in derision, 'Clemency Canning.' The Revolt had run its course by the middle of 1858, though some fighting continued in the following year. It started as a military rising, but immediately it turned into a war of independence. When the Sepoys placed themselves under the leadership of Bahadur Shah and proclaimed him Emperor of Hindustan, they began to fight for a political cause. Their struggle was then for their king and country. The Sepoys undoubtedly took up arms against their British masters for the defence of their religion, but they were also fighting for political independence as their religion was threatened by the alien government and they wanted to replace it by a political system alien to the soil.

Suryamall Mishran (NR-1868): Suryamall had started writing poetry from early childhood. He carried on the tradition of the great bard poets and composed a number of distinguished works, including 'Vansha Bhaskar'-an epic in 10,000 pages. The 1857 war of Independence had a profound effect on Suryamall. He exhorted and inspired the Kings, Princes and Zamindars of Rajasthan to fight and defeat the British. He composed another monumental work, the "Veer Satsai" for this purpose which is noted for its force and vitality, besides patriotism. The failure of the war of independence greatly affected the poet who gave up writing, and devoted his life to the service of his fellow beings.

The movement spread outside the Army and assumed the shape of a popular struggle against British rule. In many places in the North-Western Province, Oudh and Bihar, the civil population rose independently of the Sepoys. In places where the rising was confined to the Army alone its effects were temporary, but where the civil population joined, the resistance continued for a long time. In assessing the character of the revolt it would be improper to judge it in the context of the modem concept of nationalism. To assume the existence of such a conception of nationality in 1857 would not be correct, as the country was then passing through a semi-feudal stage. It would also be unfair to judge mid-nineteenth century men by the standards of today. Those who actively joined the revolt had diverse motives, but they were all united in their hatred of the British rule and in their aim to overthrow it.

The struggle was as nearly national as it possibly could be under the conditions then prevailing. It was spontaneous and was inspired by a popular impulse to break the shackles of slavery. It brought about the union of different elements and it had wide popular support from almost all classes of society. The struggle created an amazing sense of unity between Hindus and Muslims, and they fought together as brethren. The English attempted to exploit religious differences in order to create dissension in their ranks, particularly in Delhi and Bareilly, but they did not succeed.

The revolt failed in its object. That was perhaps inevitable under the circumstances. But even in its failure the struggle of 1857 forms a significant chapter in the history of India. It was the first large-scale popular uprising against British rule and the first expression of India's urge for freedom. It was undoubtedly the same urge which realised itself ninety years later. The unknown heroes of 1857 did not shed their blood in vain.

Lucknow in 1857-58: The Epic Siege

The struggle for Lucknow occupies a central place in the history of the Great Revolt. Of the major military engagements in 1857-58 the siege of the Lucknow Residency by the rebels was one of the most intense, and certainly the longest. The uprising at Lucknow and the heroic defence of the city by the sipahis and the common people constitutes a glorious chapter in the annals of the anti-colonial struggle. Not surprisingly the British had to mobilise armed force on a very large scale to crush the Revolt in the capital of the erstwhile kingdom of Avadh.

The special status of the Lucknow Residency as a sacred site associated with imperial conquest was indicated by the fact that it was the only structure in the British Indian Empire where the Union Jack was not lowered at sunset: it flew day and night, being eventually taken down only on August 14, 1947.

The origins of the Revolt may be justifiably traced to the annexation of Avadh by the East India Company in February 1856. As is well known the kingdom was annexed on the pretext of misrule. The ruler, Wajid Ali Shah (1847-56), had been asked to hand over the administration of Avadh (spelt as 'Oudh' or 'Oude' in colonial records) directly to the Company. When he refused, the kingdom was seized and Wajid Ali Shah was exiled. This political act of the Company had far-reaching military consequences since

Avadh was a major recruiting area for the colonial state's Bengal Army. On the eve of the Revolt nearly one-third of the sipahis in the Bengal army, numbering about 40,000, came from territories of the kingdom of Avadh. This kingdom was already truncated by the mid-nineteenth century. The result was that widespread discontent against colonial exploitation in the countryside (as well as in the cities, to which a large section of the rural poor flocked) could seek expression in military rebellion initiated by the Avadh 'peasants in uniform'.

Following the events of May 10 and 11, 1857 at Meerut and Delhi, and with the establishment at Delhi of an independent sipahi regime with the Mughal emperor as its nominal leader, favourable conditions for an uprising developed in Avadh. There seems to have been widespread expectation of mutiny breaking out in garrisons situated in Avadh (Avadh at this time comprised mainly the districts of Faizabad, Lucknow, Sultanpur, Rae Bareilly, Pratapgarh, Barabanki, Unnao, Sitapur, Hardoi, Bahraich and Gonda). Already there had been mutinies between May 20 and 22 in adjoining areas — at Aligarh, Mainpuri, Etawah and Bulandshahr.

On May 30 sipahis of the 13th Native Infantry (NI), 48th NI, 71st NI, and 7th Light Infantry, stationed at Lucknow, rebelled. The British authorities were able to rapidly bring the situation under control and the sipahis dispersed to the countryside, especially in the Sitapur area. Simultaneously, a mass uprising by the inhabitants of Lucknow occurred, but was quickly put down. Large scale preventive arrests were made and the situation remained relatively quiet during June.

Converging on Lucknow

Meanwhile the Avadh countryside was up in arms. At the same time neighbouring Kanpur, located at a distance of about 80 kms from Lucknow, had become a major centre of the Revolt. Rebels led by Nana Saheb had taken over Kanpur by the first week of June. After Delhi, Kanpur was at this time the other important headquarters of the rebels. The events at Kanpur had a direct fallout on the situation in Lucknow. British troops were able to recapture Kanpur by the middle of July. This prompted many of the rebels to move in the direction of Lucknow. At Lucknow mobilisation for an offensive against the colonial authorities was underway for some time. Finally, at this point many of the rebels in the districts surrounding Lucknow converged on the capital.

On June 30 a decisive battle between the rebels and the British took place at Chinhat on the outskirts of Lucknow. The rebels won a resounding victory at the battle of Chinhat. They were now in a position to take over Lucknow. British troops and civilian officials retreated to the Residency compound and were besieged. Other European inhabitants of the city also rushed to seek shelter in the Residency. In all there were about three thousand persons within the Residency compound (apart from the Residency itself this included several other neighbouring buildings; the original Residency had been built towards the end of the eighteenth century). The epic siege of the Lucknow Residency commenced on July 1, 1857.

The rebels set up a new government of their own as the legitimate government of Lucknow—in fact of the whole of Avadh—thereby proclaiming the end of the East India Company's government. They recognised the authority of Begum Hazrat Mahal who remained their foremost leader throughout the duration of the siege. Hazrat Mahal was a former wife of Wajid Ali Shah. She continued living in Lucknow after Wajid Ali was exiled. When the uprising began she declared her minor son Birjis Qadr as the ruler of Avadh. Birjis Qadr was accepted as the nominal head of government by the rebels. On July 5 he was installed as ruler in a formal ceremony. Hazrat Mahal was the regent for her son. Henceforth all official orders were issued in the name of Birjis Qadr. Recognition for Birjis Qadr was also sought from the Mughal emperor. The sipahi state in Delhi acknowledged him as the ruler of Avadh. He was granted the right to rule over the province on behalf of the Mughal emperor. All these arrangements underlined the legitimacy of the Lucknow regime, enabling it to gain widespread support in Avadh.

Political Significance

The rebels concentrated their military strength around the Residency. The siege of the Residency compound had an important political significance. This was the seat of the Company's hated administration in Avadh after the annexation of 1856. Occupying the Residency would signal the end of the Company's rule. There were at this time about 1700 combatants within the Residency. It is estimated that initially the strength of the rebel forces surrounding the Residency was about 6000. The British were led by Henry Lawrence, who had assumed the office of 'Chief Commissioner of Oudh' in March 1857, *i.e.* shortly before the outbreak of the Revolt. Lawrence was killed in the first few days of the siege, on July 4.

As there were a large number of tall buildings around the Residency compound, the rebels stationed sharpshooters on the rooftops of these buildings. Sniper fire was one of the tactics used to inflict damage on the British. Besides, the sipahis used underground mines very effectively. There were heavy casualties on the British side. We have detailed accounts of the siege from the colonial perspective, which give us a very good idea of the situation inside the Residency. In his history of the Revolt published in 1957 (Eighteen Fifty-seven), S N Sen reconstructed the details of the siege by using these accounts.

Unfortunately this made him concentrate mainly on what was happening inside the Residency rather than what was happening outside. We get to know that supplies, especially of food, were fast running out; sanitation was a major problem; Indians, mostly servants or soldiers, had to constantly face racial discrimination and were made to perform the most degrading menial tasks; and there were frequent disputes among the British. There were some peculiar problems as well, for instance the difficulty that opium addicts had in procuring the drug.

Interestingly there was a thriving blackmarket trade in opium, though all addicts could not pay the high price. Sen refers to a person by the name of Jones who found it difficult to continue without his daily dose: 'At last he decided to desert. With him went several of the King of Oudh's musicians, all native Christians [who had taken shelter in the Residency]. A number of servants accompanied them... They left inscribed on the walls in several places, "Because I have no opium"'.

Military command of the rebels was in the hands of Raja Jai Lal Singh, who had been the nazim of Azamgarh. He was a close confidante of Hazrat Mahal, and was a key member of the military council that took all major decisions. He was also the main spokesperson for the troops in their dealings with the Court of Birjis Qadr/Hazrat Mahal. Raja Jai Lal Singh was instrumental in mobilising military support from the districts around Lucknow. Another outstanding leader of the rebels was Moulvi Ahmadullah Shah, the so-called 'moulvi of Faizabad'. It would appear that he enjoyed considerable grassroots support among the urban poor. Although Ahmadullah Shah cooperated with Hazrat Mahal, there were also sharp differences between the two of them. Further, Hazrat Mahal maintained close contact with Nana Saheb. In December 1857 the rebels were reinforced with the arrival at Lucknow of Kunwar Singh during the course of his famous 'long march'. Subsequently Kunwar Singh proceeded to Azamgarh, which he occupied for some time.

Talluqdars Shift Allegiance

As the uprising progressed and British administration in Avadh collapsed, a large section of the landed aristocracy, the talluqdars, came over to the rebel cause. This is indicated by the figures worked out by Rudrangshu Mukherjee in his study Awadh in Revolt, 1857-1858. According to Mukherjee the rebels received large-scale reinforcements around the middle of November 1857 when British forces led by the commander-in-chief Colin Campbell launched a major offensive to recapture the city. At this stage there were a total of 53,350 combatants, of which 32,080 were listed as 'tallukdar's men'. In the words of Mukherjee, this 'clearly shows that the rebellion in Awadh had transcended a purely sipahi base. For one thing the fighting force was quite large and for another more than 60 per cent of the fighting force was drawn from the general rural populace. It is more than probable, given the ties of loyalty that existed in the rural world of Awadh, that the thousands of men supplied by the tallukdars were not all just their retainers but also drawn from tenants, peasants and clansmen who lived on their land'.

It may be mentioned that the Company had pursued an anti-talluqdar policy since the annexation of Avadh. This was an extension of the policy it had pursued in the adjoining North-Western Province (the North-Western Province largely comprised those territories which had been acquired by the Company in what is now Uttar Pradesh —territories other than the kingdom of Avadh). In the North-Western Province, James Thomason, who was Lt-Governor of the Province for a decade from 1843 to 1853, had steadily pursued a policy of reducing the authority of the talluqdars, had taken away their intermediary rights, had assumed some of their land, and had curbed their political and administrative power.

After 1856 this policy was extended to Avadh, but initially the newly appointed Chief Commissioner, James Outram, had moved a little cautiously in the matter of dispossessing the talluqdars. When, however, Outram proceeded on leave in May 1856, his successor C. Coverley Jackson embarked on a harsher policy, taking away the rights of the talluqdars. This gave rise to discontent among the powerful landowning classes in Avadh, and one of the reasons why Henry Lawrence had been brought in as Chief Commissioner was because he was perceived to be somewhat more sympathetic to the landed elite. But by the time Lawrence assumed office in March 1857 things had already gone too far, and then within a few months the Revolt broke out. Although initially the talluqdars were reluctant to join the rebels, once the Company's rule disappeared in Avadh a large number of them shifted their allegiance.

The British were somewhat surprised that even the peasants whom the talluqdars oppressed should have joined the rebel cause under the leadership of their respective talluqdars. Colonial officials seem to have assumed that the peasants would appreciate the Company's anti-talluqdari measures, since these were supposed to be in the interests of the peasants. However the structure of rural society and an instinctive comprehension of the exploitative nature of the colonial regime which ultimately targetted the surplus produced by the peasant, made peasants and talluqdars fight side by side in Avadh.

Regaining Lucknow

As the monsoon season came to an end in 1857, the British made a concerted attempt to regain Lucknow. By this time they already brought the area between Banaras and Kanpur under their control. This had been made possible by unleashing violence on an unprecedented scale, the most vicious campaign being that of the notorious James Neill who carried out large-scale massacres in and around Allahabad. Delhi too had fallen by the third week of September. Around this time British troops commanded by Henry Havelock (who had led the offensive at Kanpur) attempted to break through the siege. Havelock was accompanied by Outram who had returned from leave and was now asked to assume charge of the province of Avadh. On September 25, 1857 Havelock and Outram, along with a small contingent, managed to reach the Residency, but they in turn were besieged. The siege of the Residency continued.

Then in November 1857 another attempt was made to lift the siege. We have already referred to this offensive that was led by Colin Campbell (who later became Lord Clyde). Campbell's military action on this occasion was only a partial success. What Campbell was able to do was to evacuate the besieged inhabitants of the Residency. However, Lucknow itself still remained under rebel control. Eventually a massive offensive was launched in March 1857. The recapture of Lucknow was a matter of urgency; without control over Lucknow British rule could not be re-established in Avadh.

As a colonial official put it, '... the subjugation of the province will follow the fall of Lucknow as surely as the conquest of France would follow the capture of Paris'. Campbell had set up his headquarters in the Dilkusha Palace located in the Dilukusha Gardens on the outskirts of the city. Campbell's contingents occupied Lucknow on March 21, 1858.

Begum Hazrat Mahal Shifts Base

With this setback to the rebel cause, Begum Hazrat Mahal shifted her base to the fort of Baundi (district Bahraich), where she continued her struggle till she was forced to evacuate the fort in December 1858. Ahmadullah Shah too continued the struggle in the western parts of Avadh and died fighting in June 1858.

From Baundi, Hazrat Mahal moved to the dense jungles of the Tarai area. British troops pursued her, but she managed to escape capture. Subsequently she was offered refuge in Nepal. Hazrat Mahal lived on till 1879 and was buried in an Imambara in Kathmandu. Recent reports indicate that her forgotten grave has virtually been obliterated. The final significant political intervention by Hazrat Mahal, before she went into self-exile, was a forceful rebuttal of queen Victoria's proclamation of November 1858. This proclamation, as is well known, was issued after the British crown directly assumed responsibility for governance of the Indian empire (October 1858). By Victoria's proclamation all inhabitants of the empire became subjects of the crown.

The British monarch was projected as the benevolent protector of her Indian subjects. In response to Victoria's proclamation Hazrat Mahal issued a contra-proclamation in the name of Birjis Qadr in which she exposed the falsehoods of British assurances and the deceit upon which colonial rule was based. Drawing attention to the hypocrisy of British declarations, Hazrat Mahal asked, 'If the Queen has assumed the government, why does Her Majesty not restore our country to us when our people wish it?'

It is indeed a shame that in 1992 the BJP government in Uttar Pradesh temporarily renamed Begum Hazrat Mahal Park in Lucknow as Urmila Vatika. This park was originally called Victoria Park. The name was changed in 1962 to Begum Hazrat Mahal Park to honour this valiant leader of the Revolt. Not surprisingly the Sangh parivar has tried to erase the memory of the common unified anti-colonial struggle that Hazrat Mahal represented, by imposing upon this memory its politics of communal hate.

Punishing the City of Lucknow

With the military occupation of Lucknow there was swift and cruel retribution against the inhabitants of the city. The barbarities of Delhi were repeated. The city of Lucknow had to be punished so that its fate could be held up as an example of what would happen to an entire city if it opposed British rule. The objective was to strike terror among the 'subject race'. The entire layout of the city was transformed. The task of reshaping Lucknow was entrusted to military engineers led by Col. Robert Napier. A large part of the densely populated area around Macchi Bhawan, the traditional centre of the city, was demolished. Nearly two-fifths of the entire city was destroyed and the residents uprooted. The socio-religious and cultural life of the city was severely affected by the British policy of retribution.

The military occupation of the Jumma Masjid robbed the area of its life and vitality. A leading historian of colonial Lucknow observes that the area 'dwindled into a picturesque ruin on a barren eminence with an unpeopled esplanade around it. Periodic attempts at rehabilitating have failed since it now stands on the periphery of what remains of the old city and is no longer the convenient locus it once was' [Veena Talwar Oldenburg, The Making of Colonial Lucknow]. What is more, narrow winding streets that made military operations difficult were replaced with broad avenues, as for instance Victoria Street. This broad avenue, running from north to south, made it easy for the army to march from one end of the city to the other without having to encounter barricades. Thus the post-1857 policy left a permanent mark on the urban configuration of Lucknow. The city was never the same again.

After the recapture of Lucknow the British attempted to restore their authority in the Avadh countryside. For this purpose they initiated a policy of reprisals against the talluqdars, hoping at the same time to gain the support of the peasantry. In March 1858 the governor-general Lord Canning issued a proclamation confiscating the estates of the talluqdars. Only five talluqdars who had remained loyal, of whom the raja of Balrampur was the most prominent, were exempted.

This measure of Canning led to a serious crisis. Talluqdars throughout Avadh promptly mobilized themselves against the British. This was a desperate struggle on their part to hold on to their land and feudal privileges. Even fence-sitters now joined the fight. Canning's proclamation prolonged the Revolt in Avadh for several months. There was no British administration in Avadh for most of 1858, except in a few prominent towns. Canning's policy led to a complete breakdown and there were sharp differences over the proclamation. These differences almost led to the fall of the minority ministry in Britain headed by Lord Derby. In India there were differences between Outram and Canning on this question.

Canning eventually agreed to a policy of reconciliation, and Outram tried to negotiate with the talluqdars, assuring them that they would not lose their estates if they gave up the path of rebellion. It was obvious that the Avadh countryside could not be won through a military conquest. The Revolt of the people was defeated through a compromise between the colonial rulers and the indigenous landed elite. In the post-1858 period the landed elite became the main support of the colonial state. Their participation in the Revolt ended in their capitulation as a class. This capitulation was at the cost of the toiling people in villages and cities who had played such an important part in the anti-colonial struggle of 1857-58.

Understanding 1857

The Revolt of 1857 had as its opponent what was the largest colonial power of the world. It has, therefore, a notable place in the history of Imperialism, and no study of the Revolt can be separated from that of the emergence and internal mechanics of Imperialism. In a letter (27 October 1890) to Conrad Schmidt, Engels noted that while colonial powers before 1800 aspired to capture sources of imports at the lowest cost, thereafter following the Industrial Revolution, they essentially sought markets for their own industrial manufacturers. In respect to India, Marx (New York Daily Tribune, 11 July 1853) dated the change to 1813, when the Charter Act threw Indian markets open to British manufactures by abolishing the East India Company's commercial monopoly.

The results of this invasion of 'Free Trade' for India's own artisanal manufactures were disastrous. In Capital, I, (ed. Dona Torr, p.461), Marx noted that after 1833, there came about "the wholesale extinction of Indian handloom weavers", amounting to a "destruction of the human race." It must be remembered that this new source of misery was in addition to the increasing burden of 'Tribute', extracted by Britain through excessive over-taxation of the country. Marx had seen in such Tribute a special source of primitive accumulation for British capital; and this too was, therefore, an inseparable element of the new regime of Free Trade, how much individual Free Traders like Bright may have criticised it.

Not only was 'Free Trade' a vehicle for the conquest of external markets by British capitalism, a new impetus was now given to world-wide expansion of British power, so as to impose 'Free Trade' on the whole world. 'Imperialism of Free Trade' is how this new aggressive stage in British colonialism has been described by British historians, J. Gallagher and R. Robinson in an essay of this title (1953). Marx himself had never believed in the sincerity of the 'peace cant' of the British Free Traders (Tribune, 11 July 1853) and spoke specifically of the military means that were adopted for "securing the monopoly of the Indian market to the Manchester Free Traders".

The expansion of British power, both world-wide and within the Indian subcontinent imposed a still further burden on India: Annexations of princely states came one after another: Sind, Punjab, Nagpur, Satara, Jhansi, Awadh, all went into Britain's grasp between 1844 and 1856. In each state large sections from courtiers to common people lost their means of livelihood. Payment had to be made in blood as well. The Bengal Army became a major instrument that was put to use for fulfilling the sub-continental and global ambitions of British imperialism. The bones of thousands of its Sepoys lay scattered in the fields of Afghanistan, Sind, Punjab, Burma, Crimea and China, and no end to the blood-letting was in sight when the storm burst over the greased cartridges in 1857.

We can thus see in 1857 a critical juncture in the history of emerging Imperialism: the pressures it relentlessly exerted on the largest colony in the world, provoked, finally, an anti-colonial outbreak, unique for its scale in the whole of the nineteenth century. The rebellion pitted against the colonial regime over 120,000 trained professional soldiers from the Bengal Army, the most modern army east of Suez, with tens of thousands of other armed rebels, reinforcing and aiding them. In terms of the area affected, nearly a fourth of the population of British India (some five crores of people) passed under rebel control.

That the Revolt of 1857 had its roots in the pressures exerted on India by the Imperialism of Free Trade can hardly be denied; but the depth and breadth of the upheaval also raises the question of the classes and groups that became involved in it, and of their grievances and aspirations.

In his Discovery of India (1946) Jawaharlal Nehru wrote most feelingly about the slaughter and suffering imposed on the people of India by the British during and after the Revolt; and he compared the 'racialism' exhibited by the British to that of Hitler. Yet he simultaneously believed that the uprising was essentially "a feudal outburst, headed by the feudal chiefs and their followers, and aided by the widespread anti-foreign sentiment". Nehru repeats this characterisation at the end of his account of the rebellion as well.

Such characterisation, though perhaps natural with the limited amount of evidence available on 1857 at the time Nehru was writing, needs now to be reconsidered.

In the first place, the perception inexplicably overlooks the role of the Bengal Army sepoys. Coming largely from peasant and small land-owing families, they had been drilled and trained in modern warfare and, often themselves literate, were attuned to the mode of British administration with its committees and councils. They had thus no "feudal" attachments that we can think of. Yet, they remained from the beginning to the end, the firmest single component among the ranks of the Rebels. During the rebellion, they asserted their 'democratic' attitude by electing their officers (with, often enough, largely Hindu regiments electing Muslims, and vice versa). They formed 'councils' to govern their affairs, and in Delhi established the famous 'Court of Administration.' If their officers gave themselves designations, they were those of a modern army; such as "Captains", "Colonels" and "Generals"!

Another class, which we tend to overlook, is that of the educated in the towns, who were increasingly affected by modern ideas. While it is true that there was nothing comparable to the Bengal Renaissance in the Hindustani-speaking zone, at both Delhi and Agra colleges had been established, imparting modern education. In People's Democracy (April 23-29), Shireen Moosvi has given an account of weekly newspapers coming out in Delhi during the time it was held by the rebels (May-September 1857). Her account shows clearly that the rebel newspapers addressed themselves to people at large, and were not mere Mughal court bulletins.

Let us take a cursory view of the Delhi Urdu Akhbar (June 21,1857), where under the heading "Seize this Opportunity", it tells its readers that the English had been depriving India of its wealth, by taking it away to England, and remarks upon how the new rebel administration, as it extended its control over "districts" would open opportunities for men of "education and capacity." It calls upon the scions of the old aristocracy to leave their ways of idleness and take to various trades and crafts. It especially commends the ironsmiths who were manufacturing "rifles, English guns and Turkish pistols." Its appeal to Hindus and Muslims to fight the English does, indeed, make use of the slogan of saving both religions from the onslaught of the alien English, but it increasingly shifts to patriotic sentiments, addressing "fellow countrymen" and glorying in the exploits of "the Indian Army" (Fauj-i-Hindustani).

Modern methods of propaganda were also employed: a pamphlet containing an appeal to Hindus and Muslims was separately printed to be sold at a quarter Rupee per copy (issues of 5 and 12 July). Interestingly, the paper's hero consistently is not any of the Mughal princes, but the brusque "republican" sepoy leader, the Commander-in-Chief, "General" Bakht Khan. Clearly, the weekly's readership consists not just of the dependants of the Mughal court, but also a much larger educated population, which was being invited to support the rebel cause by enticing vistas of what they would gain from an Indian (not necessarily, a mere Royal) regime. The general slaughter by way of retribution carried out by the English in Delhi after its fall in September proved that in English eyes the rebel appeals to the Delhi citizenry for support had not fallen on deaf ears.

Beyond the educated class, there were the artisans whose callings the Delhi Urdu Akhbar in its issue of 21 June had so much commended. These included many who had lost their employment owing to the competition of British manufactures, especially textiles. Firuz Shah, the famous rebel leader, in his Proclamation of August 25, 1857–which reads surprisingly like a modern political party's programme–makes a special promise of giving employment to the weavers and other kinds of artisans rendered unemployed by English importations.

Such artisans formed another class that turned out to be strongly sympathetic to the rebellion. Syed Ahmad Khan then a British agent, in his contemporary memoir of the Revolt in district Bijnor (Sarkashi-i-zila' Bijnor) speaks sneeringly of how the sepoys and professional soldiers of the local rebel leader, Mahmud Khan were reinforced by "cotton-carders and weavers, who had hitherto handled only yarn, and never a sword."

While we are discussing the outlook of the rebel press at

Delhi, it may be mentioned that none of the extant issues of the three weekly newspapers display the slightest sign of Wahabi influence. Iqtidar Alam Khan's critique of the theory of a large Wahabi role in 1857 is going to be published in a subsequent issue, so more need not be said here about it. The practical absence of theocratic influence on rebel leaders, despite the constant cry of religion in danger is, indeed, remarkable.

As for peasant support for the rebellion this became so immediately apparent that already in his article in the Tribune (16 September 1857), Marx was drawing a comparison between the Indian Revolt and the French Revolution of 1789, on this, very basis. The peasants were hard-pressed by the Mahalwari system of land-tax (a consequence of the British pressure for Tribute), and the Revolt gave them an opportunity to throw off the tax-collector. The late Eric Stokes deserves much gratitude for his detailed studies of peasant participation in the Revolt. To him is owed the telling quotation from the report of Mark Thornhill (15 November 1858), where that official held "the agricultural labouring class", *i.e.* peasants, rather than "the large proprietors", as having been "the most hostile" to the continuance of British rule during the Revolt.

That large numbers of zamindars, the bulk of Oudh talluqdars and some princely courts threw their lot with the Rebels is, on the other hand, quite undeniable; and Talmiz Khaldun's suggestion that the 1857 Revolt was developing into "a peasant [and, therefore, anti-feudal] war against indigenous landlordism and foreign-imperialism" was rightly contested by P.C. Joshi in whose centenary volume on 1857 the essay had appeared. Much of the visible rebel leadership came from these elements: the reluctant Bahadur Shah Zafar, Nana Sahib and Tantia Topi, Hazarat Mahal and her entourage, Khan Bahadur Khan of Bareilly, Lakshmibai of Jhansi, and Kunwar Singh and Amar Singh of Jagdishpur, all came from what one can conveniently characterise as feudal classes. Most of them had their own grievances, over lost rights or rebuffed claims. But it needs to be borne in mind that resistance and struggle, in which support had more and more widely to be sought from among the common people, could not but force fundamental changes of outlook. One may look, for instance at two proclamations of Birjis Qadr, whom the rebels declared to be the ruler of Awadh.

The first was the proclamation of Rebel Rule at Lucknow, printed in Urdu and Hindi side by side, and issued in June 1857. Addressed to the "Zamindars and the Common People of this Country" it blames the English for their attack on the religion of both Hindus and Muslims, on their seizures of land, and on their disregard of the dignity of the higher classes by treating them at par with the meanest! There is no explicit reference to India, in the main text and, quite clearly, the interests of the landed aristocracy are given primacy. Contrast this with the last appeal to the Indian people in reply to Queen Victoria's Proclamation of November 1858. In this Appeal issued on behalf of Birjis Qadr, India (Hindustan) is in the forefront. The story is briefly narrated of how the British by force and fraud have acquired territory after territory in India from Tipu's Mysore to Dulip Singh's Punjab. The rebels are not to believe in Victoria's honeyed words, but to continue the struggle. Victoria's Proclamation shows, it asserts, that if British rule continues, Indians would remain mere hewers of wood and drawers of water. The petty matters, such as the loss of hierarchical dignity, are here quietly forgotten.

One must recognize that the overall historical orientation of the 1857 Revolt cannot be established in definitive terms for the simple reason that, because of its ruthless suppression, there is no way of knowing how it would have developed should success have come its way. But some preliminary suggestions can still be made.

Given the crucial role of the Bengal Army sepoys in initiating and carrying the Revolt forward, the Revolt at least drew on one element of the 'regenerative' process, that Marx had spoken of, in his seminal articles of 1853 on British rule. The Sepoys did not at all belong to the old world of princes and landlords. Significant also are the early traces of modern ideas and perceptions that we see in rebel journalism of Delhi and certain proclamations of the rebels. The fact that these modern or quasi-modern elements could make common cause with princely courts, zamindars, unemployed artisans and overtaxed peasants was due to a particular combination of circumstances created partly by that transformation of colonialism itself, with a discussion of which this essay had opened. To characterise the revolt as either "feudal" or "bourgeois" would be unhistorical. The time for one was past, the time for the other had not come. Such discussions have their place in attempting any understanding of how 1857 came about.

But what cannot be disputed is either the sheer patriotism of so many, whatever class they came from, or their undying defiance in the face of so brutal and ferocious a retribution as the English visited upon them. The memory of the Rebels' sacrifices in what they believed so ardently to be the cause of their country will remain ever green in our people's memory — so long, as the royal poet of 1857 said, as "the country of India endures."

Bibliography

Adikaram, E. W.: *Early History of Buddhism in Ceylon,* D. S. Puswella, Migoda, 1946.

Agrawala, V. S.: *Shiva Mahadeva: The Great God*, Veda Academy, Varanasi, 1966.

Ahmad, Imtiaz: *State and Foreign Policy: India's Role in South Asia,* Vikas, New Delhi, 1993.

Ahmad, Jamil-ud-din: *Some Recent Speeches and Writings of Mr. Jinnah,* Lahore, Ashraf, 1952.

Aiyar, R. Krishnaswami: *Outlines of Vedaanta,* Chetana, Bombay, 1978.

Archer, W. G.: *The Kama Sutra,* Unwin Hyman, London, 1990.

Ashton, S.R. : *British Policy Towards the Indian States, 1905-1939,* London, Curzon, 1982.

Aurobindo, Sri: *Vyasa and Valmiki,* Acharya Press, Pondicherry, 1956.

Avalon, Arthur and Ellen: *Hymns to the Goddess,* Ganesh and Co., Madras, 1964.

Aziz, Ashraf: *Light of the Universe: Essays on Hindustani Film Music,* Three Essays Collective, New Delhi, 2003.

Bagchi, P. C.: *Studies in Dharmashastra,* University of Calcutta Press, Calcutta, 1939.

Bahadur, K.P.: *The Wisdom of Vedaanta,* Sterling Publishers Private Limited, New Delhi, 1996.

Banerjea, J. N.: *Pauranic and Vedanta Religion,* University of Calcutta, Calcutta, 1996.

Bankimchandra, C.: *Essentials of Dharma,* Sanskrit Book Depot, Calcutta 1979.

Basu, Manoranjan: *Dharmashastra: A General Study,* Shrimati Mira Basu, Calcutta, 1976.

Beaumont, Roger : *Sword of the Raj: The British Army in India, 1747-1947*, Indianapolis, Bobbs-Merrill, 1977.

Benjamin, Joseph : *Scheduled Castes in Indian Politics and Society*, New Delhi, Ess Ess Publications, 1989.

Bhattacharyya, B.: *Nispannayogavali of Mahapandita Abhyakara Gupta*, Oriental Institute, Baroda, 1949.

Borchert, Bruno: *Mysticism: Its History and Challenge*, Samuel Wiser, York Beach, 1994.

Bose, D. N.: *Dharmashastra: Their Philcsophy and Occult Secrets*, Kali Press, Calcutta, 1965.

Bowle, John: *The Imperial Achievement: The Rise and Transformation of the British Empire*, Little, Brown, 1974.

Brockington, J. L : *Righteous Rama: The Evolution of an Epic*, Oxford, London, 1984.

Bromley, D.: *Krishna Consciousness in the West*, Bucknell University Press, Lewisburg, 1989.

Brooks, E.: *The Original Analects: Sayings of Confucius and His Successors*. Columbia University Press, New York, 1988.

Bruhn, Klaus: *The Jina-lmages of Deogarh*, MacMillan, Leiden, 1969.

Burke, Mary Louise: *Swami Vivekananda in America: New Discoveries*, Advaita Ashrama, Calcutta, 1966.

Chaudhary, M.: *Partition and the Curse of Rehabilitation*, Calcutta, Bengal Rehabilitation Organization, 1964.

Chaudhuri, Nirad: *Thy Hand, Great Anarch! India: 1921-1952*, London, Chatto & Windus, 1987.

Coomeraswamy, Ananda K.: *Buddha and the Gospel of Buddhism*, MacMillan, London, 1928.

Crawford, Cromwell S.: *Ram Mohan Roy: His Era and Ethics*, Acharya Press, New Delhi, 1984.

Dalton, Dennis : *Gandhi's Power : Nonviolence in Action*, New Delhi, OUP, 2001.

Danielou, Alain: *The Complete Kama Sutra*, Park Street Press, Rochester, 2000.

Dasgupta, Shahana: *Rani Lakshmibai: The Indian Heroine*, Rupa & Company, Calcutta, 2002.

Datta, V.N.: *Sati: Widow Burning in India*, Manohar, New Delhi, 1990.

David, M. D.: *John Wilson and his Institutions*, Mumbai, 1957.

De Bary: *Self and Society in Ming Thought*, Columbia University Press, New York, 1970.

De, Sushil Kumar: *Ancient Indian Erotics and Erotic Literature*, Firma K. L. Mukhopadhyay, Calcutta, 1959.

Deak, Istvan: *The Lawful Revolution: Louis Kossuth and the Hungarians 1848-1849*, Columbia University Press, 1979.

Dhar, Niranjan: *Vedanta and Bengal Renaissance*, Minerva Associates, Calcutta, 1977.

Dikshit, D.P. *Political History of the Chalukyas of Badami*. New Delhi: Abhinav, 1980.

Donat, K.: *Meditate the Tantric Yoga Way*, George Allen and Unwin, London, 1973.

Doniger, W.: *The Rig Veda: An Anthology*, Penguin, New York, 1981.

Duboi, Abbe: *Hindu Manners, Customs and Ceremonies*, Fifth Indian Impression, CUP, 1985.

Dwivedi, M.: *The Principal Upanishads*, Adyar Library, Madras, 1931.

Eaton, Richard M.: *Sufis of Bijapur, 1300-1700: Social Roles of Sufis in Medieval India*, Princeton University Press, Princeton, 1978.

Edwardes, Michael: *Battles of the Indian Mutiny*, London; B. T. Batsford Ltd., 1963.

Erickson, Erik H.: *Gandhi's Truth: On the Origins of Militant Nonviolence*, Norton, New York, 1970.

Farquhar, J.N.: *Modern Religious Movements in India*, Munshiram, New Delhi, 1967.

Fay, Peter Ward: *The Opium War, 1840-42*, University of North Carolina Press, 1975.

Fisher, Michael H.: *The Politics of British Annexation of India - 1757-1857*, Oxford, 1996.

Frauwallner, E..: *History of Indian Philosophy*, Motilal, Delhi, 1973.

Gambhirananda, S.: *Brahma Sutra Shamkar Bhasya*, Adavita Ashrama, Calcutta, 1977.

Gambhirananda, Swami: *Brahma Sutra Shamkar Bhasya*, Adavita Ashrama, Calcutta, 1977.

Gandhi, M. K.: *The Story of My Experiment With Trust*, Washington, Public Affairs Press, 1948.

Garbe, R.: *The Philosophy of Ancient India,* Chicago University Press, Chicago, 1899.

Goradia, Nayana: *Lord Curzon: The Last of the British Moghuls,* New Delhi, Oxford University Press, 1993.

Goudriaan, T.: *Ritual and Speculation in Early Tantrism,* State University of New York Press, New York, 1992.

Gough, A.E.: *The Philosophy of the Upanisads and Ancient Indian Metaphysics,* MacMillan, London, 1882.

Grant, G. P.: *Philosophy in the Mass Age,* Copp Clark, Toronto, 1959.

Grisenold, H.D.: *Insights into Modern Hinduism,* Oxford, New York, 1934.

Growse, F. S.: *The Ramayana of Tulasidasa,* Motilal Banarsidass, Delhi, 1995.

Gurumurthy, S. : *Hindu Heritage, Assimilative, Not Divisive,* Vigil, Madras 1993.

Haich, E.: *Sexual Energy and Yoga,* Aurora Press, New York, 1982.

Hasan, Murhirul: *Legacy of a Divided Nation: India's Muslims Since Independence,* New Delhi, Oxford, 1997.

Hasan, Mushirul: *India's Partition: Process, Strategy and Mobilization,* New Delhi, Oxford UP, 1993.

Heifetz, Hank: *The Origin of the Young God: Kalidasa's Kumarasambhava,* University of California Press, Berkeley, 1985.

Heimann, Betty: *Facets of Indian Thought,* Geroge Allen & Unwin, London, 1964.

Heinsath, Charles: *Indian Nationalism and Hindu Social Reform,* Princeton University Press, Princeton, 1964.

Heschel, J.: *God in Search of Man: A Philosophy of Judaism,* Noonday Press, New York, 1997.

Hirschman, Edwin: *White Mutiny: The Ilbert Bill Crisis in India and the Genesis of the Indian National Congress,* New Delhi, Heritage, 1980.

Hixon, L.: *Mother of the Universe: Visions of the Goddess, Tantric Hymns of Enlightenment,* Quest Books, Wheaton, 1994.

Hopkins, J.: *Kalachakra Tantra Rite of Initiation,* Wisdom Publications, Boston, 1982.

Hopkirk, Peter: *The Great Game: The Struggle for Empire in Central Asia,* Kodansha, 1992.

Hume, R.E.: *The Thirteen Principle Upanishads*, Oxford University Press, London, 1971.

Hutchins, Francis: *Spontaneous Revolution: The Quit India Movement*, New Delhi, Manohar, 1971.

Irene, S.: *Vedic Heritage Teaching Program*. Arsha Vidya Gurukulam, Coimbatore, 1994.

Iyar, K.: *Vedanta: The Science of Reality*, Ganesh and Co., Mardas, 1930.

Iyengar, B.K.S.: *Light on the Yoga Sutras of Patanjali*, Aquarian Press, London 1993.

Jacob, K.: *Religion and Ethics in Advaita*, C.M.S. Press, Kottayam, 1982.

Jafar, Malik Muhammad: *Jinnah as a Parliamentarian*, Lahore, Afzar Publications, 1977.

Jain, Kailash Chand, *Lord Mahavira and His Times*, Saraswati Press, Delhi, 1974.

James, Lawrence: *The Rise and Fall of the British Empire*, St. Martin's, 1997.

James, Robert Rhodes: *The British Revolution, 1880-1939*, New York, Knopf, 1976.

Jean, M.: *Tantrik Yoga*, The Aquarian Press, Wellingborough, 1970.

John, B.: *Mantras: Sacred Words of Power*, George Allen and Unwin, London, 1977.

John, Elsner: *Pilgrimage: Past and Present in the World Religions*, Harvard University Press, Cambridge, 1995.

John, K.: *The Origin and Development of the State Cult of Confucius*, Paragon Book, New York, 1966.

Karmarkar, D.: *Sankara's Advaita*, Karnatak University, Dharwar, 1976.

Kaushik, Asha : *Globalization, Democracy and Culture : Situating Gandhian Alternatives*, Jaipur, Pointer, 2002.

Kaviraj, G.: *Aspects of Indian Thought*, University of Burdwan, Calcutta, 1966.

Kavlekar, K.K. : *Non-Brahmin Movement in Southern India, 1873-1949*, Kolhapur, Shivaji University, 19790

Keith, A.B. : *Rigveda Brahmanas*, Harvard University Press, Cambridge, 1920.

Keith, Arthur Berriedale: *The Religion and Philosophy of the Veda and Upanishads*, MacMillan, Delhi, 1925.

Kishwar, Madhu : *Religion at the Service of Nationalism, and Other Essays*, OUP, Delhi, 1998.

Klaus, K.: *A Survey of Hinduism,* State University of New York Press, Albany, 1989.

Knipe, M.: *Hinduism: Experiments in the Sacred,* Harper, San Francisco, 1991.

Knott, K.: *Hinduism, A Very Short Introduction,* Oxford University Press, New York, 1998.

Kosambi, D. D. : *The Culture and Civilisation of Ancient India in Historical Outline,* London, Routledge and Kegan Paul, 1956.

Kottackal, Jacob: *Religion and Ethics in Advaita,* C.M.S. Press, Kottayam, 1982.

Kuiper, F.B.J. : *Aryans in the Rigveda,* Rodopi, Amsterdam, 1991.

Kuppuswamy, Sastri S.: *Compromises in the History of Advaitic Thought,* Kalyani Press, Madras, 1940.

Louis, Fischer: *Essential Gandhi: An Anthology of His Writings,* Vintage, New York, 1983.

Low, D. A. and Brasted, Howard: *Freedom, Trauma, Continuities: Northern India and Independence,* New Delhi, Sage Publications, 1998.

Maheshwari, Shriram: *Rural Development in India: A Public Policy Approach,* New Delhi, Sage, 1995.

Makhan, L.: *The Ramayana of Valmiki,* Munshiram Manoharlal, New Delhi, 1978.

Mathew, Arnold: *Culture and Anarchy,* The University Press, Cambridge, 1935.

Mayer, A. : *Caste in an Indian Village: Change and Continuity 1954-1992,* Delhi, OUP, 1996.

Mazumder, Sukhendu : *Politico-Economic Ideas of Mahatma Gandhi: Their Relevance in the Present Day,* New Delhi, Concept Pub., 2004.

Mearns, David J.: *Shiva's Other Children: Religion and Social Identity amongst Overseas Indians,* Sage, Walnut Creek, 1995.

Mearns, J.: *Shiva's Other Children: Religion and Social Identity amongst Overseas Indians,* Sage, Walnut Creek, 1995.

Mehra, Parshotam: *A Dictionary of Modern Indian History, 1707-1947*, New Delhi, Oxford University Press, 1985.

Metcalf, Thomas R.: *The Aftermath of the Revolt: India, 1857-1870*, Princeton, Princeton University, 1964.

Mohan, K.: *The Mahabharata*, Munshiram Manoharlal, Delhi 1997.

Mookerjee, Ajit: *Kali The Feminine Force*, Thames and Hudson, London, 1988.

Mookerji, Satkari: *Modern Polity and Vedanta*, Sanskrit College, Calcutta, 1972.

Moon, Penderel: *The British Conquest and Dominion of India*, London, Duckworth, 1989.

Morris-Jones, W.H.: *The Government and Politics of India*, London, Hutchinson, 1971.

Nanda, B. R. : *Gandhi and His Critics*, Oxford University Press, Delhi, 1993.

Neale, Walter C.: *Economic Change in Rural India: Land Tenure and Reform in the United Provinces, 1800-1955*, New Haven, 1962.

Nevile, P.: *Lahore: A Sentimental Journey*, New Delhi, Penguin, 1993.

Oddie, G.A. : *Hindu and Christian in South-East India*, London, Curzon Press, 1991.

Pathak, Dr S.P.: *Jhansi during the British Rule*, Ramanand Vidya Bhawan, Delhi, 1987.

Preston, Diana: *The Boxer Rebellion*, Berkley Books, 2000.

Raimundo Panikkar: *The Vedic Experience: Mantramanjari*, Longman Todd, London, 1977.

Raja, C. Kunhan : *The Taittiriya Sarvanukramani of Yaska*, Madras, 1931.

Ramamurti, A.: *Advaitic Mysticism of Sankara*, Visvabharati, Santiniketan, 1974.

Ranajit Guha: *A Construction of Humanism in Colonial India*, CASA, Amsterdam, 1993.

Renou, Louis: *The Nature of Dharmashastra*, Walker and Co., New York, 1997.

Robson, Brian: *Sir Hugh Rose and the Central India Campaign*, Sutton Publishing Ltd for the Army Records Society, UK, 2000.

Satyapal Verma: *Role of Reason in Sankara Vedanta*, Parimal Publication, Delhi, 1992.

Savarkar, Vinayak Damodar : *The Indian War of Independence* 1857 Rajdhani Granthagar, Delhi, 1988.

Scheftelowitz, Isidor : *Die Kasmirische Rezension von Katyayanas Sarvanukramani,* Zeitschrift fur Indologie und Iranistik, 1922.

Shukla, D. N.: *Vastu-Shastra,* Motilal Banarsidass, Delhi, 1966.

Singh, Birendra Kumar: *Early Chalukyas of Vatapi, circa A.D. 500 to 757*, Delhi, Eastern Book Linkers, 1991.

Smith, Col. J. T. : *Silver and the India Exchanges,* Effingham Wilson, London, 1876.

Strauss, L.: *Political Philosophy,* The Bobbs Merrill Co., New York, 1975.

Swami Vishnu Tirtha: *Devatma Shakti,* Swami Shivom Tirth, Rishikesh, 1962.

Talageri, Shrikant : *Aryan Invasion Theory and Indian Nationalism,* Voice of India, Delhi, 1993.

Tejomayananda, Swami: *Hindu Culture: An Introduction,* Chinmaya Publications, Piercy, 1993.

Thapar, Romila : *Ashoka and the Decline of the Mauryas,* London, Oxford University Press, 1961.

Thompson, Edward: *The Making of the Indian Princes,* Oxford University Press, London, 1943.

Trautmann, Thomas R.: *Kautilya and the Arthasastra: A Statistical Study,* Leiden, Brill, 1971.

Trimingham, J.: *Sufi Orders in Islam,* Oxford University Press, New York, 1998.

Utpat, V.N.: *Riddles of Buddha and Ambedkar,* Itihas Patrika Prakashan, Thane 1988.

Vable, D.: *The Arya Samaj. Hindu without Hinduism.* Vikas Publ., Delhi, 1983.

Vedalankar, Pandit Nardev : *Basic Teachings of Hinduism,* Veda Niketan, Durban, 1978.

Visvantha, K.: *Essentials of Hinduism,* Narosa Pub. House, New Delhi, 1989.

Wendy Doniger: *Siva: The Erotic Ascetic,* Oxford University Press, Delhi, 1998.

Zaidi, A. Moin: *Evolution of Muslim political Thought in India,* New Delhi: S. Chand, 1975.

Index

N

O

P

R

S

T

W

Z

□□□